Pegasus

Ken Shearwood

Oxford Illustrated Press 1975

Published by Oxford Illustrated Press
© 1975 Oxford Illustrated Press

Set in 10/12pt. Baskerville and printed and bound by
Chapel River Press, Andover, Hampshire

ISBN 0 902280 31 7

Oxford Illustrated Press, Shelley Close,
Risinghurst, Oxford

Not in growing old...
The body's sure decline towards decay...
Is tragedy.
But in the ageless heart that will not stay
Quiet in the sinking ship.
Dredging the silt of memory, the grey
Adventurer still flies his flag of dreams.

PHOEBE HESKETH

Acknowledgements

Quotations in the text have been taken from the following copyright works and acknowledgement made to :

Soccer in the Fifties
by GEOFFREY GREEN

The Edwardians
by J. B. PRIESTLEY

English History 1914–1945
by A. J. P. TAYLOR

The English Tradition of Education
by CYRIL NORWOOD

Babbled of Green Fields
by DENZIL BATCHELOR

The Double and Before
by DANNY BLANCHFLOWER

Talking Football
by ALF RAMSEY

Extracts from :
The *Times*, The *Guardian*, The *Daily Telegraph*, The *Daily Express*, The *Oxford Mail*, The *Oxford Times*, The *Evening Standard*

If I have failed to ask permission of the holders of the copyright in any articles I have used, it is an error of omission, and I ask pardon for it.

I am indebted to Martin Moriarty, my old friend and Oxford colleague, who read the book in typescript. To Ted Maidment who perused the book at regular intervals and offered sound advice. To Mrs. Yvonne Griffiths who too read and sifted through the typescript. And finally, to my dear daughter, Vanessa, who typed it all and was such a help and encouragement to me.

Contents

Foreword

Scarcely forty-eight hours have elapsed since I finished reading the first and last words of Ken Shearwood's absorbing book about Pegasus, the Flying Horse of combined Oxford and Cambridge University football whose flowing tail so many romantics caught for a brief but magic trip over the rainbow of the early 1950s.

But in spite of all the joy, and high hopes of an inspiring concept at the start it is with a sense of impaled sadness that one reaches the end. For here, like some Greek tragedy, is the story of what might have been a powerful marriage that was doomed; the rise and fall of a family rich in promise but finally torn by dissension; twin religions with a common stem which, in spite of it—or perhaps because of it—became irreconcilable.

It is time for the story to be told. The departed years have lent perspective and Ken, I believe, has told it fairly—objectively and with an understanding that neither shirks the facts nor blinks the many-sided truth as it was seen at the time.

Though the central theme is Pegasus, this is more than the mere history of an original football venture, offspring of Centaur and Falcon, which soared like a brilliant comet and died within a crowded decade and a half, victim of its own early success.

Across these pages are woven a wider human pattern: esoteric days at Oxford, the trials of parenthood, of cricket in high summer, the growing pains of a schoolmaster at Lancing. And through it all moves a cavalcade of people who in the end provide the real currency of life.

For me in a strange way it all has something of the elusive quality of a 'Brideshead Revisited'. Not an Evelyn Waugh novel in shape or form, of course, but a raking of dormant senses, of footsteps retraced, of events recreated and relived by one who was at the eye of the storm.

Curiously, too—though separated in time by the wastage of the 1930s when many of us failed to heed the fateful march of time—I find several points of contact with the author.

Generations apart, we both played centre-half for Shrewsbury and for our universities, he dark blue, myself a lighter shade of pale at the other place; we both played cricket and read history, each painfully scraping a Third almost at the eleventh hour, having sensibly decided that Jack was not going to be a dull boy at any cost ('Any of you chaps tell me who the Franco-Prussian War was fought between?' had inquired a Hockey Blue at one of four critical last ditch working breakfasts at Pembroke in the good days); we both duly became schoolmasters, Ken fully fledged, myself briefly at a preparatory school while awaiting the next turn of life's wheel; we both fished mackerel off Mevagissey in our separate dawns. And so on. These at least will suffice as a working L.C.M.

Above all, however, remain the bitter-sweet memories of Pegasus and jaunts with them as they scaled the heights of Wembley twice within three seasons. They touched the imagination of the country then, refreshing the appetite of the simple man for the glory that once was Corinth.

At the heart of it all was 'Tommy' Thompson, who in another age might have been the N. L. ('Pa') Jackson of his day, a visionary and realist able to split atoms and opinions with equal facility; sensitive, talented Denis Saunders, the captain, who rode Pegasus from start to finish; and Ken himself. All these and others wore victory and defeat like a garment.

'Who knows?' writes Shearwood in conclusion. 'Who knows?' Who, indeed. Yet maybe one day again . . .

GEOFFREY GREEN.

London, January 1975.

Preface

For a long time I have wanted to write something about an amateur soccer club called Pegasus, but have been daunted by the fact that we live in an age of professionalism, particularly in soccer where there is now no distinction, rightly so I hasten to add, between amateur and professional. And once persuaded that there could be some justification for a book, I had to ask myself whether anyone would be interested in reading the history of a club which only existed for a decade and a half. And even should an interest exist, could it possibly be sustained by a factual account of a series of matches? I thought not.

Eventually, and at the risk of appearing egotistical, I came to the conclusion that the only way to tackle the thing was to tell the story autobiographically, linking the events of Pegasus with my own personal experiences, first as a married post-war undergraduate at Oxford studying history, then as a schoolmaster at Lancing. In this way I hope the reader will see the club in perspective, share its humour, growing pains, disappointments and successes.

Today its members have all grown older, perhaps a little wiser, certainly a little thicker round the middle. Occasionally we meet with our wives for dinner. I don't think any of us dwell unrealistically on the past. We do not consider that we were better than comparable sides of today. In any case such comparisons are invidious and quite impossible to gauge. I am an optimist and my own view is that all things go forward, no matter what, and soccer today has improved at every level. Had we been competing now, our skills and techniques would have been found wanting, as in similar circumstances would our contemporaries of the professional world.

I mention this just to lay a certain bogey that critics might seize upon, for it is never my intention to make out that we were a particularly great side then, or in the light of today. All is relative, and if we are to be judged at all, it must be in the context of the fifties.

We did hit some highlights, and we did derive a great deal of pleasure from the soccer we played and our company. Often we were absurdly casual and light-hearted in our approach, but we could also be serious. There were personal clashes and internal problems, and we tasted the sweetness of success and the bitterness of defeat, all part and parcel of the story. My credentials for writing it? 172 games for a club whose brief history I believe is worth telling.

KEN SHEARWOOD.

Sanderson's, Lancing, Sussex.

1 A First Tutorial

Whenever I spot a pheasant in the countryside, I mentally doff my cap, inwardly give thanks and recall yet again how much I am indebted to these handsome creatures. For had Rob Tillard, Wykhamist and regular army captain in the 60th Rifles, not elected to go shooting one particular Saturday in November 1947, I would probably not have had the opportunity to play soccer against Cambridge three weeks later, nor perhaps have enjoyed all those subsequent years with Pegasus.

I was twenty-six and married when I came to Oxford after four and a half years in the Navy, followed by a financially unprofitable, though far from unrewarding, eighteen months of inshore-fishing down at Mevagissey in Cornwall.

In June month of that lovely summer I had come up from Cornwall and sat three entrance examinations and made a 'pig's-ear' of them all. At the interview Dr. Stallybrass had given me a kindly introduction to the assembly of Brasenose dons seated round the table, and finished by remarking that I had recently been fishing for a living. A brief silence greeted this piece of information and then I heard someone asking me politely what flies I had been using. It was my cue and I began to tell them about dog-lining and how we had worked a thousand hooks a man and that fishing was hard graft and long hours in all weathers, often for scant reward. I spoke of the nights of pilchard-driving and the excitement of looking down and seeing those first silver pilchards glittering in the water beneath the fishing lights. I told them about the superstitions of the fishermen and what it was like to unhook fifty score of dogfish and how, when lining, the tide was the killer.

It seemed to do the trick, for several days later, returning in the late afternoon from a day's spillering out on those great sandy stretches of sea bed that lie some twelve miles south-east of Point Head where the whiting come in the summer months, I found a letter from Dr. Stallybrass informing me that I had been accepted at Brasenose College to read for an honours degree in history.

1

Years later, 1963 to be precise, Eric Collieu, writing about that interview in the college magazine, *The Brazen Nose*, in an article entitled, 'Admission Procedures of the Past', wrote :

The marks gained by the successful candidate on this occasion are still preserved in a tutorial file, but they constitute one of those journalistic confidences, rather than violate which the Editor of this magazine would prefer to suffer a long term of imprisonment.

In fact he did give the game away when he wrote and asked my permission to quote the account of that interview which I had recorded in *Whistle the Wind*. In his letter he said :

I may disclose, incidentally, that after I read your book, I looked up my examination records and found I gave you delta for history, with the comment that you appeared to know none. But you did a respectable General Paper, and that, combined with your close resemblance to a former pupil of ours, whom we greatly liked and who was killed in the war, got you in!—I may add that we never had any regrets at our decision.

It was very kind of them all and we were delighted.

And so my wife, Biddie and I, got there and our immediate task, a by no means easy one, was to find accommodation. Eventually we found a bed-sitting room above a fishmonger's shop out at Botley, and there with our Labrador, Kim, we began our times at Oxford.

Very well do I remember that first tutorial with Kevin O'Hanlon, a tall, highly intelligent Irishman, for it proved a most disquieting affair. Attired in our short commoners' gowns, we sat upon an enormous settee that was covered in a loose fabric of gold hopsack and listened as Edgar Stanley Cohn outlined the course of study for the term, gave us a bibliography and advised us what lectures to attend.

'Of course we expect that you know all the facts and events of history,' he remarked casually, standing before his elegant fireplace in a room lined with books, its mellow old walls and ceiling panelled in oak.

I hastily nodded my assurance, but I found his words neither comforting nor particularly easy to hear. For Stanley Cohn had a habit of speaking in low musing tones, almost as though we weren't there. And then without warning he would break off, glance down as if suddenly aware of our presence once more and smile benignly.

He was a small man, dark and slightly Jewish-looking, and when he smiled his eyes narrowed, his mouth curled upwards and his whole face creased in puckish humour. He wore a hound's-tooth brown jacket, dark flannels and neat suede shoes and he rocked gently to

2

and fro, his heels on the hearth, while he stared thoughtfully over our heads at the long windows overlooking the quad.

'Well,' he said at length, addressing O'Hanlon, 'I think you'd better write an essay this week on the . . .' and I watched Kevin's aquiline features as he scribbled something down on paper.

And then it was my turn and although I could hear his voice, for the life of me I could only distinguish one word, Northumbria. I pretended to be writing it all down, for I had not the courage to ask him to repeat himself.

'Right,' he said softly, dismissing us with the slightest of nods and another brief smile, and we got up to go.

Outside the door I followed Kevin down the narrow spiral steps.

'Did you manage by any chance to catch the title of my essay?' I asked him as we went out into the sunlit quad.

He shook his head. 'Something to do with Northumbria I think.'

'Yes,' I said, 'I got that bit too.'

'Well, we've a whole week to do it in,' he remarked cheerfully as we parted.

But I found it difficult to see what difference a week or even a year would make to the predicament I now found myself in.

Most of that following week I spent at Iffley Road striving for recognition in the soccer trials held for freshmen. Those interested had written a short account of their previous performances to Colin Weir, the Oxford captain and goalkeeper, who stood all of six foot six.

My own experience had been two years in the Shrewsbury eleven and a year captaining Mevagissey football club in one of the junior leagues of Cornwall. Apart from a game in Greece against the crew of the *Ajax* and an officers' match against the ratings in Messina, in which the officers lost not only the game but a good deal of their prestige as well, my very earliest football experience had consisted of being shown at the age of six how to lace my boots at Miss Maltby's establishment in Derby, by Sammy Crooks, the tiny England and Derby County right-winger, and sitting with my father in the directors' box watching the *Rams* perform in the latter half of the Thirties.

As far as I was concerned the trials were not a success, for I found myself playing at left-back, a foreign position, and marking a neat, fleet little right-winger, Jimmy Potts.

At half-time, Laurie Scott, the current England and Arsenal right-back who was coaching the university side that year, spoke to us and told us what we were doing wrong and what he was looking for.

I saw Rob Tillard, who had played with fearless ferocity, listening attentively and noticed a short stocky player whose hair was silver-grey, Tony Pawson. Slightly behind Laurie Scott, watching the proceedings closely, his grey eyes hooded and unwinking, stood the honorary treasurer of the O.U.A.F.C., an old Blue, a fair, curly-haired man in a raincoat, a cigarette in his mouth. His name was Dr. Harold Thompson M.A., F.R.S. and he was a fellow of St. John's College, Oxford. I was acquainted with only one other person in the room, Tony Peet. He was the secretary of the O.U.A.F.C. and we'd met that summer playing cricket together for Cornwall against Devon.

The mood was all very competitive and not particularly enjoyable and I returned disconsolate to Botley and Biddie.

Three days before my next tutorial I decided that there was no alternative but to visit Stanley Cohn and find out the title of my essay. So mustering my courage I climbed the spiral staircase at five o'clock one dull afternoon and knocked on his door. I heard a muffled voice call out and entered.

Stanley was reclining on his enormous settee, the warm glow from a solitary lamp lighting the pages of the book he was reading. He glanced at me over the top of his spectacles.

'I'm extremely sorry to trouble you sir,' I began, still standing in the doorway, 'but I didn't quite catch the title of the essay you set me.'

'Oh,' he said, frowning slightly, 'I've set a lot of essays over the past few days.'

I nodded uneasily and waited while he thought.

'Well,' he said at length, 'you'd better do an essay on ...' and I watched his lips moving, drank in the scene as though mesmerized and heard his words as from a far distance, and then his voice suddenly tailed off and he had picked up his book and begun reading again.

'Thank you very much sir,' I said, coming to, and backed out of the room.

Outside the door I stood stock still, appalled. Exactly as before I had caught only that one wretched word, Northumbria. I was no further on. I considered knocking on the door and saying, 'Look, I'm very sorry but I simply cannot hear what you are saying; would you

4

please speak up and tell me again what you want me to do.' But my courage failed me and with sinking heart I retreated slowly down the steps and out into the quad.

I visited the Camera and tried to find out all I could about Northumbria. The following day I wrote my essay in our bed-sitting room.

At the appointed hour we entered Stanley's room and sat down. For a moment or two our tutor studied us reflectively.

'Well now O'Hanlon, let's hear what you've written,' and Kevin gave the title of his piece of work and began to read.

I listened to the words of his essay with mounting apprehension, for though its content meant little to me it nevertheless sounded impressive.

When he had finished Stanley nodded his approval and asked one or two questions which Kevin answered confidently.

Then I could feel Stanley's eyes turned in my direction.

'And what have you got for us?' I heard him say, and taking the bull by the horns I mumbled a few incoherent words and at the end let fly in a firm voice my single trump card, 'Northumbria' and without waiting began to read. As I came to the end of my first page Stanley moved over to the window.

I read on, my discomfiture increasing at every word, until at last I had finished.

Stanley had not returned to his usual see-sawing stance before the fireplace. I half turned in my embarrassment. He was still standing gazing out of the long window.

At last he spoke, his voice low, but this time I heard him clearly.

'I think you might safely commit that piece of work to the flames.'

I looked at the empty fireplace and folded my worthless sheets of paper in two.

But I caught just a flicker of a smile which gave me some slight consolation.

Nearly every afternoon we would train at Iffley Road and there was usually a Centaurs' match, which was very well organized by Jim Hornby, during the week for those not playing in the university side.

I made friends with Jimmy Potts, who was married to a charming girl called Toni, and David Carr who had been badly wounded in his right arm while serving with the Royal Norfolks in Normandy.

Despite eighteen months in plaster and an eighty per cent disability pension he played football and cricket most effectively. Both were reading history. Travelling to away matches we would discuss the subject in a jocular fashion—in my case it couldn't really be in any other manner—and they were always most curious to know about the current essay I was doing. Much later Jimmy Potts was to be of considerable help to me.

Another who played in those early Centaur games was Denis Saunders, a tall, gentle soul who came from Scarborough. He had long thin legs and seemed to have all the time in the world to collect and do what he wanted with the ball. Despite his big feet he had immaculate control and I never saw him bettered in the air. I also never knew a player with a calmer disposition.

And as each Tuesday morning came round, sitting on the big settee alongside Kevin O'Hanlon, I would read out my essay to Stanley, and when the ordeal was over repair to Fullers or the Kardomah or the Kemp and drink a cup of coffee and breath a sigh of relief.

I attended only two lectures. On the first occasion Vivian Hunter Galbraith, a fine old gentleman with magnificent white locks, was lecturing on the Anglo-Saxons. There was such a crowd that I had to sit on the floor, my discomfort slightly obviated by the fact that I was inconspicuous. I recall one of his sentences, for he repeated it several times, as he pattered to and fro on the dais shaking his mane from side to side. 'Anglo-Saxon justice was nothing less than unmitigated barbarism', and I quickly wrote it down in my note-book, feeling that I had at least achieved something.

The second lecture I attended given by W. A. Pantin, was on church history. This was an embarrassing experience, for unlike the first there were no more than half a dozen people in the lecture room and I felt exposed. Not infrequently I caught the lecturer's eye and whenever I did I tried to look knowledgeable, and ever so slightly inclined my head to assure him that it was all going in. The lecturer was quick and competent, but as I had no basic framework of history with which to relate his words I found it all quite meaningless and nothing went in.

So I went once more to Fullers and drank yet another cup of coffee.

Those were the only two lectures I ever attended during my three years at Oxford.

The term was rapidly drawing to a close when, on going into the college one morning I found in my pigeon-hole at the porter's lodge a card from Tony Peet to say that I had been selected to play for the university that Saturday against Epsom at centre-half, it being the occasion of Rob's prior engagement with the pheasants. So I promptly hastened back to tell Biddie the good news, for I had almost given up hope of being selected.

It was a good time to come into the side. There were only five more matches to go before we met Cambridge. Of the seven games already played the Oxford side had won only once, beating the Corinthian-Casuals. They had lost to the Army, Bromley, Oxford City and to selected sides from Tottenham Hotspurs, Arsenal and Wolves. It was my chance.

Of the match I remember very little, except that we won 4–1 and Colin Weir and Dr. Thompson—the latter came to all our matches and was known to us as Tommy—seemed reasonably satisfied with my performance.

The following Tuesday, 18 November, we played a very strong F.A. side captained by Leon Leuty, the Derby County and England centre-half. There were two other first division players on view that day, Len Goulden, the England and Chelsea inside-forward, and J. McCue of Stoke City. Leon Josephs, Phipps, Hopper, Stroud and Topp, were all then or later amateur internationals. My task, to mark Ron Phipps of Barnet and England, was not as difficult as Rob Tillard's : he had to mark the cultured Len Goulden. Mark him he certainly did, particularly his ankles, as Len in all good humour testified later.

Although we lost the match 2–0 we acquitted ourselves well enough; the press gave us a good write-up and thought we had a fair chance of winning against Cambridge.

After the game I asked Leon Leuty how he coped with Tommy Lawton in the air. 'Tommy?' he said, drily, 'you go up with him, but you don't win it often.'

That Saturday we beat the A.F.A. 3–2. Our forward line, although very small, was reasonably tidy and beginning to combine well. Alan Hunter at inside-right had a good shot. Jimmy Potts at outside-right had flair. Stanley Thomas, tiny and humorous (he was reading politics, philosophy and economics), fiddled around at inside-left, mesmerizing himself and all around, though to be fair not always without effect. Tony Pawson on the right wing, with tight control, was fast and

7

dangerous, but couldn't head. Jerry Moss at outside-left was neat but a bit on the slow side. Our defence seemed settled. Denis Saunders was the inspiration, Rob Tillard was ninety minutes of honest endeavour, and I did my best to obliterate the centre-forward. Tony Peet at right-back was a strong competent player, while at left-back John Rae, an old Blue, was experienced but rather slow on the turn. Colin Weir in goal took care of all the crosses and despite his enormous height was remarkably quick on the low ones.

On the 26th we travelled to Portsmouth to play the Royal Navy at Fratton Park, and beat them fair and square 3–0.

Tony Peet, Rob Tillard and myself stayed for the night as guests of the officers' mess. I was particularly intrigued to find myself face to face with an officer whom I had last met when, as ordinary seaman D/JX 286602, I had joined the destroyer *H.M.S. Foresight*, up at Scapa Flow in January 1942. I reminded him how we had been 'fell in' on the iron deck and informed in no uncertain terms that we would be expected to work harder and better than anyone else on the mess deck. We were H.O.'s (hostility only) men, and he had looked at the five of us standing there, weary and dishevelled after an all-night train journey to Thurso followed by a wicked crossing of the Pentland Firth, with all the distasteful contempt of the professional for the amateur. We'd had a rough time aboard that ship, and ten weeks later, after docking at Grimsby for a major refit and de-ammunitioning ship, we'd been found wanting, for some reason never explained to us, our seatime discounted, and sent back to barracks for redrafting. We felt bitter and disillusioned. But had we known it, we were the lucky ones. Three weeks later the ship sailed from Grimsby and went straight on a Russian convoy where she was heavily outgunned and severely hit in an engagement with bigger German destroyers. Shortly afterwards she was sunk in the Mediterranean.

I'm not sure he recognized me or even remembered the incident, but my hackles had risen and since we were now on an equal footing, I couldn't resist remarking with mock surprise what a poor show the Navy had put up that afternoon : surely they were capable of better things? But he only laughed and bought me a stiff drink, so I buried my memories in a bibulous evening.

On 6 December 1947, we met Cambridge at Champion Hill, Dul-wich, and were decisively beaten. When they came out they looked to me business-like and confident in their light blue shirts, white shorts and light blue stockings. I have always preferred their kit to ours.

And on the day they were much the better side. Norman Kerruish, Hubert Doggart, Barry Abbott, Doug Insole and Trevor Bailey were all good players. Trevor Bailey in particular caused us a lot of trouble, cutting inside and outside our left-back, sleeves flapping, rapping the base of the upright late in the second half and crossing the ball dangerously to his tall, powerfully-built inside trio of forwards. Despite a good performance by Colin Weir in goal and some fine individual attempts by Tony Pawson and Jimmy Potts to penetrate the Cambridge defence we lost the game 2–0.

But I thought at the time, and so did some of the papers, that the outstanding player on both sides was Denis Saunders. Elegant and poised, he did everything possible to set things going for us.

Two days later, our disappointment behind us, we all met at Euston Station to catch the 3.45 boat train for a tour of Eire and Northern Ireland. We played the Bohemians first in Dublin. Then on to Derry City, where the crowd behind Colin Weir pelted him with mud balls and anything else they had to hand, all of which he ignored with noble and lofty disdain. In a match that should have been cancelled, but in fact inexplicably went on for 110 minutes we then beat the Irish universities in dense fog. I left before the final game at Cliftonville to captain the Old Salopians against the Old Reptonians in the first round of the Arthur Dunn at Repton, a match which the Old Salopians won convincingly despite the balding head of Dickie Sale, the Derbyshire cricketer, now headmaster of Brentwood School, who did his best to stem the goals.

And so home to Biddie and Christmas at Derby, and the New Year at Evesham. I had taken a pile of books with me and plenty of resolution, but somehow the days slipped quickly by and in no time the Hilary term was at hand.

2 Tommy's Plan

Back once more in our room above the fishmonger's shop out at Botley, I found on going into Brasenose at the start of our second term at Oxford that I had been given a new tutorial partner, another Irishman.

Martin Moriarty was a gentle person, with a certain passive acceptance of life which gave him an air of vulnerability. He spoke in moderate tones, each word carefully selected. He was not tall and his face, rugged and seamed, had the quality of one who had seen much and learnt to endure patiently. Before coming up to Oxford he had worked for a publishing firm in America and there had been a tenuous connection with the radical movement. We soon discovered we shared one thing in common, a mutual apprehension of our weekly confrontations with Stanley Cohn.

Martin, it seemed to me, lacked confidence, and would always denigrate his intellectual capabilities, which were considerable, with a quick wry smile and a slow shake of his head. In fact he had literary style, a critical mind and was widely read. I knew that he had nothing but his grant to live on and that books meant more to him than anything. He managed his affairs quietly and never complained. Looking back I now realize how much of a struggle it all must have been for him and yet it was only many years later that I discovered how different his background was from that of the average undergraduate of those times. From an elementary Roman Catholic school he had won a scholarship to the local grammar school, headmastered by one Arthur Hope, a Brasenose man, a fact that came up at his interview. He was aged forty when he came to Oxford and we were to see much of each other in the next three years.

The new Oxford soccer captain for the Hilary term of 1948 was John Tanner, a Carthusian who had already played as an amateur for England and Huddersfield, and under him we began to build our side.

John was an independent cove, unpretentious and neat in style and looks, his freckled features even, his smooth dark hair never out of place on his rather round-shaped head. I had first played against him as a schoolboy when he came to play at Shrewsbury for the Charterhouse side one Saturday in 1938. They were supposed to be a good side, and, unwisely, as it turned out, stuck up an enormous teddy bear by their goalpost. We knocked ten in to their one. The second time I met him was in an Arthur Dunn match against the Old Carthusians at Charterhouse in 1946. Biddie and I had come up from Cornwall and I remember the game well for two reasons.

Firstly, John played at outside-right and destroyed our left flank. I was drawn from the middle time and again to cover the left-back. His technique never varied. He used sheer speed to beat his opponents and he certainly had this most valuable of assets. He would take the ball up to an opponent, show it him and make his break when in striking distance to do so. On one of the many occasions he had rounded the back, I had gone across, balked him rather badly and he had fallen flat. Picking himself up he had followed me into the middle as the free kick was being lined up. 'That was quite unnecessary', he remarked, and I agreed with him and laughed. We lost the match.

Secondly, Biddie had somehow allowed Kim to dig, apparently unnoticed, yet under the noses of everyone including the headmaster, a spectacular hole in the hallowed precincts of their immaculate ground.

Our last match of the season was against Bournville Athletic in the Midlands. I cannot remember whether we won or lost. All I recollect is that Tony Pawson had to rush away immediately after the match without a bath to catch the boat for a fishing holiday in Ireland, and that sitting in the train on the way back to Oxford, Tommy began to tell us about his plans for entering a combined Oxford and Cambridge eleven to play in the F.A. Amateur Cup Competition.

'That's if we can get permission!' he said ruminatively, coughing for quite five seconds as though to emphasize his point. 'Won't be easy,' he reflected, 'there'll be a lot of opposition,' and regarding us with those slightly brooding, unquestionably calculating eyes, he began to explain what these difficulties were.

To begin with, in order to enter for the F.A. Amateur Cup, a club had to have its own registered ground. His proposed new club had no ground of its own. The Grange Road pitch at Cambridge belonged

11

to the University Rugby Club, so it looked as though it would have to be the Oxford ground at Iffley Road.

Then there was this question of gaining exemption from the earlier rounds of the Amateur Cup which otherwise would have to be played before December. The Oxford and Cambridge match is not played until early December and throughout the preceding months of the Michaelmas term each university has its own standing fixtures given up to preparation for this game. In Tommy's eyes it was vital that we had this exemption. I thought at the time though that it was extremely unlikely that the F.A. Amateur Cup Committee would grant us such a request, for it seemed to be asking an awful lot.

'What's the club to be called?' someone asked.

'Well,' said Tommy after another long cough and much falling of ash (he'd seldom remove the cigarette from his lips) 'my wife has thought of a name, she suggests we use the combination of the Oxford Centaur and Cambridge Falcon and call the club Pegasus, the winged horse of classical mythology,' and after a moment's pause to consider his words, we all thought it an excellent idea. Then, lighting another cigarette, Tommy sat back and gazed thoughtfully out of the window while the train rattled on towards Oxford.

Towards the end of the term came the knowledge we were to have a child and the prospect delighted us. But we also had a problem on our hands—to find somewhere to live. We had an even bigger problem, a financial one, for we had nothing in the bank. My grant was a little over three hundred pounds a year, which did not go very far. The six hundred and eighty pounds I had received on selling my fishing boat had dwindled away. I had no other resources. Biddie's mother came to the rescue. She had been left some money of which three thousand would eventually be ours. She let us have it now, and after a good deal of searching we found Laburnum House in Woodstock, for exactly this amount. The house was three centuries old, at the end of a row of tall semi-detached houses set back on the left at the top of the steep decline which one approaches when heading north for Chipping Norton.

There was a big open fireplace in the sitting-room, and the tiny kitchen had French windows leading to a narrow path flanked by a high mellow old stone wall. There was an ancient apple tree and a few flowers on each side of the path which served as a right of way for two elderly Welsh spinsters, the Miss Parkers, whose abode lay at the back of Laburnum House. Above the kitchen was the bathroom and lavatory, and when the wind blew from the north the branches of the old apple tree brushed against the window panes of this small, weird-shaped room with its thick, crooked walls. There were two bedrooms on this floor. Through a latched door and up another very steep and narrow flight of stairs were two beamed attics which could serve as bedrooms. From one of the windows facing north could be seen the great column on which the first Duke of Marlborough stood in high and solitary splendour, surveying the acres of his palace, Blenheim. Beneath the kitchen and down a very short steep flight of steps lay a cellar, and on entering the front door one came straight into the hall which served as our dining-room. It was our first home and we grew very fond of it.

That Easter holiday, after we had moved into our new home we went back to the West Country to see our old fisher friends down at Mevagissey. How good it was to be with them once more and see at night the Mevagissey fleet of pilchard-drivers, their fishing lights, scattered specks of gold, flickering in the darkness of the Bay. You never see them now.

I'd taken my football boots with me in anticipation of a game, and sure enough the committee invited me to play that Saturday.

Eagerly we drove up Tregony hill and along the narrow familiar twisting lane, the high thick hedgerows full of primroses, the small stunted hawthorn bushes prickly and white as snow, till we came at last to that preposterous, rough sloping field set high above Mevagissey where the players were already assembled. They handed me a green and yellow shirt, number five, which I slipped over my head before running on to the pitch. There were shouts of encouragement from the fishermen on the touchline, and in particular from Catherine, my most loyal supporter of the previous season, when I'd captained the Mevagissey football side, and the game began. I was fit and confident and determined to show them that I really could play a bit.

Ninety minutes later when the whistle finally blew and we had lost the match, I was not so sure that I had achieved my object. By the middle of the following week I knew for certain that I had failed, for a note arrived from the committee politely informing me that they thought it better to keep the team as it was and hoped I would understand.

13

A week before the start of the summer term of 1948 I had been invited to attend the early nets in the Parks so that the Powers that be could assess the cricket form of the newcomers as well as the established.

I was a wicket-keeper and my enjoyment was not particularly enhanced by one Garth Wheatley, a wicket-keeper and Blue himself, who, standing behind the net in which I was keeping, remarked caustically, 'Snatching a little bit, aren't we?'

I did not impress and was not chosen for the trials. But I played a lot of cricket and became an Authentic, and later a Harlequin.

Sometimes of an afternoon, if it was sunny and warm, Biddie and I would go to the Parks and watch Tony Pawson hook, cut and glide with praiseworthy control, now and then nudging the ball into the covers to scamper for a quick single, for he was no exponent of the off-drive. He had some good players in his side : Philip Whitcombe who twice clean bowled Len Hutton that season and played for the Gentlemen, Haffiz Kardar of Pakistan, Clive van Ryneveld of South Africa, Geoffrey Keighley of Yorkshire, Tony Mallett of Kent, and Hughie Webb, who hit an unbeaten 145 against Cambridge at Lords that summer. There was also the enormous Australian Jiker Travers, the Oxford rugger captain. I liked the story of the previous season when he'd been bowling his medium pace in the nets to Martin Donnelly, who'd been hitting him all over the place in his own inimitable style and classic abandon. At length Travers had rapped Donnelly on the pads and let fly one of his stentorian nasal shouts, 'Ow's that?'

'Not owt, you big bum,' came the even more emphatic reply from his wife who, unnoticed, was approaching the nets while out walking in the sunshine with her children.

It was the summer that Bradman's Australians came and went with the Ashes, their side at Oxford captained by Lindsay Hassett, the only team that year to defeat Tony Pawson's eleven. For of the nine county sides played, Oxford had beaten Middlesex and Somerset, and drawn with Gloucester, Yorkshire, Hampshire, Warwickshire, Lancashire, Sussex and Surrey. Finally at Lords, just to round it all off nicely, Cambridge had been defeated promptly at three o'clock on the last day by an innings and eight runs, despite Doggart, Dewes, Insole and Bailey.

We went to a May Ball at Pembroke College (not one of those all-night affairs) and enjoyed ourselves hugely. In the still early hours

14

we jogged slowly through the slumbering city back to Woodstock in our little old box-like Morris Minor which we had acquired after selling the Jeep. As we let ourselves into Laburnum House Kim came forward and greeted us with sleepy warmth, returning to his slumbers in the kitchen. Before climbing the narrow stairway to snatch a few hours sleep we made ourselves a cup of tea and sat and watched through the French windows as the first streaks of dawn imperceptibly lightened the darkness outside.

And every week Martin and I would meet for our tutorials and somehow I'd manage to get something down on paper to read out. I would go into the Camera and sit for an hour or two and try to work, or browse at Thorntons, or Parkers, or Blackwells, those excellent bookshops in the Broad. But I found it heavy going and I knew I was making little headway. In the end I'd seek out all the conclusions and summaries that I could find, to obviate ploughing through the lengthy bibliographies that were presented to us.

Often of an evening Martin would come out to have supper with us, and later I would walk with him to the stop outside Roadnight Carter's Antique Shop where I would gaze through the window at the old bits and pieces inside, chatting with Martin while we awaited the arrival of the last bus back to Oxford.

So the summer days passed and our first year at Oxford came to a close with a Commem' Ball at Brasenose, an all-night affair this time. It was enjoyable enough, chatting, eating, drinking and dancing our way through the night hours, but by five-thirty in the morning we were glad to set off for home. Tony Peet, Jimmy Miskin and Michael Morton came out with their girls to have breakfast with us, which Tony Mallett and his wife-to-be, Vivienne, set about cooking with a will. Since it was a lovely morning we took our plates of eggs and bacon and hot cups of coffee and sat in the warm sunshine outside the front door of Laburnum House, the girls gay in their finery, their chatter every so often drowned as an early lorry struggled up the hill.

Eventually we bade farewell to our friends, who climbing into two rather battered-looking cars set off for Oxford. We watched till they were out of sight and then turned to go in. The sun was well up and hot, the sky cloudless. It looked as though it was going to be another perfect day, a fitting start to the long vacation.

15

3 Oxford v Cambridge 1948

We began the summer vacation by visiting our respective homes and at each I tried to do some serious reading. I attempted unsuccessfully, to achieve a comprehensive grasp of English history from Anglo-Saxon times to the end of the twentieth century, embracing all those facts and events that Stanley had so rashly assumed I knew. I consoled myself that at least I was now aware that 'Anglo-Saxon justice was nothing less than unmitigated barbarism' and remembered that Stanley seemed particularly interested in something called the *writ praecipe*.

But at length I closed my books and climbing into our 1932 Morris Minor, Kim in the back with my cricket bag, we set off once more for the West Country where I played several games of cricket for Gorran and went pilchard-driving on the *Margaret* with Edgar Husband and his crew.

'Never mind about Oxford University and its soccer side,' shouted Edgar over his shoulder to me in the wheelhouse, at the same time lying back and hauling in the headrope, 'starboard your wheel, come on, keep her up to the net man,' and pausing momentarily, he glanced swiftly round at the lights of the rest of the fleet before hauling again. 'You never were any damned good for Mevagissey soccer. You know very well you only had one damned supporter and that was Catherine,' and he shook with silent laughter. 'Never any damned good at all,' he said even more emphatically than before, and he laughed so much that he had to cease hauling, while George Pearce on the leech emitted a great snort of mirth, and turning his head sent a stream of spittle across the boat as he thrashed the heavy net against his yellow oilskin, the silver pilchards showering into the fish-berth. And all the while the gulls hovered in a white cloud above the boat shrieking their derision, the beat of their wings fanning our faces as the black dripping net shimmering with fish came up out of the water and over the clicking roller. At such moments it didn't really seem to be very important that I knew so little history.

16

Early in September we returned to Laburnum House, Woodstock. The town, really no more than a village, was full of history and fine old houses. There were two excellent inns, the Bear and the Marlborough Arms, and a very good fishmonger, Pitts—more of him anon. Almost next door to the Marlborough Arms was a rather exciting, dowdy antique shop. Amongst all its junk there could be found the occasional very good antique. It was owned by an ancient whose name, Roadnight Carter, was displayed in faded gold above the unimpressive glass door alongside the shop's bay window. I often dropped in to see the old man and his pieces and in the course of time bought an old oak chest of handsome rich patina, and a warming pan.

Living at Woodstock had other advantages. In no time we could be walking in the country and just round at the back of us, past the Bear Inn, one could enter the grounds of Blenheim by the north gate and look down the gentle green slopes to the great sculptured lake and the palace beyond. There we would often stroll with Kim. Dogs were supposed to be kept on the lead but occasionally, when no one was looking, Biddie would let Kim off. The Duke did on one occasion materialize from nowhere to enquire whether she had read the notice.

One day towards the end of the long vacation I received a letter from Archie Smith, the Gorran cricket captain, who was later to captain Cornwall, asking me to go down and play for them in the cricket final of the *Western Morning News* Cup. I knew Archie well, and had played quite a lot of cricket with him, including a minor county game for Cornwall against Devon, when I'd got seventy and a badly bruised finger wicket-keeping. I had played for Gorran the previous year in the cricket final against Penzance at Camborne, and made fifty out of a total of a hundred. I'd hit two sixes, one of which had cleared the crowd and gone straight through the headlight of a car owned by a Mrs. Tregaskes, who lived at Gorran. I only discovered this fact twenty years later, and apparently she has never again parked her car inside a cricket ground. We had lost the final decisively.

It was a difficult decision to make. I had already begun soccer training and we were preparing for a pre-season tour of Cornwall. The October term was threatening and I felt I must get down to more reading for there were Collections (informal examinations at the start of a term) to be faced. I'd played only a few matches that season for Gorran. There was the expense of a long train journey and I could well go the whole way down and make nought. Above all it meant

17

that a regular player would have to be dropped from what was the most important match of their season.

I wrote and explained all this. Back came a letter from Archie saying that they had held a committee meeting and decided to pay all my expenses. I wrote and thanked them profusely but still felt I should not go. Back came another letter saying that I could have a taxi all the way down at their expense. Finally Archie telephoned, and it was all I could do to stick to my guns. I was very touched. I had a great affection for the little Gorran cricket club with its Whetters, Hurrells and Bunnys, and all the others that kept it such a force in the Eastern league of Cornish cricket. I loved too the picturesque grounds that they played on, none more so than Boconnoc where the wicket lay in a glade, and deer would wander from beneath the trees, nibbling their way amongst the deep bracken which formed the boundary. It was there that a Gorran player was given out when struck on the pads yards down the wicket.

Astonished the Gorran man had held his ground. 'I'm not complaining,' he said, 'but I couldn't have been out L.B.W.'

'No,' said the umpire, 'you're quite right. I'm giving you out for obstructing the wicket-keeper.'

Sadly they lost that 1948 final of the *Western Morning News* Cup and I still have a long letter from Archie telling me of the match and explaining that if I had kept for them they would have won. Who knows? All I do know is that I enjoyed my cricket with Gorran as much as any that I have played.

Before the Michaelmas term of 1948 began, the Oxford side under John Tanner set off by bus for a tour of the West Country. Tommy came with us and it was all very happy and highly successful for we did not lose any of the three games we played. We stayed at Newquay and there one morning, playing football on the sands, Rob Tillard lost two front false teeth as he bent to retrieve the ball from the white bubbling fringe of surf. We all searched unsuccessfully, laughing the while, at the same time doing our best to commiserate, for Rob was most concerned about his new appearance. Early the following morning we were astonished to see Rob still searching for his two teeth, a lonely figure on that great expanse of clean sand swept smooth by the big Atlantic breakers. Needless to say he never found them.

On going into Brasenose at the start of the new term I called on

18

Eric Collieu, my tutor for the foreign period, 1789–1870. He was a slight man with a thin, sensitive face and a very sympathetic manner. He spoke beautifully in a quiet voice, his words seemingly selected with effortless ease, each pause significant, each sentence smooth, faultless and proffered with disarming thoughtfulness. I liked him very much.

I don't think my essays had improved much, but I began to enjoy reading about the French Revolution, though the more I did so the more complicated it seemed to become. With Stanley we tackled some political science, in particular Aristotle, Hobbes and Rousseau. We discussed the teleological approach, the problem of 'ought', and why man was born free yet was everywhere in chains. I saw a glimmer of light.

Most afternoons we'd catch a bus, or walk down the High and over Magdalen Bridge to Iffley Road where we'd do our training. Twice a week we'd play a match and afterwards have tea upstairs, served by Ben Standen, senior common room steward at Corpus and his wife, while Tommy would buttonhole the press and comment, not always as discreetly as one might have hoped, on the afternoon's performance.

I grew rather fond of the pavilion at Iffley Road, which was a homely off-white stuccoed architectural monstrosity, but the ground was excellent. The pavilion was equally ugly inside, but when the weather grew cold, we'd have a big glowing coke fire in the changing room which did something to compensate for the splintery floors, the two huge Victorian baths, antiquated showers and row of basins stained with age and use.

There, on a match day, standing on the balcony at the top of the pavilion in belted mackintosh, trilby tilted slightly over one eye, Tommy would watch the proceedings with all the wariness of a successful Chicago gangster. For those plans that he had first spoken of some seven months back when returning in the train from playing Bournville Athletic had now come to pass.

At a meeting held at the East India and Sports' Club in St. James' Square, London, on 2 May 1948, Biddie's birthday, representatives of Oxford and Cambridge with members of the Corinthian-Casuals in attendance and formed the Pegasus Football Club, its object, 'the encouragement and improvement of Association Football at the universities of Oxford and Cambridge by the formation of a joint team'.

In principle Pegasus sides were to be selected from members in

19

residence at either university, but the constitution granted the selection committee a right to call upon players who were in residence during the previous season. Tommy, the founder and inspiration, had become the first honorary secretary; the Rev. K. R. G. Hunt, of Corinthians, Wolverhampton Wanderers and England fame, the first president; A. G. Doggart, the first honorary treasurer; and a committee was to include the captains of the university football teams and the secretaries of the Oxford Centaurs and the Cambridge Falcons.

There was no money in the bank or in sight, and until matches were played the only income was from the 2s. 6d. life subscription payable by the joining members. Nor was there any support to count upon. It was just a belief, little more than a dream held by Tommy and several others that this new club, this winged horse of mythology Pegasus, might fly to the very heights of amateur soccer and in so doing stimulate the game in the schools and universities.

But there yet remained the difficult question of exemption, and preliminary enquiries from the F.A. had not proved very hopeful. Understandably there were those who thought that new entrants for the competition should prove themselves before any sort of exemption be granted. Nevertheless, despite this lack of unanimity the F.A. Amateur Cup Committee, considerably influenced by Mr. Andrew Ralston, to whom Tommy had sent a long and detailed memorandum, decided to grant Pegasus exemption until the fourth qualifying round which was to be played at the end of November. They further empowered the new club to ask its opponents to defer the tie until a week after the varsity match.

We had drawn the Athenian Club Enfield at home in the fourth qualifying round, the match to be played at Iffley Road, Oxford. But Enfield agreed to postpone the date only provided the match was played on their ground and not at Oxford. We had no alternative but to accept, and I do not blame Enfield one bit for what they did.

And so throughout that term Tommy could be seen up on the balcony, often with Penelope at his side, or down with us in the changing-room, smoking, plotting, coughing; laughing one moment, the next planning with deadly intent some Machiavellian counterstroke against occasionally real, often imaginary, enemies of his beloved winged horse. And when his prophecies of doom reached outrageous proportions and we would laugh outright, he would pause and regard us in some astonishment before remarking with slow deliberation and knowing shakes of the head, 'Well, don't say I didn't warn you. You'll see, you'll see I'm right.' And maddeningly he often was.

And he was up there now of course, not only as treasurer of the O.U.A.F.C., but as secretary of Pegasus, very much aware that just a week after the 1948 varsity match a team would have to be selected from the two university sides to represent Pegasus against Enfield.

Meanwhile the Oxford side had improved steadily and towards the end of November, when we played an F.A. eleven, it was settled. I had a difficult task that afternoon marking Charlie Vaughan, the Charlton Athletic centre-forward. Playing at centre-half for the F.A., I saw for the first time Vic Buckingham of Spurs, a most cultured player who seemed to have all the time in the world to contain the speed of John Tanner and distribute the ball. Derek Richards at right-back had to contend with Finchley's outside-left, George Robb, who later turned professional and played for Spurs and England against the great Hungarian side of 1953. He had a difficult afternoon. John Tanner justifiably suspected his fitness and decided to put him through his paces before selecting him to play against Cambridge. He took him at speed round the Iffley Road running track. Derek, who was married with children, knew that if he didn't measure John lap for lap he would not play against Cambridge. He was a slow mover and John, who was exceptionally fit and fast, taxed him to his limit. He managed to keep pace with John but the poor chap was very sick at the end of it all.

So, after a good deal of early experimenting at full-back and inside-forward the side was ready for the annual combat with Cambridge. We had a good goalkeeper in Roy Lenton, who though a little on the short side was agile and confident, catching the ball early and quick to come out of goal. Derek Richards, though he had sound control was slow and would use every wile in the book, and some that were not, to contain his winger. Geoffrey Pass on the other flank was tall and dependable, but again a little slow on the turn. Our half-back line was the same as the previous year. Denis was playing as skilfully and calmly as ever. I could read the game and usually hold the middle, while Rob's endeavour, if anything, had become even more ferocious. Tony Pawson, now at right-wing, John Tanner at centre-forward and Jimmy Potts on the left-wing were our three match-winners. Dick Rhys at inside-left could take on a defence

21

while Stanley Heritage at inside-right, good in the air, collected and worked the ball unceasingly, looking for his players all the time.

It was an excellent, well balanced side, and on 4 December, on the Spurs' ground at White Hart Lane, before a crowd of 12,000, we defeated Cambridge 5–4 in a gripping match.

Cambridge had M. J. Hardy in goal. At back A. R. Butterfield and Mike Bishop, the latter a huge fearsome Reptonian who was to become a doctor. In mid-field, Cyril Tyson, a tiny, stocky and very competent half-back, whom I was to see much of later as a schoolmaster, Ralph Cowan, an excellent centre-half dominating in the air, and W. R. Sheret. In their forward line they had E. R. Jackson at outside-left with Hubert Doggart inside him, big, awkward, high-stepping and snorting all the while as he bore down on any ball that he considered his. T. McGurk at centre-forward was elusive, and quick off the mark, giving the ball early and going fast for the return. At inside-right, Doug Insole, the Cambridge captain, was a heavy deliberate sort of player with a tremendous shot in either foot, who'd get hold of the ball and hold it; outside him Johnny Dutchman, leggy, tall and dangerous, was a footballer through and through.

It had all the ingredients for a good match and on the following Monday *The Times* Correspondent, beneath a headline 'Oxford win a fine match' wrote :

The sixty-fifth meeting of Oxford and Cambridge, and the first at White Hart Lane, brought Oxford victory by five goals to four on Saturday in what must surely have been the most exhilarating university match for many years.

It was a game that produced a record total of goals in the whole series, but it was not so much the harvest as the way it was gathered that left us warm and comforted. Such a score might suggest poor defence. That was not entirely so. Rather, it was one of those occasions on which attack, backed by first-class shooting, broke loose to bring life, colour, and a sharp excitement to the afternoon.

The fun soon began. With only 20 minutes gone we had had four goals and Oxford led 3–1. The expected pattern had begun to take shape : a good Oxford side was going to walk away with it we thought. Yet events were to prove otherwise. It was Potts, after six minutes, who set things on the move, and there was Rhys up quickly to shoot a low centre into the Cambridge net. Dutchman almost at once put Cambridge level, but the impression that this was merely incidental was strengthened when Tanner, at the end of 17 minutes, completed a closely linked sortie down the middle by Rhys and Heritage. Scarcely had Cambridge recovered from this blow than Tanner again was through, this time on one of his darting runs that left Hardy helpless as the ball was flicked home from close range. Here was quality and splendid individualism and Cambridge, three goals to one down, apparently already out of the hunt.

Certainly during this phase Cambridge had looked to be at sixes and sevens. The Oxford attack, well supported by the quick tackling and passing of Saunders and Tillard, was moving smoothly. Tanner, Rhys, and Heritage were making good use of Pawson's speed and Potts's footwork, and, hard though Cowan, Tyson, and Butterfield were working in the Cambridge defence, all now seemed plain sailing for Oxford.

But soon a sudden transformation came over the game. Insole and Doggart—and particularly Insole—began to break free in mid-field, and one or two of Jackson's long cross passes to his opposite wing were seen to catch the Oxford backs on the wrong foot; Tyson, too, was doing the work of two men at left-half. At the end of half an hour came a goal that confirmed the Cambridge revival. A quick pass from Tyson reached Insole, and the Cambridge captain ended a strong dribble with a magnificent shot from 20 yards that gave Lenton no earthly chance. It was just what Cambridge needed and, with Cowan now getting the measure of Tanner, their long sweeping movements clearly began to disturb Oxford.

Five minutes before the interval, however, a cross pass from Rhys found Potts's head as he moved inwards and the left-winger, with the accuracy of a Lawton or a Mortensen, guided the ball from fully 12 yards into the far corner of the net. Oxford were two goals ahead once again. But there was more to come, and before half-time arrived Insole, taking a pass from Jackson, sent another arrow speeding to its mark beyond Lenton—a fine goal to add to the others. It was 4–3 now and a great change. Oxford only just had their noses in front.

The interval, with its animated chatter between old and young, partisan and neutral, seemed something of an intrusion. However, they were soon at it again, and at once Cambridge, amid great clamour, were level when Lenton fumbled a shot by Jackson. But Oxford, to their eternal credit, survived the crisis. From the beginning they had struck one as the more scientific side, and steadied by Shearwood, they regained their earlier poise finally to snatch a deserved victory. The deciding goal came 29 minutes from the end when Pawson, taking a forward pass by Heritage, showed Cambridge a clean pair of heels to finish his run with a powerful shot. After that, on a rising note of excitement, Jackson twice missed golden chances for Cambridge, but it was Oxford who now carried the greater thrust down the wings and only some flying saves by Hardy, especially from Heritage and Pawson, kept them out.

It had been a fine game, made possible by Cambridge's inspired performance against a good Oxford team. We had seen attack and counter-attack, splendid shooting and noble recovery from both sides. Each man on the field will be proud to remember the part he played, especially Insole and Pawson. But the pity of it was there had to be a loser.

The teams were :—

OXFORD – R. Lenton (Quarry Bank H.S. and St. Peter's Hall); D. M. Richards (Salesian College, Battersea, and Queen's), L. G. Pass (Gossop G.S. and Hertford); J. R. Tillard (Winchester and Trinity), K. A. Shearwood (Shrewsbury and

23

Brasenose), D. F. Saunders (Scarborough H.S. and Exeter); H. A. Pawson (Winchester and Christ Church), H. R. A. Rhys (Shrewsbury and Wadham), J. D. P. Tanner (Charterhouse and Brasenose [captain]), S. G. Heritage (Holloway County School and Exeter), H. J. Potts (Stand G.S. and Keble).

CAMBRIDGE – M. J. Hardy (Repton and St. Catherine's); M. H. H. Bishop (Repton and Clare), A. R. Butterfield (Bolton School and Caius); W. B. Sheret (Wellingborough and St. Catherine's), R. Cowan (Chorlton H.S. and Queens'), C. Tyson (Darwen G.S. and Jesus); J. A. Dutchman (Cockburn G.S. and King's), D. J. Insole (Monoux G.S. and St. Catharine's [captain]), T. McGurk (St. Peter's, Glasgow, and Christ's), G. H. G. Doggart (Winchester and King's), E. W. N. Jackson (Chorlton H.S. and Queens').

As we came off, the crowd gave both sides a great reception. And it was auspicious that it should have been such an excellent match, for of those who had played, eleven would in a week's time be doing battle with Enfield.

4 A Spreading of Wings

Biddie had not watched the match. Though fit and well she had been advised not to attend, which was just as well for four days later, on 8 December, early in the morning, Paul was born.

We had arranged for a nurse to come and stay. Everything seemed prepared. Her mother Winnie was staying with us and we were to notify the nurse as soon as was necessary, which we did. And then everything went wrong. It was a long labour and at four o'clock in the morning on the third day Winnie urged me to summon the doctor despite the assurance of the nurse that all was well. When the doctor, hastily attired, arrived twenty minutes later and went upstairs he was down almost immediately asking if my wife had ever had fits. 'No', we both said shocked.

'Well then you'd better ring for an ambulance,' and seeing my concern added, 'I don't think your wife's in any immediate danger, but I'm worried about the child.'

I was very alarmed. I lifted the receiver and flashed the operator. There was no reply. It was an old telephone. I flashed again. There was still no reply. I heard a lorry rumbling up the hill and then, unable to wait any longer, rushed out to the Miss Parkers' house at the back of ours and banged on their door. Astonished, they allowed me to use their telephone, their white pekingese snapping at my heels.

In surprisingly quick time a very old ambulance arrived with two young attendants, who seemed no more than boys. Somehow they got Biddie down those impossible stairs on a stretcher and set off for the Radcliffe.

As if in a nightmare, with Biddie's mother sitting beside me, I drove the eight miles into Oxford following the ambulance. Forewarned, the hospital staff was ready and waiting. A little later, halfway up the stairs of the maternity wing (I don't know how I got there) I met our doctor, who reassured me and disappeared up the stairs again. I was too bewildered to say anything and went down and walked outside oblivious of the cold winter morning, while Winnie sat inside and waited. After what seemed a very long time the doctor came down

25

and told us that Biddie was under a deep anaesthetic and we had a fine healthy son.

Quite exhausted we got into the car and drove back to Woodstock. In the afternoon I returned to the hospital and peeped at Biddie through the glass doors of the darkened room where a nurse sat by her bedside. She had suffered from eclampsia and I was told that it was important that she be brought back to consciousness very carefully.

That same day Pegasus played their first match against the full Arsenal Combination side and won 1–0, the winning goal coming from a header by Barry Abbott, the Cambridge centre-forward of the previous year, from a cross by Tony Pawson.

After the match, the selectors, Guy Shuttleworth, John Tanner, Doug Insole and Tommy, having canvassed opinions, selected the side to play against Enfield. It would hardly have been surprising had they picked the side that had just done so well against Arsenal's Combination side. In fact they moved Barry Abbott to inside-left and played John Tanner, who had been injured, at centre-forward, and dropped Hubert Doggart. The new forward line read : Tony Pawson, Doug Insole, John Tanner, Barry Abbott and Jimmy Potts. Surprisingly, they brought me in at centre-half and moved Tony Peet to left-back, dropping Geoffrey Pass at right-back for Ralph Cowan. I say surprisingly, because I thought Cowan, the Cambridge centre-half was a better one than I was. He was taller, more accurate and commanding in the air, and a much better distributor of the ball. I was probably faster, as good positionally and as hard, but little more than a purely destructive stopper, and I believe it was in that capacity they selected me for the fourth qualifying round of the Amateur Cup. The half-back line read : Guy Shuttleworth, myself, and Denis Saunders. At left-back was Tony Peet and in goal Ben Brown, who never got a Blue. He was at Oxford doing research, had the reputation of being an excellent goal-keeper, and so was selected to play, the selectors' decision no doubt being influenced by the fact that Colin Weir was going down from Oxford that summer. I could not make up my mind as to whether I should play, so I went to talk it over with Tommy.

'You might just as well,' he said after careful consideration. 'There's nothing you can really do,' which was quite true. So I took his advice and played.

26

John Tanner captained Pegasus that afternoon and the match was televised.

At half-time the score was level. As we sat sipping our tea, saying little, there wasn't one of us that didn't know we now faced a formidable task. Tommy came round and spoke a few words of encouragement, but I could see he was worried. We needed a professional to take control, reassure us, give us some quiet words of advice, lift some of the weight from our shoulders. There remained forty-five minutes to prove ourselves and vindicate the F.A. Amateur Cup Committee's decision to grant us exemption. If we failed now there would be no exemption next year and that would mean the end of Pegasus and Tommy's dreams.

The referee's head had appeared round the dressing-room door. 'It's absolutely crucial that you score an early goal,' said Tommy as we went out for the second half. Ten minutes later Enfield had scored. As the ball was brought back to the centre I felt a sudden wave of panic well within me, which I tried hard to dispel by looking fixedly at the opposing centre-forward, who, alert and ready to challenge, was watching the referee, waiting for him to blow his whistle. I tried hard to rid my mind of the alarming prospect of those precious seconds slipping away. They were ahead now and would fight like hell to keep their lead. Who wouldn't? My heart thumped. I felt dismay and forced myself to keep calm and not worry about the time factor. But it wasn't easy. The sharp blast of the whistle did the trick.

And then there came one of those turning-points well on in the game, an incident that I recall most vividly. Jack Rawlings, their powerful international inside-right, after a lot of Enfield pressure, broke through ominously and hit a tremendous shot from outside the penalty area. It passed me close by, going too fast to intercept. I just had time to turn and watch, a helpless spectator as the ball flew low and true towards the right hand corner of our goal. It was on target all the way, the final nail in our coffin. I had no doubt of it, nor had anyone else as I afterwards discovered. And then, impossibly, Ben Brown was diving horizontally to his right and instead of turning the ball round the corner, actually catching and holding it clean as a whistle, and I for one thanked the Almighty as we breathed again.

Reprieved, and with less than a quarter of an hour to go we suddenly began to play a bit. Tony Pawson and Jimmy Potts, taking on their backs, opened up the middle for John Tanner's quick thrusts. Twice

27

he broke clean away and scored typical goals, using his speed and driving the ball home low each time. He was a deadly finisher and watching from defence I would always feel that if he could get his shot in, with either foot, it would usually be there and abouts. Seldom would he hit one over the top. Finally a penalty sealed it for us, Doug Insole crashing the ball home. Then the whistle blew and it was over.

As I shook hands with their centre-forward and saw his dejected face, I felt for him; it could so easily have been the other way round. But then that's what cup football's all about. It's a cruel business; a case of sudden death; them or us; ninety minutes of tension at the end of which you're in, or you're out, either on top of the world or lying at the bottom sprawled in an abyss of gloom. This time it had been us.

So we went through to the first round proper, having won, on reflection, the most important cup-tie Pegasus ever played.

Tommy was in tremendous form as I drove back with him and Penelope in their Wolseley, which Tommy drove extremely fast, as he always did. On the way we stopped to see some friends of his and I can see him now, all beams and smiles, a drink in his left hand, his right arm flung protectively round some female shoulder, as bending slightly, he expanded on Pegasus and how the lady in question must come to the next match. And so into the car again and on to Oxford, even faster, where on arrival, I was able to peep through the window at Biddie who was still lying in a deep sleep, a nurse by her side, before going out to Woodstock.

I talked at length on the telephone with my father, a wise general practitioner of much experience, and he urged the importance of Biddie's being kept very quiet and not quickly dismissed from hospital. I attempted to put all this tactfully to the specialist without causing offence and was informed with courteous gravity, 'You can rest assured Mr. Shearwood, your wife will not leave here until she is completely well'.

A week later we were told she could be taken home and eagerly I drove in from Woodstock early one cold December afternoon to fetch her. We had a great log fire burning merrily in the open fire-place of our sitting-room and the house was warm and welcoming. As we brought the tea in I suddenly saw Biddie seated by the fire begin to shake violently. There was nothing we could do to stop the rigor and eventually I carried her in my arms upstairs and sent for the doctor. She had a temperature of over a hundred and four and was ill for the next three months with acute pyelitis. They were trying days and we owed much to both our mothers who came to the rescue and looked after us all so well.

Before, throughout and after that Christmas of 1948 Biddie was far from well, but it was very good to see our son in his cot beside her and know our family was complete. Kim too would spend a lot of his time lying quietly on the landing upstairs. And at nights when the December winds blew cold round the house, we'd listen to the sound of approaching lorries rumbling up the hill, hear them change gear as they came to the steep bend, then draw away past the Marlborough Arms where they'd change gear again before heading on towards Oxford.

I did no reading. There was no real excuse for not doing some but there seemed such a lot to do about the place. And little by little as the days went by Biddie grew stronger, but it was slow progress. A gale of wind finally blew the old year away, and caused the branches of the ancient apple tree to rattle the bathroom window panes.

On New Year's Day Pegasus played Headington United and won 3–2. The following week we defeated Barnet on their ground 4–2 and now we were ready for our next opponents, Smethwick Highfield, a Midland side whom we had drawn in the first round of the Amateur Cup, the match to be played at Oxford. We made one change from the side that had played Enfield, bringing Hubert Doggart in for Barry Abbott. We won 4–1, John Tanner scoring three, Doug Insole one, and the size of the crowd and measure of support astonished us.

We awaited our next opponents and when the third round was announced, knew we faced our stiffest task to date, Willington from the north who had been finalists in the last season before the war and were to win the cup in 1950. Before we took them on we travelled to Merthyr Tydfil, a mining community that had suffered severe unemployment in the early thirties, where the women carried their children over their shoulders in shawls. There we played the Welsh F.A. and lost 2–3. It was a hard game in every sense of the word and when the final whistle blew, their centre-forward, who had a face of granite and a handshake of steel, growled some fierce unintelligible words of Welsh which I wasn't sure sounded all that complimentary. But it was good preparation for Willington.

When we met them the following week we made two changes. John Tanner was injured, so Barry Abbott came in again at centre-forward and Geoffrey Pass took over at left-back from Tony Peet who had gone into the Colonial service. Ninety minutes later we had beaten Willington 3–2, our goals scored by Stanley Heritage, Barry Abbott and Tony Pawson. As the crowd of nearly seven thousand streamed contentedly away down Iffley Road and across Magdalen Bridge we sat in the changing-room which was now suddenly full of people all talking at once.

Tommy was going round laughing, telling us he'd told us so, coughing his head off then retreating into a corner with Harvey Chadder and Graham Doggart, his face suddenly serious, no smile now for he was seeing where nobody else could, to far beyond the horizon where unseen and terrible dangers loomed in wait for us all. But he couldn't keep it up and once more all smiles, he disappeared up the stairs and began to commiserate with the Willington officials and players who weren't in the least bit keen on being commiserated with.

A stocky, beaming supporter, inarticulate with excitement had somehow got inside the changing-room and was going round cutting off segments of orange for us with a penknife, his hand shaking so dreadfully that on accepting the proffered piece one was liable to severe injury. His name was Chedder Wilson and we were to see much of him and his oranges in the future.

Upstairs in the midst of the noisy, jostling tea-nudging throng, Sir Stanley Rous, the Secretary of the F.A., and our President, the Reverend Kenneth Hunt, stood talking together, a head and shoulders above everyone else, apart from Colin Weir. I found myself alongside a distinguished elderly gentleman, who spoke quietly and most knowledgeably about the game. In the years to come—Guy and Helen Pawson seldom missed a cup match—I was to find their unobtrusive presence and wise counsel a soothing antidote to those tense moments before, and sometimes after a match, when all had been lost and there seemed nothing worth living for.

So on we went into the fourth round of the Amateur Cup, one of the last eight remaining clubs left in England to go into the hat for the quarter-final draw.

And by Monday we knew who it was to be : Bromley, one of the strongest sides in the country, at Oxford. And suddenly the name of

30

Pegasus was on everyone's lips and wherever we went people were stopping us and talking to us and wishing us luck and saying they were coming to the game.

We had a fortnight in which to prepare, the Oxford contingent training at Iffley Road, the Cambridge one at Grange Road. There was no question of our getting together and working things out as a unit. We had no coach, so no tactics were laid down. It was term time and both universities were still playing, so it was not possible to have a match before the quarter-final took place. Added to all this there was doubt about John Tanner's fitness. Barry Abbott had played very adequately for us. He was big, strong and good in the air, if a little predictable. But John had the happy knack of scoring goals and in the end it was he who played.

On reflection he should not have done so. But it is easy to be wise after the event. He had seen a physiotherapist in the morning who had pronounced him fit. He should then, however, have been put through a rigorous fitness test before the match, but there was no one to do this. He did give himself a good work-out an hour before the game on the Christ Church fields at the back of the pavilion, but the weight of decision was finally his and in such circumstances it is hard on a player and too much to ask.

Of the team that was finally selected, eight of us were resident at Oxford, three at Cambridge. The die was cast.

Just under twelve thousand people packed into Iffley Road that last Saturday of February 1949 to watch the cup-tie with Bromley, a record crowd for any Oxford sport.

By one o'clock a hundred coaches had converged on Oxford, bringing the Bromley supporters. Everywhere buses, cars, and crowds of people were streaming towards the ground. Arriving early we watched the scene from the changing-room windows facing the pitch, around which four temporary stands had been erected. Long before three o'clock the ground was full.

The referee had come in. There was five minutes left.

Nothing had been said. We had joked and laughed and talked as we changed, but not about football. We were keyed up. There was much at stake. Now it was time to go.

As we emerged a roar greeted us and shouts of, 'Come on the Pegs!', 'Up the Pegs!', 'Come on the Lillywhites!' Cries that were to become so familiar, now came from all around the ground.

31

There was another roar, less loud, but significant none the less, and Bromley were coming out in their hooped blue and white shirts and black shorts with white flashes down their sides. I took a good long look at them and I thought they appeared a thoroughly professional lot.

The whistle had blown and Guy Shuttleworth was shaking hands with Charlie Fuller, the Bromley centre-half and captain, and then we were off.

I could tell at once that they were good, for they began to move the ball around effectively and confidently as one would have expected from a side with four current England players in their midst and more to come.

I'd studied my opponent, big George Brown, their international centre-forward, who had already seventy-three goals under his belt that season. I quickly discovered that he screened the ball well and moved wide and deep for crosses. I found him particularly good in the air and I determined not to let him get on the back of me.

Things were going well. We were coming at them on the flanks, both Tony Pawson and Jimmy Potts worrying the Bromley backs with their speed and skill. Jimmy Potts in particular was having a good game, killing the ball quickly then sending his full-back one way and going outside. He was explosively quick over a short distance, but could be caught over a long run. Now he was making his breaks where they counted most, deep in the Bromley half, getting in behind their right-back.

Tony Pawson on the other flank was a more direct player and ultimately more dangerous for he could sustain his speed. He was also, despite his lack of height, very difficult to dispossess, for besides having tight control he was tenacious and particularly strong of limb.

It soon became apparent that we had a problem on our hands. John Tanner was limping and whenever he tried to accelerate, it was obvious to all that he was carrying his leg badly. It was a serious blow, for it took the pressure off Charlie Fuller and gave him time to move forward and create.

And then, after twenty-five minutes had passed, Tony Pawson, from a corner, dropped an away swinger into the far part of the six-yard area where Stan Heritage found space and headed an excellent goal.

Our elation was short lived however, for five minutes later Bromley had equalized through George Brown. Ruddy, their outside-left, beat

Ralph Cowan and cut in to the goal-line. As I left George Brown to challenge Ruddy he slipped the ball back to the Bromley centre-forward who side-footed the ball first time into the left-hand corner of our net. Looking now at a photograph of that goal it would seem that I had hardly left the side of Brown. In fact the centre-forward had checked in his run in, timing it to perfection and Ruddy, looking for him, had knocked it across early. So simple, so effective.

But then their elation was short lived, for within two minutes we were ahead again.

A quick, retaliatory break down our right found Bromley's defence stretched. Pawson shot. Cornthwaite could only punch the ball away, but not cleanly. The ball bounced awkwardly for the Bromley right-back, and Potts, beating him in a race for possession, shot into their empty net as Cornthwaite came out. A somewhat fortuitous goal, but it put us in the lead and by half-time we were still one up.

As we sat in the changing-room, everyone delighted, I cannot recall any constructive advice being given. But there was plenty of encouragement, not least from Chedder Wilson, who had somehow got in and was going round armed with his orange and that lethal penknife.

Five minutes after the restart Bromley had drawn level again. Tommy Hopper, their England inside-right, seizing upon a loose ball had, in a flash, hit an unstoppable twenty-five yarder. Now, aided by the strong wind, our opponents began to pressurize us in earnest. Their style of play differed from ours. We tended to push the ball about more and keep it on the ground. They tended to use the long ball, sweeping it out to their wingers or thumping it up the middle to George Brown, whom I found increasingly difficult to hold in the air.

And then it happened. A dangerous swirling cross came over from the left and I went up for it. Even as I jumped I knew I had mistimed it badly. I knew also that Brown was right on the back of me and the roar of delight that rose from the Bromley supporters told me the worst: he had made no mistake. My heart sank and I cursed myself for being the victim of such an elementary mistake, one that I had been so determined not to make.

But they weren't ahead for long. Again Cornthwaite could only parry another fierce cross from Tony Pawson and John Tanner was on hand to make the score three all.

Five minutes from time they took the lead yet once again through Martin their outside-right, and now things were really desperate for us. Even so we weren't finished. Jimmy Potts, looking for chances and as lively as a cricket, fastened on to the ball some twenty yards out and let fly with his left foot, the ball smashing the goal post. An inch to the right and we would have been level again. Nor was that the end of our challenge. Right on time a brilliant bout of short passing brought our forwards and wing-halves swarming into the Bromley penalty area. A fierce cry for hands rose spontaneously from the crowd behind the goal.

But the match was over. We were out. And as I shook hands with George Brown I knew exactly how the Enfield centre-forward had felt.

It remained but to ponder on what might have been and wait for the press reports on the morrow. There was naturally a strong sense of anti-climax and disappointment, the taste of which seems always particularly bitter on waking the following morning. But it all passes and we had much to be thankful for and to look forward to.

Tommy had proved his point beyond doubt. We had won the respect of the amateur world of soccer and would gain exemption next year. The press had said some very nice things about us all. Despite my mistimed header I had been favourably compared with Charlie Fuller and there was mention of international honours for some of us.

As for Bromley? They went on to play at Wembley before a crowd of 93,000 and won the Amateur Cup of 1949.

And Pegasus? Why, we had spread our wings and taken flight.

5 Aspects of Amateurism

Well before the spring of 1949, Biddie had regained her health and strength and we were able to walk together once more in the grounds of Blenheim, pushing Paul in his pram, accompanied by Kim.

That Easter I went with the Oxford side to Holland, where we stayed in Amsterdam at the hotel Krasnopolsky. There we took part in a tournament comprising the now famous Dutch side Ajax, Le Stade Dudelange from Luxemburg, the Swiss side Biel, and ourselves.

On paper it all looked rather formidable. In practice it certainly was. To make matters worse, John Tanner, who had played in an Arthur Dunn match just prior to the tour, had again been troubled with the same injury that had plagued him in the Bromley cup-tie. Since we were short of forwards and Tommy was anxious that we should make a good impression in our first match against Biel, he persuaded John to play, much against the latter's inclination, having first taken Denis, Tony and myself aside, and given us his considered opinion that Tanner was fast becoming a neurotic.

In the light of events we did well to draw with Biel, but John, who somehow got through the game, ruptured the quadraceps of his right leg so badly that the muscle never properly knit together, but built up round the side of his thigh.

There was much muttering of 'nicht fair play' overheard later that night from the Swiss contingent who were staying in the same centrally-heated oven of an hotel as ourselves and had sampled Rob at his most ferocious.

Walter Crook, once captain of Blackburn Rovers, now the Ajax coach, gave us all the help he could, which included a hard training session without a ball. But in the end we were no match for Ajax, who won the tournament while we finished up with the wooden spoon. On the last evening, all four teams sat down to a big dinner at which Tommy made a speech in German that was not only well received but did a little, I thought, to compensate for our somewhat undistinguished performance.

So the season ended and we returned to England and the summer term, feeling more than a little weary, none more so than Denis Saunders.

As in the previous year, I was invited to attend the early cricket nets, this time with more success. The new Oxford captain was a South African, Clive van Ryneveld, and coaching in the nets was George Pope.

'Watch for the back of his wrist. He can't bowl a googly without showing it,' said George, seeing I was having difficulty keeping wicket and spotting Clive's 'wrong 'un'. 'Well, watch his elbow then,' he called from the bowler's end, as I went the wrong way again. 'He can't bowl a googly without bending his arm,' and he came down behind the net and read each ball that Clive bowled. He could read and play the spinners as well as anyone in the country.

I had first met George when he'd bowled to me in the Derbyshire nets in the late thirties, when the county had such players as Tommy Mitchell, Stan Worthington, the two Pope brothers, George and Alf, Dennis Smith and Harry Elliot, to mention a few of that championship side.

As boys we would go down in the Easter holidays and be coached by the Derbyshire players under the eagle eye of that dour, terrifying little old cricketer, Sam Cadman. He would wear an old-fashioned cap with a small peak which did nothing to hide a fierce face, mottled and purple. I was happily walking one fine morning in 1938 down the long unattractive approach to the Derbyshire cricket ground with a friend, John Keatinge, who was to become Senior Commoner Prefect at Winchester and win a scholarship to Cambridge. Very sadly he never reached the university for he was killed near Caen in 1944 when the turret of his tank received a direct hit from an 88 millimetre. He had just gained his commission and was serving as an officer with the Second Armoured Battalion of the Irish Guards.

I suppose, to be more accurate we were just sauntering along on this occasion, carrying our bats and pads over our shoulders, when suddenly Sam Cadman (looking like an enraged Mr. Punch) assembled the Derbyshire players hands on hips roared in our direction, 'You just take your time gentlemen, don't you trouble to 'urry yerselves.' We hurried then all right. Myself straight into a net where I had a most uncomfortable half-hour trying to obey Sam Cadman's repeated instruction to, 'Get yer foot to the ball, get yer head over it', as I

36

strove to play a young and lively fast bowler, Bert Rhodes, who eventually changed to a leg spinner when Tommy Mitchell gave up.

George Pope did all he could to help me in those early Oxford nets, and before he left assured me that I should get into the side. How much influence he had I'm not sure, but I was selected to play against Gloucester in the first match and fared none too badly. I caught two, stumped two and made 28. But I still found Clive van Ryneveld's googly difficult to read, and to facilitate matters he'd give me a pre-arranged indication of when he was going to bowl it.

I played in the next match against Worcester and then, out of the blue, I had an invitation to go as one of three reserves on an F.A. tour to the Channel Islands, the first since the war. I was in a quandary. The F.A. side was a strong one, containing four top professionals, Len Duquemin of Spurs, Jim Taylor and Joe Bacuzzi of Fulham (the Fulham side had just won the Second Division Championship) and George Curtis of Arsenal. Both Len Duquemin and Jim Taylor had been capped for England. Denis Saunders and Jimmy Potts had been selected to play and were going, so I would have company. The tour was from 7th May to the 12th, bang in the middle of the next match against Leicester. I sought Tommy's advice and he urged me to go on the tour as he thought it would stand me in good stead for an amateur cap. So after informing Clive, I decided to go, hoping that it would not jeopardize my chance of getting back into the Oxford cricket side.

Unfortunately, the F.A. lost the first match against Jersey, and the selectors, not unnaturally, decided to keep Jim Taylor in at centre-half for it was imperative that the F.A. put up a better show against Guernsey, which they did, winning narrowly. Our trainer, Jack Jennings, advised me not to go on and play out of position for half a match, which was what it would have meant. So heeding his advice, I sat on the touchline for both matches and on reading the paper discovered that Ian Campbell, who had come in as wicket-keeper, had scored 43 against Leicester. When I read a little later an article in the *Daily Telegraph* stating that Oxford could well have a trump card up their sleeve in Ian Campbell, a big, bold hitter, I knew I'd had my chips. Apart then from two enjoyable sea passages, the presentation of a small replica of a Channel Island urn, and my dubious assistance to Joe Bacuzzi in judging a beauty competition, I neither achieved nor contributed very much to that tour.

I never got back into the Oxford side, though I made a few runs,

37

including a 65 out of 140 for a strong 'A' eleven against Jim Swanton's Arabs.

Now Jim Swanton, as everyone knows, is as good a writer and authority on cricket as anyone in the world. He is a big, dominant character, and in 1949, as cricket and rugby correspondent of the *Daily Telegraph*, he wielded considerable influence at Oxford, and to me epitomized the establishment in these two sports.

I remember particularly one evening having coffee in the top room of Vincent's Club when Jim came in.

'Tell me now, Ken,' he began, his presence filling the room, 'what's all this I hear about Pegasus?'

I don't think that he meant to be patronizing, but he knew and I knew, that for many years soccer had not had the same status at the universities as rugby and cricket, and in this context I felt he was having a slight 'dig', and I felt irritated. 'Well, Jim,' I said, 'it's a club composed of Oxford and Cambridge players who have just been knocked out of the quarter-finals of the Amateur Cup before the biggest crowd that has ever watched a match in the history of Oxford.' He looked at me for a moment.

'Quite something,' he said with sonorous amusement, and somehow that did it.

'Yes,' I replied, now truly nettled, 'it was. And what's more Jim—who knows? Perhaps one day we might win the Cup, and if we do we shan't be playing at jolly old Twickenham, but at Wembley, the premier stadium in the world, so you'd better come along and see for yourself.'

'I will indeed,' said Jim with another deep chuckle which promptly started me off again.

'It's about time cricket took a leaf out of soccer's book because otherwise the game's soon going to be as dead as a dodo. You want to have a knock-out competition on an over basis with a Cup Final at Lords so that the crowds can come and take their shirts off and wave their rattles and banners and shout and enjoy themselves.' And this time he laughed me out of court, assured me with the utmost confidence that it would never happen, and promptly bought me a drink.

I wanted to go on and say a lot more, but it would have taken too long, and at the end I would probably not have made my point. However, I hope the reader will bear with me now if I digress for a moment to reflect just why soccer in 1949 did not have the same status as rugby and cricket at Oxford and Cambridge. The short and immediate answer of course is that in soccer the professional had got under way and the amateur had been outpaced. But that is only to state the obvious and ignore the great part that the amateur had played in the game. So briefly, back to the beginning.

From the 1860s to the 1880s, the amateur clubs such as Oxford University, the Old Etonians, Old Carthusians, the Wanderers, the Royal Engineers, the Swifts and Clapham Rovers, reigned supreme, having won the F.A. Cup regularly between 1872 and 1883, the last victory of all in that year going to the Old Etonians. After that the great amateur clubs of the south never again got their names on the trophy, for the F.A. Cup's entry had increased in that first decade from 15 to 100 clubs. The professionals had arrived; from then on it was to be their Cup.

However, this was by no means the end of the matter for in 1893–4 the amateur was revived and given a new interest by the institution of the F.A. Amateur Cup. In that first final of 1894 the Old Carthusians beat the Casuals. In the following year Middlesbrough (the same Middlesbrough that we know today, but then amateur) beat the Old Carthusians. The Carthusians won again in 1897, but after that, apart from the victory of the Old Malvernians over Bishop Auckland in 1902, the old boy sides disappeared even from this new competition.

So, as the years passed the old boy clubs and the universities, who had been the founders and once masters of the game, superseded by professionalism, now found themselves in competition with a 'new' type of amateur, the working-class player as opposed to the middle and upper-middle-class. And feeling that the Amateur Cup had become the be-all and the end-all for certain types of clubs, sixteen of them banded together in 1903 to form their own exclusive old boy competition, the Arthur Dunn Cup.

There were now three strata in the game. The professional; the school, university and old-boy type of player; and the working-class amateur, the 'shamateur', imitating the professional with varying results, and often given some form of remuneration.

Upon this developing scene the Corinthians made their great impact and contribution to the game. Founded in 1882 and composed of old boy and university players, they became the most powerful side in the country. Had they entered the F.A. Cup there is no doubt that they would have run away with the trophy more than once in those days when the rest of the amateur clubs had fallen behind. But rule seven of their constitution read : 'the Club shall not compete for any challenge cup or prize of any description whatever.'

So strong were these Corinthians that in 1894 their complete side represented England against Wales at Wrexham, winning 5–1. Perhaps the most famous victory of all was their 10–3 defeat of the full Bury side, the Cup-holders, on 5 March 1904, Bury having beaten Derby County in the final of the F.A. Cup 6–0.

In 1923 the Corinthians altered their rules and entered the F.A. Cup for the first time, but without much success. The most sensational and thrilling game they played was against Newcastle United in the fourth round of 1927, having previously beaten Walsall 4–0. Fifty-six thousand spectators in the old Crystal Palace ground saw the cream of the amateur game, leading by one goal with fourteen minutes of the match left, lose 3–1 to the cream of the professional world, who were at that moment leaders of the League First Division. But by the thirties the slide was well on and all the glory that was Corinth had crumbled away, a sad end to a great saga.

Somewhere along this line the soccer public schools and Oxford and Cambridge were very slow to adopt a more professional approach and seek advice from their new masters. I am tempted to suspect, particularly in the thirties, that the distinct working-class connotation of soccer had something to do with it all. Most public schools had cricket professionals to help in the coaching, but then the amateur in cricket was still in command captaining his county and country, for command still remained as in most walks of English life an amateur occupation. And rugby? They have never had any problem in this respect. Abhorring professionalism, they have set their own standards, their own ceiling, an artificial one, but truly amateur. And this is the crux of the matter. The perfection of rugby as it now stands is a myth. Association football by its professionalism has left rugby behind in the fullest exploitation of the game as an art. Here lies the great difference between soccer and rugby as played at their top levels.

To imagine in 1949 that an Oxford or Cambridge soccer Blue might possibly be selected for the full England professional side was as absurd then as it would be today. Yet an Oxford or Cambridge rugby Blue has always had every chance of playing for his country. Had one over the years compared the standard of soccer and rugby as played in the public schools and universities, there would have been little difference one way or the other.

40

In the mid-twenties and throughout the thirties there began a new development. A number of schools turned from soccer to rugby, a trend coming upon Cyril Norwood's proposal to the Headmasters' Conference that all schools should change to rugby. In 1929 he followed this up with an extraordinary attack on association football in his book, *The English Tradition of Education*, in which he wrote :

When rugby becomes 'rough' or 'unfair', the game is ruined; it is one of its many merits that it can only be played by those who are in the real sense of the word gentlemen. It is a test of character.

There are those, however, who would raise the claims of the rival code of association football as the best, because at present it is the most popular game, and who deplore the fact that more and more schools desert association for rugby on the ground that it is bringing class distinctions into a national game. Association football is a good game, but it is not so good a game as rugby for the education of boys; it does not require the same speed, endurance, courage or chivalry. It has, as a game, been almost entirely ruined by the professionalism which dominates it, and professionalism is the complete antithesis to the English tradition of sport. What is to be desired in the interests of the true athletic tradition of the country is that more and more schools should take up rugby, prove themselves morally and physically fit to play the game in the spirit in which it should be played, and never on any consideration whatever allow a breath of professionalism to come into it.

Of course those in education are bound to have their own views on the relative merit of soccer or rugby as a school game—though it is astonishing that even today the choice of rugger is often justified on grounds of expediency : thirty boys to a pitch instead of twenty-two!

However, I cannot help but feel that somewhere lurking behind Cyril Norwood's dogmatic and harmful assertion lay a deep sense of alarm that soccer had been so eagerly and successfully seized upon by the mass of the population. J. B. Priestley, in his book, *The Edwardians,* writes critically of that large section of the upper-middle-class, who both before and after the First World War preferred rugby to soccer, because the 'latter game had been enthusiastically adopted by the working class'.

The social implications of the relation between the two games are there for all to see. It is not surprising therefore that the universities in the thirties and the forties—middle class to the core—made rugby their game. Fortunately soccer has succeeded in losing its class connotation. In the words of A. J. P. Taylor, it has proved to be 'the most democratic game' which 'united all classes'. Perhaps we at Oxford

41

in 1949 couldn't so clearly see this process in operation and felt unjustifiably patronized by the rugby pundits.

It was against this background Pegasus emerged.

Good cricketers were ten-a-penny at Oxford and Cambridge during those years. To mention but one, D. B. Carr in 1949 scored nearly five hundred runs in his first three matches against Leicester, Gloucester and Middlesex, and three years later the Cambridge side contained no less than six test players. There was never any question of either university not being able to hold their own in the world of professional cricket, so very different from the university soccer situation.

One explanation for this is that there are far fewer professionals in cricket than in soccer and the opportunities to play cricket are not equally distributed. Middle-class boys are well equipped and well coached, first at their preparatory schools, then at their public schools, where the conditions and the coaching advantages are infinitely superior to anything that the state schools can hope to offer. Another indisputable fact is that it requires money to play cricket, thus putting the game beyond the reach of naturally talented working-class boys, always of course excepting those in Lancashire and Yorkshire, who reach the game through their distinct league system. Had there been more facilities, money, and coaching available, as well as a more realistic approach at the top—akin to those counties already mentioned—the standard of English cricket would have risen and the amateur been eclipsed, just as surely as he had been in association football.

I had kept wicket a few times for the Derbyshire second side and towards the end of June 1949 played my one and only first class match for the county against Gloucester down at Bristol. I found myself staying in a different hotel from the rest of the team along with the two other amateurs in the Derbyshire side, David Skinner, the captain, and Laurie Johnson. During the match we changed in a different room and ate at a different table, though I think the food was the same.

As for the match—it was a disastrous affair and we lost by an innings and one run, my contribution, a single crude blow for four off Tom Goddard, which promptly caused the Gloucester captain, B. O. Allen, who was fielding at silly mid-on, to belch loudly in my left ear whereupon I was bowled the next ball. However, the crowd

42

did get its money's worth once when a swarm of bees descended around the fiery head of Bill Copson who, flailing his arms and using fearful expletives, set off at an astonishing rate for the pavilion, urged on by cries of 'Windy! . . . windy!' from a delighted crowd. Surprisingly, I was invited to play in the next match against Kent, at Ilkeston, but declined as we had tickets for a Commemoration Ball.

Looking back on it all, I now rather regret that I did not take the game more seriously, though I would not have enjoyed the extraordinary segregation of amateur and professional that was still in existence. But I had too much on my plate really. I was a married undergraduate with a child. I'd already played a great deal of football and cricket at Oxford, and there was a good deal more football still to come; it was my first love. And always nagging away quietly at the back of everything was the fact that in nine months' time I had to sit my Finals.

I tried hard to work seriously that long vacation, sitting in one of the rooms at the top of the Lodge, the old house where Biddie's mother still lived and where we stayed for most of that summer.

Through the open window I could hear the distant sound of tractors and see across the vale of Evesham to the Tower on top of Broadway Hill. I read and noted and put in the hours, but I seemed to make no headway. As the days and weeks slipped by, my efforts served only to make me increasingly aware of my appalling ignorance, and how short was the time that lay ahead.

6 The One-Year Rule

Refreshed from a short holiday in the West Country we returned to Woodstock in September 1949 to learn that Denis Saunders was in the Osler Hospital at Headington with chest trouble.

I rang Tommy at once.

'Hello,' his voice was as flat and expressionless as ever.

'Ken here.'

'Ye . . . s,' he never made the running in a telephone conversation.

'How's Denis?'

'We . . . ll,' and there followed a good deal of coughing at the other end. 'I'm afraid he's not at all well.' He spoke in solemn, measured tones, his words almost a drawl, his Yorkshire inflection unmistakable. 'He'll certainly not play football this year and I think it's very unlikely he'll ever play again.'

'Oh dear,' I said.

'Ye . . .s,' said Tommy, 'it's all most unfortunate; we'll just have to wait and see,' and he began coughing again.

'And how's Penelope?' I asked.

'Oh, she's all right . . . but I've not been at all well.'

'I'm sorry to hear that Tommy.' I smiled, this was routine stuff.

'And I'm not at all happy about the way things are going with Pegasus. I'm convinced we've got to get rid of this one-year rule if we're ever going to do anything as a club. Still we'll talk about all that later. You and Biddie all right?'

'Yes, we're fine.'

'That's good . . . g'bye,' and before I could reply he had hung up.

I went into the sitting-room and sat by the fire which we had lit, for the evening was chill.

'Any news about Denis?' Biddie asked.

'Not really. He was X-rayed and they found a spot on his lung. It's now a question of rest and treatment.'

'Poor Denis,' she said.

And I nodded and began to think how much we would miss his quiet personality and skilful control in midfield. And then I considered

Tommy's words about the one-year rule, which had first been questioned at an Extraordinary General Meeting of the club, held on Saturday, 9 April 1949, when the club still had no rules.

It came up again shortly afterwards when Tommy had received a letter from the wife of the club's president, dated 26 April, in which she wrote :

Edgehill,
Heathfield.
April 26th 1949.

Dear Dr. Thompson,

My husband is still in bed after his pneumonia and so will be unable to attend the meeting on Saturday. He wants me to say that he feels very strongly that the rule of qualification for only one year after going down should be altered at once, otherwise the club will die a natural death in a very few years. He asks me to ask you if you will convey his congratulations to the team upon the magnificent start they have made.

With kind regards,
Yours sincerely,
C. May Hunt

On the 27th the Reverend Kenneth Hunt died.

Two days later, the committee met at the East India and Sports Club where Graham Doggart took the chair and spoke of the very sad and unexpected death of our first president. After this it was agreed unanimously to invite A. H. Chadder to become the new president until the next Annual General Meeting. And then Tommy read out the letter he had received from Mrs. Hunt, and the cat, so to speak, was well and truly out of the bag.

There followed a long discussion on the eligibility of players, and at the end it was agreed by the Cambridge members, who at first wished to retain the one-year rule, that there was a good case for its removal. In order to allow members further time for consideration the matter was deferred to the next meeting at the East India and Sports Club, where on 16 June 1949, a memorandum from the Corinthian-Casuals F.C. was submitted by W. H. Webster. Once again it was decided to defer the whole matter for later consideration at the next meeting to be held in October.

In fact the committee met on 17 September, without the presence of Tommy, who was in America, or Graham Doggart. John Tanner took Tommy's place as acting honorary secretary.

Again the one-year rule was thoroughly discussed and views aired. Hubert Doggart thought that it was necessary to ensure that the undergraduate influence in the club was retained and that it remained essentially a university rather than an ex-university organization. Jimmy Potts and Ralph Cowan felt that there was a good case for allowing those who had been down for more than one year to play for the club in cup-ties where this was advisable, for the sake of securing the best club side possible and where the position of the Corinthian-Casuals was not affected. F. G. I. Packington and W. H. Webster both thought that there was reason in this argument, but asked for assurances that their club (the Corinthian-Casuals) would be specifically protected in any change of rules which might be made.

But by the end of the meeting still nothing had been decided. All that was clearly and rather painfully emerging was a steadily growing difference of opinion concerning this question of the one-year rule.

Such was the situation at the start of the Michaelmas term of 1949.

We played our first match of the season against Aylesbury Town on a bone hard ground. Jimmy Potts had taken over from Denis Saunders as captain of the Oxford side and I was secretary, not a very effective one, though it was not altogether my fault, for an injury put me out of the game for six weeks.

I had gone up for a ball and received a severe blow on the side of my head; I think it was an elbow. I recall a bright flash and momentary bewilderment. But I was able to carry on all right and went home with nothing more than a considerable swelling and a dull ache.

The following day I still had a headache and feeling listless and tired I went down to Iffley Road in the afternoon to train and perhaps get rid of it that way. It was raining hard and I did a few laps to start with. As I jogged slowly round behind the goal a ball came over and automatically I went up and headed it back on to the pitch. It shook me considerably, for the ball was wet and heavy.

When I awoke next morning my headache was no better and I could not sleep. That afternoon the doctor called and I was examined and told I had concussion and was to stay in bed. Two days later I was still no better and sleeping badly. I began to wonder whether perhaps I had something worse than concussion and with this in mind I turned to the *Home Book of Medicine* to see what light that could throw on my condition. Reading the chapter on head injuries and the brain, my consternation mounted in leaps and bounds till finally I came to the alarming conclusion that I was suffering from nothing less than a brain tumour.

46

'What do you think's the matter with me?' I asked our pleasant but rather serious Wykhamist doctor when he called the second time.

'I'm not sure,' he replied truthfully.

'Could it be a tumour?'

His eye caught sight of the *Home Book of Medicine* lying on the floor at the side of our bed. And suddenly he was not at all amused. 'So you've been reading that rubbish,' he remarked angrily, kicking the book under the bed.

I nodded and smiled weakly. 'But why doesn't this headache go?'

He looked at me gravely for a moment, and somehow I rather wished I had not asked him.

'You could have a blood clot,' he said quietly.

'Good God,' I said, now thoroughly alarmed.

'I'm going to send you by ambulance this afternoon to see a "nut-cracker", a brain specialist,' he explained. 'I shouldn't worry if I were you,' he added, leaving the room.

But then of course he wasn't, and I certainly did worry. I worried all morning, bemoaning my fate and predicting to my long-suffering wife that this was it and I probably would never make the return journey.

'Of course you will,' she assured me, as I was lifted into the same old ambulance that had conveyed her to the Radcliffe nine months earlier.

On arrival at the hospital I was taken on a stretcher and put behind a curtain on the other side of which someone was either having a baby or some sort of a fit. My heart beat madly and my imagination ran riot as I lay and listened, and suddenly I wasn't at all sure whether I had a headache or not. After what seemed a very long time they wheeled me away to have my head X-rayed, after which I was trundled back to my curtained compartment where I was asked some more questions and eventually allowed to go. Greatly relieved, I was just being pushed back into the ambulance when somebody rushed out and said they wanted to re-examine me.

So once more I found myself back in the curtained-off area. 'We'd like to see you tomorrow,' said the man in the white coat when he'd finished his examination, and then I was taken out and pushed finally into the ambulance.

That night, propped up in bed, I slept very little and my headache was severe.

The following morning I was duly carried off again to the Radcliffe where this time I saw the key 'nutcracker' himself. He examined me quietly and with immense authority which impressed me deeply.

'You've got a bruised brain, Mr. Shearwood,' he said when he'd finished. 'It will take time. Could be a few days, could be a few weeks, could be even longer. Just like any other internal bruise it will eventually disappear. When it does you can carry on quite normally.'

'I can play football?'

'Yes. As soon as it goes you can play. But until it does, stay at home and take things quietly.'

Very relieved I thanked him and was carried back to the ambulance.

Later that evening the telephone rang.

'How is he?' asked Donald Carr.

'He's fine,' said Biddie, 'they've X-rayed his brain and found nothing there.'

'What—nothing at all?' remarked Donald, incredulous and delighted.

'No, nothing at all,' she assured him, which startling piece of news promptly spread through Vincents and elsewhere.

For four long weeks I suffered a severe headache and crept about the house feeling ill and weak and thoroughly wretched. The nights were the worst. I could do no reading. Tommy, Jimmy Potts, John Tanner and others came out to see us and tell me how the Oxford side was faring. And as the days and weeks passed I began to wonder if I ever would play again. And then one night I fell into a deep sleep and when I woke it was as though my head had suddenly been released from the grip of a steel band.

'It's gone,' I said to Biddie, 'it's completely gone. I feel a new man.'

'I know,' she said coming into the room with Paul in her arms. 'I watched you sleeping, you've had a really good night.'

And I put on my dressing-gown and went down and made a cup of tea.

I had just over three weeks to get fit before we played Cambridge, so I began training straight away. I also began trying to catch up on my work. Eric Collieu had been in touch and insisted that I was not to start unless I was really feeling all right. I never told him just how much his kindness meant.

By 3 December I was fit again, and ready to play against Cambridge at Tottenham where this time we drew. The match had hardly begun when I received a severe blow on the head trying to win a ball in the air, and just for one awful moment I wondered if there was not to be a repeat performance, but all was well.

Jimmy Potts, who had already won a cap for England, had a very good match jinking away on the flank, nibbling at their defence, but I knew I had not particularly distinguished myself. For Cambridge, Ralph Cowan played beautifully at centre-half and I admired his mastery. But there was little doubt we missed the cool influence of Denis in mid-field, and when the final whistle blew I felt we were slightly fortunate to have drawn the match.

Later that afternoon an Annual General Meeting of the Pegasus F.C. was held at the Public Schools' Club, and there the rules of Pegasus, which had been drafted and circulated by the committee on the 17th of September, were discussed and amended in such a way as to clarify the position of players who had been down from their universities for more than one year. Many members expressed their views that players should be free to play for either the Corinthian-Casuals or Pegasus, according to their personal wishes, and the rule was modified to read as follows :

All members shall be eligible to play for the club, but it shall be the policy of the selection committee to choose primarily those players who are either resident in their university or who went down the previous season. It shall be clearly understood that the Corinthian-Casuals F.C. shall have the prior right to request the services of players who have been down from the universities for more than one year and who are members of both clubs, in the event of the selection committee wishing to play them. The final decision rests with the player himself.

Much was to hinge on that last sentence.

Five days later Paul celebrated his first birthday and before we knew it Christmas was upon us and another year was drawing rapidly to its close—but not before we had spent its last few days on a football tour based at Torquay, in preparation for our next venture in the Amateur Cup. The club had played only three matches since our defeat by Bromley the previous February. The first was against the Cup-holders, on their ground. We lost 2–0. We won the other two games against Moor Green and Henley Town.

The tour began with a win against the Amateur Football Alliance at Finchley. I had badly turned my ankle and could not play in this game. But at Barnstaple, where we lost 3–1 on the last day of 1949, I strapped it up and captained the side. I should never have played. The ankle was thick and full of adhesions and I sweated every time

49

I touched the ball with my right foot, let alone tackled. That night, donning our dinner jackets, we danced the old year out and the new year in.

The following morning we gathered round a billiard table with Tommy, Graham Doggart, and Harvey Chadder, to discuss tactics. There was a good deal of talk and demonstration with billiard balls, which became not a little out of hand, particularly when Mike Bishop hurtled the pink across the table to jump the pocket, narrowly missing Tommy, who had to be persuaded later that it was not a personal attempt on his life by the Cambridge contingent.

I made a suggestion that we should appoint a professional coach who should dictate policy.

'We never had a coach,' said Graham Doggart smiling, his manner was gentle and courteous as ever. I never saw him put out. He and Harvey Chadder had played at the end of the great Corinthian era, the latter marking and holding Hughie Gallacher, the famous Scottish international in that Corinthian versus Newcastle United cup-tie of 1927. But I could not see the logic of Graham's statement and suggested again that if we had a coach it would end any tactical differences of opinion that might exist amongst the players. Tommy had that old foxy look about him and I could see he was not going to commit himself. Not surprisingly we got nowhere.

I could not play in the last match of the tour against Torquay United, which we lost 4–1. But when I got back to Woodstock, Biddie, by profession a masseuse, worked on my ankle and I was able to play against Morris Motors in the Oxfordshire Senior Cup, a match which we won by six clear goals.

A week later we met Erith and Belvedere in the first round of the Amateur Cup on their ground. Of all pitches that I have played on this was the stickiest and heaviest. In such conditions the ball has got to be whacked about; too much of the short frilly stuff courts disaster. That day we tended to play some of this and very nearly paid the penalty. Only a single goal by Tony Pawson kept us still in the Cup.

I was so tired that I could hardly pull myself aboard the bus. As the game wore on it had become a physical effort to lift one's feet from the cloying mud. Our forwards were small and we relied on the strength of Doug Insole and the skill of Norman Kerruish to spray the ball about. Above all we missed the penetrating thrust of John Tanner, who was injured.

50

On the next Saturday before a capacity crowd on the Oxford City ground (the Iffley Road ground was having a running track put round it and being levelled), we defeated Erith and Belvedere in the replay 5–2, Potts and Tanner scoring two apiece and Insole one.

In the second round we drew Walthamstow Avenue away—a really stiff hurdle—and Doug Insole, who had played for Walthamstow, was able to give us a lot of information about the London side. But on the day it availed us nothing. Despite an early goal by Tanner, we lost 3–1 and were out with a bang. Once again I had allowed Turner, their centre-forward, to get on the back of me to score with his head from a Lewis cross.

I had played against Walthamstow two years earlier when on tour with the Yorkshire Amateurs and marked Doug Insole, but my chief impression then and now had been the skill of this semi-professional side and the ugliness of their ground, dominated at one end by a great towering block of flats which did nothing to alleviate my sinking spirit as we made our exit from the Amateur Cup of 1950 on that bleak afternoon at the end of January.

But we still had something to play for—the Oxfordshire Senior Cup—and this we went on to win, defeating Osberton Radiators, Headington United (now Oxford United), and Chipping Norton 5–0 in the final, though only after a replay, both games played on the Iffley Road Rugby Ground. It was our first trophy.

7 Finals

Barely five months now remained before I sat my Finals and only too painfully I was aware of the fact. The very thought of entering those grim Examination Schools and writing for twenty hours and more sent shivers down my spine and filled me with alarm and despondency. My scalp literally prickled when I reflected how little I had done, how little I knew, how much lay ahead.

I'd been gently reminded of the last fact by Sonners (Dr. W. T. S. Stallybrass), the Principal of Brasenose College, at that first Collection in 1947, when every undergraduate appeared in the hall before the Principal and Fellows to hear his tutor report publicly on his progress.

I met Sonners only once more, this time informally on a week's cricket tour in Devon with the Strollers, his Brasenose side of undergraduates. I remember the tour chiefly because, celebrating after making 80 against Sidmouth in the first match, I was apprehended, along with Tim Whitehead and Nevill Acheson-Gray, the following evening in the village of Beer by a friendly and bucolic member of the Devon constabulary. I was charged with having purloined a 'shrub in a tub', and driving it away on the bonnet of my jeep—a charge I could not in all honesty deny.

Later, when facing a belligerent and slightly alcoholic Sidmouth sergeant of police, who began with a long and lurid account of what Sir Archibald Bodkin, the magistrate, would have in store for us at the local bench, the six legal brains of the Strollers, who had accompanied me to the police station, rose magnificently to my defence. Summoning their wits and using every conceivable form of legal jargon, they so impressed the astonished and bemused sergeant that in no time a compromise had been reached, all was forgiven and the undamaged 'shrub in a tub' duly conveyed once more on the bonnet of my jeep back to its proper place of residence by the side of the Sidmouth Hotel's front door, with abject apologies to the management.

Tragically, on 29 October 1948, Sonners mistakenly opened the carriage door when returning on a late London to Oxford train and fell to his death, an error attributed to failing eyesight and extreme fatigue.

Now, two years later I faced Hugh Last (Sonner's successor) at my last Collection before Finals, and was reminded once again how much lay ahead, how short was the time that remained. It was a warning I acknowledged with as much assurance as I could muster, in a vain attempt to hide my acute embarrassment and feeling of real despair—for at that stage I did not even know for certain which king succeeded which.

I was faced with two alternatives. Carry on as I had been doing, nibbling away at the subject but never getting anywhere, or make one great assault on the work. I decided on the latter and made my plans.

First I determined that each day I would write down exactly the number of hours and minutes that I had sat reading. My target was to work six hours a day without exception. If I could do more, so much the better, but on no account was any day to be missed, Sundays included. I would start at seven each morning, do two hours before breakfast, have a break, do another two between ten and twelve and a couple more between two and four in the afternoon. That left plenty of time to find several hours more in the day if I felt like it. But above all the routine must never be broken. On paper it looked easy.

Next I had to organize an up-to-date but minimum bibliography that would cover the syllabus thoroughly. I had no time to read round the subject. Every corner must be cut. Here Martin Moriarty was a great help and so were Tony Pawson and Jimmy Potts, the latter particularly so, for he generously allowed me to borrow his book of essays for a week, each essay beautifully written in immaculate longhand. I wanted to copy them all out but it would have taken hours and there just wasn't the time to spare. So I called on our solicitor in Woodstock and asked if I could borrow his secretary.

'She's doing rather a lot of work for me at the moment,' he said, 'but I can get them done for you.'

'Within a week?'

'Yes.'

'Then go ahead.'

Back they promptly came, typed in triplicate, complete with a bill that I had not bargained for. Twenty-six pounds!

I decided to do all my work up in the top attic, seated by the window from where I could perhaps gain some solace and inspiration from the distant statue of Marlborough. I began the assault immediately on our return from the New Year Tour.

Each morning the alarm went off at half-past six and well before seven I was up in the attic doing the necessary reading to cover the first paper of English history.

At first my task seemed insurmountable, but gradually I got into the swing of working and ever so slightly I began to make some progress. But there were often ugly moments of black despair when I felt I was getting nowhere and the centuries of reading that lay ahead stretched interminably. At such times I would get up and go for a walk or take a bath before going back to the books.

And ever so gradually I found I was beginning to enjoy my work and when at the end of each day I came to write down the exact hours and minutes I had sat reading, I even began to feel slightly virtuous!

A genuine six hours of reading and noting I quickly discovered took some doing, but in no time I was managing eight hours a day and more, only easing off on a Saturday if I had a match. Even then I would manage several hours in the morning and probably an hour or two in the evening. Sundays were no exception for I was determined that I would have not one day's rest until the examinations were over.

Soon I actually looked forward to climbing the steep flight of narrow wooden stairs at the start of each day. And as the mornings grew lighter, the birds sang earlier and the first green shoots of another spring appeared, came hope and a growing confidence that despite the acres of reading that still lay ahead, I might yet digest the pile of books that surrounded my chair in time to pass my Finals.

At most week-ends Martin Moriarty would come out and we'd discuss the Chartists and the Docker's Tanner and Keir Hardie as we walked along the road that leads north to Chipping Norton. I learned much from Martin, who was interested in the early days of the labour movement.

I never went near the Parks or opened my cricket bag, and as I sat on the top of the bus on my weekly tutorial visit to Oxford I'd take from my inside pocket a packet of white postcards that I always carried with me, on which I had made neat précis of all Potts' twenty essays. These I would read, committing to memory, only putting them away when the bus reached the tree-lined Woodstock Road, for then I liked to look down at the big square houses, their gardens now colourful and summery beneath the various shades of fresh foliage.

I read, noted, and re-read Rousseau, Hobbes, and Aristotle, until

I understood something of the philosophy and flaws of their arguments. And the more I worked the more virtuous I felt until I could almost feel the halo about my head! I had now reached the stage when I wanted to put myself to the test. I no longer feared the examination, in fact I looked forward to it.

May was drawing to a close. John Tanner, much to his disgust, had got a third in history and was now working at the Oxford Appointments' Board. I knew he was mildly curious about my outcome. I hadn't seen much of Denis Saunders, but the news was encouraging. Donald Carr was making runs in the Parks and Ben Brown, who had got a first in science, was now doing research work at Oxford. Tony Pawson, who had just missed a first, was teaching at Winchester, without much enthusiasm; Rob Tillard had returned to his regiment with a third in history. Several times Jimmy and Toni Potts came out to see us with their year-old daughter Janet, and while our two wives pushed their respective offspring in the park, we'd talk history and I'd impress Jimmy by giving him detailed and analytical answers to various questions he'd put to me about subjects on which he'd written essays.

'You seem to know quite a lot,' he said astonished, unaware of course that I possessed copies of all his essays, which I had now memorized. He was extremely able and those who knew about such matters considered he'd get a first—not quite so in my case.

June arrived and I made my final plans. I decided that each day I would have a taxi into Oxford and a taxi back and I organized my revision in the following manner.

The evening before each examination day I would revise between eight and ten for the following afternoon paper. Promptly at ten, come what may, I would pack up and go to bed. On examination day the alarm would go off at half-past five and I would be at work well before six, revising for the morning paper which began at nine-thirty. Biddie would bring me my breakfast on a tray and I would work as I ate. At half-past eight the taxi would arrive and I'd set off sitting at the back still working. A friend had arranged that I should have a room at his digs in Longwall Street, conveniently close to the Examination Schools. A cold lunch would be laid ready for me when I came out at twelve-thirty. I would then work through the lunch period revising for the afternoon paper which started at half-past two and ended at half-past five. That completed I would return to the digs

55

in Longwall Street where the taxi would be waiting and drive straight back to Woodstock.

So came the first day of the examinations, and dressed in a blue suit, white tie, commoner's gown and mortar board, I kissed Biddie goodbye, climbed into the back of a big comfortable old Austin and set off for Oxford. On the way in I glanced through Sayles' *Foundations of Medieval England*, and had a look at a couple of Potts' essays. As a last-minute stand-by I had taken with me a thin little book entitled *History Helps*—not found, I hasten to add, in any of the university's libraries!

My friend and host, Michael Wrigley, a very tall, erect and assured Harrovian, now in the Foreign Office, greeted me with his customary air of benign condescension. I'd kept wicket to his fast bowling on occasions, when he had displayed a splendidly cavalier approach to the game that had appealed to me. He had a whirligig action—all arms and legs—and an uncanny adroitness at dropping the easiest of slip catches at the same time making them appear the most difficult. But he hit the jackpot all right in 1949 when he took eight New Zealand wickets for fifty-one runs.

'All ready Shearwood?' he now said, looking down at me with that amused, slightly twisted grin of his, 'know all about the Anglo-Saxons?'

'I know that their justice was nothing short of unmitigated barbarism,' I replied.

'Very impressive too,' he said, laughing and showing me my room where I dumped my books. 'I've laid on your lunch and a stiff gin—we shall both need it.' Then we set off down Longwall Street, the high stone wall of Magdalen College mellow and bright in the June sunshine. Dodging the High Street traffic we reached the other side, where serious-faced undergraduates in short gowns were converging from all directions on the open doors of the Examination Schools. We entered the building and joined the general scrimmage. 'See you later', said my companion above the hubbub, and I went up the broad stairway and into the examination room where I found my desk. Glancing round I caught sight of Jimmy Potts. I saw no one else that I knew. And then we were off and I picked up the paper and began to study the twenty-three questions from which I had to answer four.

Three hours later I handed in my paper and emerged blinking into the sunlight. I ate my lunch, drank my gin and revised hard for the afternoon paper.

56

'Time we went,' said Michael still grinning away and we walked the short distance back to the Examination Schools.

At five-forty I climbed into the back of the waiting taxi and closed my eyes. I was very tired but satisfied, for I had not disliked the two papers and felt that I had coped adequately with the eight questions I had attempted.

'How did you get on?' Biddie greeted me when I got back.

'Not too bad,' I told her, sipping a cup of tea before taking a bath. At seven I had supper and when I had finished I went up top and worked till ten when I promptly went to bed.

All week I kept this up, working twelve hours a day and then suddenly it was over and we were drinking champagne at the top of Vincent's. That night I went to bed early and slept for twelve hours. When I awoke I had a feeling that I should be up in the attic working, for the sense of purpose that had motivated me for the last five months was still present. I felt slightly flat.

I felt also that I had passed, for I had found none of the papers beyond my powers. In fact I had quite enjoyed doing them, particularly those on political science. My family too had played their part nobly, Biddie by her quiet, unfailing support and undemanding nature, Paul by never keeping me awake at night during the examinations, something which might have proved disastrous. For several days I felt drained and I could not forget the books and the attic.

Weeks later, sometime in July, when I had long forgotten all about the examinations and what I had written, I was called by the Examining Body for my 'viva'. Sitting outside, waiting to be called, dressed once again for the occasion in blue suit, white tie and gown, I felt somewhat apprehensive though at the same time intrigued. All the work that I had done had now become something of the past, almost unreal. The night before I had glanced through some of the books in the attic for an hour or two, but the spark had gone. I had written the papers and as far as I was concerned they were either good enough or not.

When I went in I was asked to sit at the centre of a long table facing a group of dons and one woman. They were in no hurry and I could see they had my papers before them. I cannot remember a great deal about that viva but I do remember that they asked me what the Chartists wanted and I was able to give them all six of their demands. Then I was asked if I would mind going down to the end of the table as somebody wanted to put a question to me on paper three.

It was about something I had written on Gladstone and Disraeli and I found myself in some difficulty, my plight made no easier by the distinguished historian Miss Hurnard, a cousin of Stanley Cohn, who sat opposite me, one elbow resting on the table, eyes closed, hand to brow in what I could only suppose was an attitude of prayer or great sufferance; I suspected the latter. And then I was thanked politely, God knows for what, and rising clumsily I walked to the door and closed it behind me.

Now there was only the waiting for the lists to be put up in the Examination Schools to see who had got firsts, seconds, thirds, the rare fourths, and fails.

I was not particularly worried. I had done what I could so I just forgot about it all, opened my cricket bag and played for Blenheim Palace, a side which I had captained the previous season. The ground at Blenheim is a beautiful one and I had first played there at the beginning of the war for Shrewsbury against Malvern, who were evacuated to the Palace. It was said that if you could break a Palace window when batting the Duke would pay you a fiver. I don't think it has ever been done but I had a few goes on that occasion and hit 67.

One evening I was playing cricket for the Brasenose side of college servants somewhere in the heart of the Oxfordshire countryside, trying to keep wicket in the gathering twilight. At last, as the stars were emerging we finished the match and adjourned to the village pub. Chatting and drinking our pints of beer, I suddenly saw Charlie making his way towards me through the crowded little room with outstretched hand.

'Congratulations,' he said, 'you've got a third.'

'I have?'

'You have,' he nodded smiling and twitching his nose. 'I've been and verified it. Your name's there. It's all quite true. Now drink up and I'll get you another,' he said making his way to the bar before I had time to reply.

Good old Charlie, I thought. He'd no need to have done it. He had watched all our Pegasus matches and that's how I had first met him. He had also been a great help to me when I had been short of money, taking me with him on jobs clearing houses, drawing up lists for the big auction sales which were to follow, joking about the various items, twitching his nose at great speed like some frightened rabbit sensing danger, as he skilfuly sorted through piles of pictures, books, chairs, curtains, carpets, kitchen utensils, telling me as he did so what this would fetch and that wouldn't. During the lunch breaks we'd often talked of Pegasus and on occasions I had spoken to him about my academic fears.

Somehow that afternoon he must have heard that the results were out and gone down to the Examination Schools to see whether I had passed. He had rung Woodstock immediately and told Biddie the good news and she had given him the information that I was out playing cricket for the college servants. She was unable to tell him where so he had promptly gone to the Lodge at Brasenose college and found out. Good old Charlie. I hope he reads this book. We all had a few drinks that evening.

'You've passed,' said Biddie delightedly when I got back. 'You've got a third.' And then we made some telephone calls.

'Let's go down to Cornwall,' I said that night, 'I want to smell the sea again.'

Two days later we set off for the West Country.

8 On the Way

Earlier that year I had applied to the Oxford School of Education to do what is called a 'Dip. Ed.' and been accepted. I had as yet no real plans for the future, though Colin Weir had sown some seeds when tentatively sounding me out as to whether I would be interested in going to teach at Lancing College. What really appealed to me about taking a Diploma in Education was that it gave me another year at Oxford and the chance to play some more football and captain the university. At any rate on the credit side I now had an Honours degree in history, if only a third, with which to face the future.

Returning from our holiday I immediately went up to Tottenham with Stan Heritage, the Oxford secretary, to meet Vic Buckingham, who was to coach us in the forthcoming season. Over lunch it was agreed that he would coach us on Mondays and watch our mid-week matches. The physical fitness of the side he intended leaving to us, which was quite right.

Vic was tall, good-looking, debonair and charming and I could see as he coached us that season with his own brand of amused, almost casual authority that he was enjoying himself every bit as much as we were enjoying his coaching. He would laugh quietly at our awkwardness as he worked with us, correcting and encouraging, watching closely and assessing us shrewdly. He wanted us to play it simple and quick, push and run stuff, give and go, our wingers coming right back and collecting the ball from defence, everyone playing a part and taking responsibility: 'This fellow Ramsay at Tottenham' he would say, 'he's so good at taking responsibility. Even in the six yard area he'll want the ball and try and start something going. He's as slow as an old cart horse, but what a player, what positional sense!'

And when each session was over, Stan and I would discuss with him the selection of the side for the mid-week match, which he would come down and watch.

After the initial success of our pre-season tour of the West Country, when we had defeated the Cornish F.A. twice and the Dorset F.A. our results were disappointing. Of the fifteen matches that followed

60

we lost nine, drew four and won only two, those against London University and the Metropolitan Police. We had a lot of difficulty finding a goalkeeper and tried amongst others, two cricket Blues, Christopher Winn and George Chesterton. The latter, on his one and only appearance against Wolverhampton Wanderers, was forced to retrieve the ball five times from his goal. In desperation Vic brought the England and Spurs goalkeeper, Ted Ditchburn, down to try and help us find a 'keeper. In the end we plumped for Bernard Boddy who had played the previous year at back. He had a good eye, was big and strong and had what we thought were a sound pair of hands.

When the side was finally selected, four Salopians were included, John Clegg, Dick Rhys, myself and Miles Robinson, the latter chosen in place of Derek Richards. It is never a pleasant business dropping an old Blue but on balance I thought Miles was the right choice. He was not as good a player on the ball as Derek, but he was bigger, stronger and faster and I thought better equipped to contain the threat of the Cambridge right-winger, Roy Sutcliffe. To our great delight Denis Saunders was fit and able to play again. He had gradually eased himself back into the game and was as good as ever. With Gordon McKinna and Denis we were strong in the middle of the field. Up front we had two good wingers, John Clegg and Donald Carr, and a very experienced player at inside-right, Stan Heritage.

But Cambridge too were strong mid-field, with such players as Reg Vowels, Ralph Cowan their captain, and Jimmy Platt. They had two good inside-forwards, Jack Laybourne—who was later to play for Spurs—and Peter May, and on the flanks Lionel Boardman and Roy Sutcliffe. They would be no push-over.

In the official programme notes of that 1950 Oxford and Cambridge match played again on the Tottenham Hotspur ground, Vic Buckingham wrote :

I feel sure that the respective playing records of both universities this season in no way reflects the strength and capabilities of the teams. It would seem from the respective 'goals against' columns that this game to-day will be a high scoring one—it may be so especially if conditions are treacherous—but in the main many matches by both universities have been played with teams depleted by injuries, and often experiments have been undertaken. The past two or three weeks have seen both sides taking the field with more or less settled teams, and two 'footballing sides' should be on view here this afternoon.

With colleague Bill Nicholson at Cambridge, and myself coaching Oxford, it was obvious to me that we would both press for the simple and quick style of the Spurs. I had toyed with the idea of surprising both Bill Nicholson and the Cambridge team with an 'Arsenal pattern' or style of play, but Mr. Whittaker

61

would not lend me Leslie Compton. So be it. Two Spurs happily trying to advance certain Tottenham methods into two teams playing on the Spurs' ground, and before many, I hope, Spurs' supporters.

Oxford, under their admirable skipper, Ken Shearwood, are a happy group of fellows. The exuberance and whole-hearted endeavour always associated with these matches has, I feel, been controlled in some measure. Knockdowns there will assuredly be, taken and given in the true sporting spirit, but over-riding it all will be the accent of football—simple, quick and progressive. I shall not be disappointed.

The result? Oxford to win.

Wrote Bill Nicholson :

I think the chief characteristic of the Cambridge team is determination. The way these boys play whole-heartedly for the full ninety minutes with each one giving maximum effort for the success of his team is a delight to see.

But these fellows will try to play good football too. Naturally you will not expect to see it played with the same brilliance that you associate with First Division football but you should see a good standard, with method win through. There is so much rivalry between these teams, and so much tradition and fidelity to uphold.

The result? Cambridge to win.

It was my fourth and last varsity match and I chiefly recollect an incident towards the end of the match which our opponents felt had robbed them of a goal. In the heavy slippery mud Bernard Boddy fumbled a close-range shot from Lionel Boardman and in a trice the Cambridge winger had followed up and banged the ball out of his groping hands into the back of our net. Immediately our goalkeeper had fallen flat on his face and remained motionless. It was difficult to know quite what was wrong. I tried to get a response and find out if he was injured. Or was he just mortified by what had happened? Our man with the sponge, Leslie Laitt, was on his way out, trilby on head, running through the mud. Cambridge meanwhile had taken the ball back to the middle and were lined up impatient to start again. There was no doubt in any of their minds that they were now one up.

'Kicked it out of his hands ref,' said Leslie arriving on the scene and puffing indignantly at the referee, Mr. J. H. Lockton, who seemed momentarily at a loss to know what to do or say, 'kicked it out of his hands he did,' and bending over the recumbent Boddy (excuse the pun) he held a wet sponge to the back of his neck.

'I know,' said the referee quietly, 'it's not a goal,' and he signalled to the Cambridge players to return the ball, which did not please them one bit.

And then Bernard began to stir and after several moments rose shakily to his feet. Leslie Laitt left the field, I took the free kick from the goal line, and play resumed. Twenty minutes later the match was over, a goalless draw.

'The magic of a cold sponge and silver-tongued oratory had saved the day for an Oxford side that began on its toes but ended on its heels,' concluded *The Times* correspondent. But then I ought to remind the reader that Geoffrey Green, besides being a Salopian, was also a Cambridge soccer Blue.

The following morning, Sunday, the customary Pegasus meeting was held and Tommy and Graham Doggart were appointed to the selection committee for the season 1950–51. Then Graham dropped a bombshell by proposing that players selected for the coming tour should be limited to those in residence or for one year thereafter, his proposal seconded by Peter May.

At once Tommy strongly opposed the proposal, pointing out that apart from any other considerations a few senior players had held themselves available for Pegasus rather than playing in cup-ties for other clubs. Whereupon Graham at once withdrew his proposal and the meeting ended with Denis Saunders being appointed captain for the coming season.

I was present at that meeting, as I had been for many others, and could see how wide the rift was growing. Graham Doggart, a Cambridge and Corinthian player, had naturally many friends and connections with the Casuals and was in an unquestionably difficult position. His son Hubert had just come down from Cambridge and the Cambridge contingent led by Doug Insole were coming out into the open more and more as supporters of the one-year rule. Sadly, and inevitably it seemed, a major difference of opinion over the interpretation of the rules and future of the club was becoming a chasm too wide by far for any bridge to link the two universities. In all sincerity Graham believed that the Cambridge point of view was the right one. And in equal sincerity Tommy and the Oxford contingent believed that unless the club used its resources to the full, it could never make the necessary impact to stimulate the game at the universities and, as the Reverend Kenneth Hunt had so bluntly predicted in his letter, 'the club would die a natural death in a very few years'.

This was the position when we set off on the New Year tour of 1951 with a party of eighteen players, twelve from Oxford, six from Cambridge, plus wives and officials to play three matches against Winchester City, Salisbury Town and Jersey with Vic Buckingham, much to my delight, as the club coach.

We beat Winchester City 4–1, lost to Salisbury 0–3 and ended up with a fine win against Jersey, 5–1 when Johnny Dutchman scored four goals and John Tanner one. In the heavy conditions the side 'clicked' and Vic Buckingham was delighted. I had particular cause to remember the Jersey centre-forward Le Mesurier who had been with West Bromwich Albion for a spell and was sharp and mobile. I stuck to him closely—perhaps too close—for backing into me to make good a ball laid to his feet, he brought his elbow back into my midriff with a short vicious jab that knocked the stuffing out of me for a minute or two.

But in all it had been a very successful tour and when we got back (Biddie had come on tour with me), the telephone rang almost as soon as we had opened the front door of Laburnum House, and there was Jerry Weinstein on the other end wanting all the news.

Jerry was at Brasenose. Having taken a good degree in jurisprudence, he was reading for a B.C.L. I'd really got to know him that Michaelmas term when he was reporting our matches for the *Isis* magazine. I had liked him at once. As a Japanese interpreter in the Far East during the war, he had caught polio, which had left him severely crippled. Black-haired and blue-jowled, tinted glasses bridging heavy Jewish features and wearing a long airforce officer's overcoat, he would limp slowly and lop-sidedly across the High, grim of visage, holding the oncoming traffic at bay with stick aloft, occasionally stopping to tap the bonnet of any car that ventured too close. Once he was safely across his features would suddenly break into a huge grin, engaging and infectious. He had come to Oxford as a scholar from St. Paul's. He was fluent in four languages, had a rapier mind, witty and devastatingly fast. Since he was no longer able to play, he watched and wrote with insight about the game and not only contributed a great deal, but became as much a part of the Pegasus scene as anyone.

'Gosport will be no push-over,' I heard him say, 'I've watched 'em and they've a useful centre-forward, Albert Mundy. He's turning professional for Portsmouth at the end of the season. You'll need to mark him tight. How's Tommy?'

'Pretty good form.'

64

'Might pop over and see you tomorrow evening.'

'Why not have some supper?' I suggested, and he accepted.

Ten days later, having defeated the Home Air Command 5–2, we journeyed to Portsmouth and after lunching together caught the ferry across to Gosport to begin our next venture in the Amateur Cup along with sixty-four other clubs and a mighty close affair it turned out to be as *The Times* made clear :

Pegasus reached the second round of the F.A. Amateur Cup competition when they beat Gosport Borough Athletic at Gosport on Saturday by four goals to three, but they scarcely took to their wings in doing so.

Indeed, on the general run of the play Gosport perhaps were a shade unfortunate to lose a match which was lifted above mediocrity only by the home side's gallant rally after half time and by a thoroughly exciting climax to the sunny afternoon. At the interval it had seemed to be all over, for Pegasus, after conceding an opening goal to the opposition, had largely found their feet and their touch to establish a comfortable lead of 3–1. The rest appeared no more than a formality.

But Gosport to their undying credit came out for the second half with no such thoughts. By hard, quick tackling and bustling methods they succeeded in knocking Pegasus completely off their game to take control of affairs and all but save their skins. Six minutes from the end the score was still 3–1. Then the game leapt forward with a sudden jerk. First Gosport took a step nearer their opponents to make the score 3–2. In a twinkling Pegasus, with the equivalent of a fast uppercut that should have put Gosport out for the final count, strode away again to 4–2. But Gosport, like heroes, refused to lie down. A minute from the end they scored again; Pegasus were now ahead merely by a whisker at 4–3 and the end found them hanging on for dear life and counting the seconds, each one of which must have felt like an eternity.

That dying convulsion left the deepest impression on an afternoon that was otherwise largely undistinguished. True, Pegasus, after taking a long time to get into their stride against the sharp tackling of Stares, Ramage and Sanderson—Fisher, too, played gallantly—did show us something of their undoubted quality for some 25 minutes before the interval. But that was all. Only for short spasms afterwards did they slip into their smooth attacking rhythm and because Gosport could bring little else to the game but their fire and enthusiasm, the play deteriorated into a confused pattern of stray ends.

A fine shot on the turn by Loman five minutes after the kick-off not only put Gosport's tails up but seemed to disturb Pegasus unduly. Slowly, however, the cool defence of Cowan and the midfield promptings of Platt and Saunders —a thoughtful player—were seen to be having their effect. The Pegasus forward line, clearly so full of goals once given the service, began to flower, even if Carr and Dutchman were not always using Potts and Pawson to the fullest advantage against backs who tended to stand square. The through pass inside the defender was what was really required and three times Potts moved for the forward touch that never came.

At the twenty-second minute, however, a clever piece of combination between Tanner and Dutchman was splendidly consummated by Carr with a fast left-foot shot on the turn. Once level a heavy load seemed to drop from Pegasus. At the half hour they went ahead after a quick advance down the left between Potts and Carr, Tanner taking the inside's well-timed square pass to slash home a low shot past Farquhar. The pattern we had expected began to take shape at last and became even clearer a few moments later when Tanner, after some stuttering in the Gosport goalmouth between himself and Carr scored the third Pegasus goal after Pawson's dash and square pass had provided the prelude.

So it was 3–1 to Pegasus, rightly, at the interval. Plain sailing now, we thought. But we were wrong. As at the beginning, so again Gosport shook their opponents out of their measured stride. The Pegasus defence now began to show its limitations. The root cause of the trouble was Bowyer's inability to check the youthful Dimmer, whose footwork sent his opponent in all sorts of directions. Nor did Bowyer help himself by granting the winger the freedom of Hampshire in which to do his work. The defensive ills seemed to spread outwards from this sensitive spot. Saunders began to tire; Shearwood, good with his head, began to make some faulty and untidy clearances on the ground. Cowan and Platt, however, stood reasonably firm. This was the time when the full defensive support of two experienced inside forwards would have been invaluable. Carr and Dutchman played their parts in this fashion manfully enough but showed in effect what they were—players out of their true positions. With Potts not the Potts we know—understandably enough, for he had come straight from a bed of influenza—only Pawson and Tanner held promise of a further Pegasus goal in a few breaks-away. Yet for all their control Gosport had not a sufficiency of skill to press home their point.

So we came to that lively finale. A weak clearance by Shearwood was punished even further as Brown misjudged Dimmer's cross lob to the far corner —3–2 now, Dimmer running wild and the crowd on the tip-toe of excitement. Almost at once though there came a sudden break by Pegasus and Carr had volleyed them to 4–2. But Gosport went down finally with their colours flying when Cole beat Brown with his head as time all but stood still. The teams were:

GOSPORT BOROUGH ATHLETIC – J. Farquhar; A. Wilson, F. Fisher; J. Stares, E. Rammage, R. Sanderson; D. Dimmer, J. Cole, A. Mundy, J. Loman, K. Mason.

PEGASUS – B. R. Brown; R. Cowan, R. E. Bowyer; J. Platt, K. A. Shearwood, D. F. Saunders; H. A. Pawson, J. A. Dutchman, J. D. P. Tanner, D. B. Carr, H. J. Potts.

'Well,' said Tommy when it was all over and we were on our way home, 'I think we were very lucky.' And that week he sent out a notice to twenty-four players warning them of the need for maximum fitness which had seemed in question against Gosport and not to underestimate Slough Town, our next opponents on 27 January:

Reports on the Slough team in their game against Eastbourne yesterday

(Slough 2 Eastbourne 1) are being prepared for circulation. It seems, as expected, that they are a strong fighting team, with clever forwards. They have this season knocked out of the F.A. Cup Oxford City, Banbury Spencer and Headington United (Southern League at present 6th), but if we can play our best we should beat them. It may prove our crucial match. I visited the Slough ground to-day, and found it a somewhat miserable Greyhound Stadium, hard but sticky surface, not very well rolled, fairly flat but rather bumpy surface, rather a tough sort of atmosphere, but not as bad as it might be. They are (according to their Secretary) pretty self-confident.

I would like to have seen that meeting of Tommy and the Slough secretary.

Jerry Weinstein drove Denis Saunders, Donald Carr and myself to the game in his black Hillman especially converted for his needs. He drove fast and generally well, but on this occasion not quite well enough. I was sitting in the front.

'You're driving too close to his tail Jerry,' I said.

'D'you want to walk?' he retorted and Donald laughed. The road was narrow and windy and Jerry was impatient to pass.

Suddenly, the car in front, which was being driven irritatingly slowly, braked with no warning and began to turn left into a hidden drive. And just as suddenly we ran straight into its back. There was a sound of rending metal, tinkling glass, and hysterical laughter from Donald and myself.

In a trice Jerry was out, and looking his most menacing he limped towards the other driver's window and leaning upon his stick, let fly a legal tirade of such spectacular length and vehemence that it seemed to leave whoever was on the receiving end quite speechless. Finally an arm shot out and a gloved hand thrust a driving licence into Jerry's face. He stared at it blankly for a moment, before turning and limping toward us.

'The man's a Pole,' he said quietly. 'He can't have understood a bloody word I've been saying,' and he leant on his stick doubled up with silent laughter.

'Just as well,' said Denis wiping the tears from his eyes, and when addresses had been exchanged we set off again, minus a headlight and with a damaged wing.

'And if you say "I told you so" Shearwood you can still get out and bloody well walk to Slough,' said our driver, which set us laughing again.

67

As we drew near Slough, however, we became increasingly pre-occupied with our own thoughts. I was thinking of Clements and what I knew about him as a centre-forward from the report we had been sent. I began to sweat slightly anticipating the game and the movements of the man I would soon be marking for ninety minutes. And then we were at the ground and there was Tommy and Graham and Harvey Chadder and Sir Stanley Rous and I caught sight of Denis Compton, who had come to report the match and lots of friendly Oxford faces in the crowd outside the ground. Inside the cramped changing-room Leslie Laitt was putting out our kit with trilby still on head. He was never without it and some of us, Jerry in particular, were of the opinion that he wore it in bed.

Over six thousand watched our unchanged side defeat Slough Town 3-1, all four goals scored in the first twenty minutes. Said Denis Compton :

It was half an hour of incident-packed football. Slough had no counter to the speed of the Pegasus attack. Tanner was fast, and his two goals were beauties and Dutchman opens up the game and is a good forward. But the Pegasus defence is not so sure and confident, and though it looked better after the interval one felt that a top class attack would have riddled it earlier on. It is here where changes will have to be made if Pegasus are to go forward, and they can win the cup if the defence is tightened up.

Coming out for the second half we heard above the noise of the crowd the pleasant strains of the Eton Boating Song, sung by a group of college boys who had come over to watch the match. It became our theme tune and we were to hear it on many more occasions.

After the match the three of us again drove back with Jerry to Oxford, stopping to have a meal on the way. Much later, entering Oxford, we passed the road where Leslie Laitt lived and decided to pull up. A ladder lay outside; a light was on upstairs. Carefully, though somewhat unsteadily we placed the ladder against the front of the house and Donald, singing the Eton Boating Song, began to climb. Half way up, the window opened.

'Hello Leslie,' said Donald.

'Is he wearing his hat?' enquired Jerry from the foot of the ladder.

'You'll wake the neighbours,' warned our man with the sponge, good humouredly, 'you'd better come in and have a cup of tea.'

Before the three of us parted that night we telephoned Tommy from a public call box.

'Ye . . . s,' came the guarded drawl.

68

'Swing, swing together,' we sang down the phone and waited for a response.

'We ... ll,' he said, completely ignoring our singing. 'I've been giving the game a lot of thought and I don't think we're going to get much further unless we do something about the defence. I'm not at all happy about Ted Bowyer. He's a very nice fellow, but he's not the answer. And I'm still very concerned about the club's constitution and the one-year rule. There's a great deal of hard thinking to be done. I don't think any of you quite realize the sort of difficulties that lie ahead.'

'Swing, swing together,' we sang back and there was a slight chuckle at the other end followed by a bout of coughing.

'It's time you three went to bed,' he said and hung up.

'At any rate Tommy's in his usual fine form,' said Jerry emerging last from the call box.

We were drawn away to Brentwood and Warley in the next round and neither Tony Pawson, who had pulled a muscle, nor myself could play. I had eaten something that had disagreed with me and felt ill and weak and very disappointed. I was just about fit enough to travel to the game with Jerry and watch the match.

Ralph Cowan, who had already won a cap for England, took over at centre-half and held the defence together brilliantly. Roy Sutcliffe came in at left-wing, Jimmy Potts moved to his international berth at right-wing and we had two new backs, John Maughan and Derek Richards.

It was a match memorable for the dreadful conditions. Two goals down at half-time, we again failed to adapt to the heavy mud, tending frequently to pass short and square. But for twenty minutes of the second half we pressed strongly and Potts reduced the lead after a Sutcliffe-Tanner move. And then the minutes began to tick away fast until there were only ten of them left and onlookers could do little more than hope. The equalizer came with a pass from Tanner, and Potts was through to score. And suddenly Brentwood disintegrated, as can happen sometimes when a side has sensed victory only to have it wrenched from their grasp. For the last five minutes we had them by the throat and could have scored several times. Sutcliffe got our third and winning goal with a clever lob, and for the second time in three years we had reached the quarter-finals of the Amateur Cup.

Yet again we were drawn away from home, but in a way this cup-tie was at home, for we'd drawn our neighbours, Oxford City, who in the previous round had defeated the redoubtable Crook Town in a replay.

And immediately the coming game was the talk of Oxford. It was Town versus Gown and yet not quite—for five of the Pegasus side were to come from Cambridge.

'You can do it—of course you can,' said Doug Margates, friend and staunch supporter, who lived not thirty yards down the road from us and had never missed a match. Doug worked at Morris Motors, getting up every morning well before five. He was a small wiry man who cheerfully accepted life's lot. He didn't seem to need sleep for he never went to bed before midnight. He had made a great flat plywood flying horse attached to a pole which came to all our matches. 'Up the Pegs!' he would greet me, and we'd discuss the prospects of the next game and I'd get tickets for him and his friends from Tommy. Often of a morning his young daughter would come and play with Paul. They were a very kind family.

That Easter I started my term's practical teaching at the Woodstock Secondary Modern School, a low, prefabricated building. It was very convenient and I felt the only really valuable part of the educational course I was doing. The theory of education is a splendid sounding phrase but has little bearing on the practical business of teaching a class—as I soon found out.

The headmaster of the school, Percy Thompson, was a diminutive Yorkshireman, full of personality and vigour and a great cricket enthusiast. He had kept wicket in the Yorkshire League and proudly showed me his broken fingers. One morning I was teaching a big class, well over forty, girls one side, boys the other, trying to give them some idea of what the French revolution was all about, when the door opened and in walked Percy.

'Aye,' he said looking at the blackboard curiously, where I had written a few names, Lafayette, Mirabeau, Danton, Robespierre, 'what have you got up there, Ken, the runners for the three-thirty?'

'Oh, we're just doing a bit of history,' I told him.

'Aye, now let's see,' he said taking over and addressing the class. 'Who's best batsman in't world?'

'Bradman,' came a voice from the back.

'Can't hear,' Percy pretended, leaning forward and putting his right hand to his ear.

"Utton,' came a few more voices.

'Still can't hear you.'

'Len 'Utton,' came the concerted shout.

'You're right,' said Percy. 'Now then, which county did he play for?'

'Yorkshire,' came the prompt reply.

'Right again,' said Percy. 'And who were Yorkshire's great enemies?'

'Lancashire,' sang out the class, warming to the subject.

'And didn't they each have a flower for an emblem? I think the girls could answer this one.'

'A rose,' whispered several shyly.

'A rose,' repeated Percy, 'and wasn't there once a war called the War of the . . .?'

'Roses,' roared the class.

'Right again,' said Percy triumphantly, and turning to me and dropping his voice, 'got the idea, Ken?' and he went out and left me to it.

I learnt a lot at that school and was greatly helped by the geography master, who was an excellent teacher, and had been a Chief Petty Officer in the Royal Navy. I wasn't in the least surprised to learn that shortly afterwards he was appointed a headmaster.

I used to sit in and watch the technique of the masters when I wasn't taking a class myself. There was a young Scot who couldn't keep order at all and he asked me if I would mind not attending his classes, a request to which I readily acceded.

The master who took the metal-work classes however had no trouble in keeping order. I would stand talking with him while the class got on with their work, banging away at the metal until some of them began to wander about and get up to mischief believing their master's attention to be elsewhere—which was very far from the case.

'Jenkins,' he would shout abruptly, 'what the hell are you doing with that bloody hammer?' and he'd glare at the offender for several long seconds before continuing talking, his eyes alert.

Suddenly he'd break off again. 'Just a minute,' he'd say lowering his voice, 'just look at that little bugger over there,' and moving stealthily forward he'd catch the unsuspecting boy a fourpenny one which made the rest of the class titter until they felt his eyes turned in their direction. Coming back poker-faced he'd give me a wink and carry on talking as though nothing had happened.

The most skilful teacher I've ever listened to was the mathematics master. He was a veteran and an artist and a lesson to anyone in how to use the voice. It was a to and fro business. He'd put a simple fraction on the board and build it all up from there with questions whispered to his riveted audience. He never hurried, he never raised his voice and he never lost their attention. He knew his trade and they knew he did.

I was in the common room one afternoon doing some marking, when the geography master entered. 'There's a parson and two ladies outside who are asking to see you. Apparently they're something to do with the Oxford Educational Authority and have come to hear you teach.'

'Well they're out of luck,' I said, 'I'm not in.'

'I think you'd better go and see them,' he advised. So I opened the door and went out.

Across the hall a parson and two formidable females wearing spectacles were standing together talking. As I approached them, the concern on my face—I learned this afterwards—caused the parson, the Very Reverend Jerry Weinstein, to begin shaking uncontrollably with laughter while the two females, also Brasenose undergraduates, unable to contain their serious expressions any longer, followed suit.

'We'd hoped to catch you teaching,' said Jerry. 'We were going to sit at the back of the class and ask you one or two awkward questions.'

I enjoyed that term's teaching at Woodstock and whenever I ran out of words, a not infrequent occurrence, I'd get straight on to the subject of football, and Pegasus, and who was going to win the Cup. I couldn't really go wrong.

There was a tremendous demand for tickets to see this all Oxford fourth round cup-tie, and letters signed 'Disgusted', 'Bitter Sweet', appeared in the local press from some of the unsuccessful applicants.

Tony Pawson failed a pre-match fitness test and John Tanner had a groin injury. So Roy Sutcliffe kept his place at outside-left, Jack Laybourne came in at inside-right and Johnny Dutchman moved to centre-forward. I took over again at centre-half and Ralph Cowan moved to left-back. In the Oxford *Green 'Un* Syd Cox had this to say :

After a thrill-packed first half, in which the honours were even, Oxford City

72

fell away against Pegasus in the quarter-final of the Amateur Cup before a crowd of about 9,500 on the White House ground this afternoon.

The Times concluded :

For the first twenty minutes of the second half the Pegasus forwards and wing half-backs, playing delightful football simply carried all before them. J. S. Laybourne opened the scoring heading in a well-taken corner by H. J. Potts and D. B. Carr followed with another clever goal from D. Saunders's free-kick. After R. Sutcliffe scored Pegasus's third, following a perfect bout of passing, it was obvious that the City were a well-beaten team.

So we reached the semi-final—and Tommy was delighted, but not for long.

9 Two Semi-Finals

Before we played the semi-final against Hendon at Highbury the Lent edition of a Cambridge university magazine called *Light Blue* came out, in which Doug Insole wrote a critical article on Pegasus, giving his views, which at the time I could appreciate but not share. I quote his article in full because it throws a light on the widening split between the Oxford and Cambridge members of the club over the one-year rule. The article can only really be judged in the context of the whole of the club's short history; I leave the reader to form his own conclusion. Calling the article 'Pegasus', he wrote :

The ideas behind the formation of a joint universities' football club in the first instance were, at least in the minds of Cambridge people, to provide some sort of interest for varsity soccer players in the Lent term, to enhance the reputation of university soccer, which had for so long been at rock bottom, and provide a little financial assistance for the varsity clubs.

Prior to the forming of Pegasus, a joint side from Oxford and Cambridge played an annual fixture against the Universities' Athletic Union, and it was after a match in this series, played at Woking, that the first concrete ideas about forming a club to play in the Amateur Cup were put forward. On the occasion in question we beat a very strong U.A.U. team 7–2, and played really well in doing so.

It was decided that the possibilities should be investigated, and during the varsity cricket match at Lord's in 1948 Dr. Thompson, the Oxford Treasurer, and Denis Saunders, Oxford's Captain, met Hubert Doggart and myself, secretary and captain of Cambridge, and it was decided to go ahead with the formation of a club. At once a small committee was formed, the club was christened Pegasus, and we set about drafting a constitution.

It was the constitution which was, and indeed still is, the main cause for dissension in the club. Before we could go to the F.A. and ask for exemption in the Amateur Cup, to enable us to start playing in the competition, we had to be a club with a name, a ground and a set of rules. It was evident, I think, from the very first meeting, that whereas we in Cambridge visualised the club as one for university players, and I mean by that men actually in residence, the Oxford people were looking for something with a much broader base. It was eventually agreed, however, that men who had been down not more than one year might be allowed to play, and this proviso meant that Guy Shuttleworth could skipper the side in its first season.

It is the breaking away from this original constitution which has caused the split which now exists in the ranks of Pegasus. The reasons for our insisting that players should actually be in residence were, first, that the club was formed with a view to improving the standard of university soccer; and, secondly, that to include old players would inevitably cut across the Corinthian-Casuals, who were struggling to keep going, and who might be expected to benefit, eventually, from any improvement in university soccer standards.

It must be said, too, that all the original moves towards the formation of the club were made in consultation with members of the Corinthian-Casuals' committee, and that we had received every encouragement from them. It has since transpired that had the F.A. Council not been assured that the Corinthian-Casuals approved of Pegasus, and had the one-year rule, as we call it, not been part of the constitution, we should not have been given exemption in the Amateur Cup, as, in fact, we were after a prolonged struggle.

In that first season we were drawn to play away at Enfield in the fourth qualifying round of the Cup, which was to be played in mid-November. This was two weeks before the varsity match, and we had to ask Enfield to postpone the match for three weeks so that both universities could complete their normal programmes. This Enfield very sportingly agreed to do, contrary to the advice of the other clubs in the Athenian League. We beat Enfield 3–1 after a very thrilling struggle, and were lucky enough to be drawn at home in the following three rounds, against Smethwick Highfield, Brentwood and Warley, and Willington, who won the Cup last year.

By playing entertaining football we managed to arouse a good deal of enthusiasm among the populace at Oxford, and when we were again drawn at home, to Bromley, in the fourth round, it became necessary to erect extra stands to cope with the people who wanted to watch. We lost this match by 4 goals to 3, after what was said to have been the best game seen in Oxford for many years, before a record crowd for any varsity sporting event in Oxford.

Thus ended a gallant attempt to win the Amateur Cup at the first attempt, and I think that we were a little unlucky not to get into the semi-final at least. Had we not enjoyed such a successful first season the question of extending the constitution to admit anyone who had ever been at Oxford or Cambridge as a playing member would probably not have arisen. However, the Oxford contingent were most anxious that, having started so well, Pegasus should provide for a possible falling-off in varsity soccer standards by making sure that its 1948–9 side was available at all times, and at the Annual General Meeting the constitution was extended by a majority vote.

This may seem democratic enough, but it appeared to the Cambridge element to be a breach of our agreement with the Corinthian-Casuals, and to be working against the original idea of the club, which was to improve university soccer standards. We could, in fact, visualise the day when there might be no resident member of either varsity playing for Pegasus.

This move did in fact cause something in the nature of a split between the Oxford and Cambridge elements in the club, and as a result much of the great team spirit and will to win was missing last season, and accounts, in my view, for the comparative lack of success of the club, which lost 3–1 at Walthamstow in the second round of the Amateur Cup after beating Erith and Belvedere at the second attempt in the first round. In the event the Cambridge members,

75

and one or two Oxford stalwarts, have stuck by the original arrangement, and have not played for Pegasus after they have been down for one year.

At the time of writing Pegasus have battled into the fourth round of the Amateur Cup by means of a fine win away from home against Brentwood and Warley. On paper Pegasus are the best side in the competition, and quite capable of winning the Cup. Many people, and they may well be right, regard this fact as a sufficient justification for the playing of several players who have been down from the varsity for more than one year. My own view is that the attraction and glamour of Pegasus left the club when it became just another club, and ceased to be a varsity team.

I was a founder member of Pegasus, and am proud of the fact. Moreover, at that time I had never played for the Corinthian-Casuals, so that my defence of them at the time of the drafting of the original constitution was not promoted by any especial allegiance to them. I much regret the strong differences of opinion within the Pegasus Club, but it would seem to me that the element which has tried to retain an exalted position in the amateur soccer world by breaking an agreement, but which has found time to protest to the F.A. about the signing of Walton and Slater by Bishop Auckland, has turned a glorious experiment into something of a blot on university sporting traditions.

Strong words, and not unnaturally there was a good deal of talk within the club. Tommy, of course, was at his best, confiding his concern to us at Oxford that the article was a deliberate attempt to sabotage the semi-final. 'I've a good idea who's behind this. We've got to have a meeting as soon as possible.' He loved meetings. And when Denis gently suggested that perhaps it wasn't really as bad as he was making out, Tommy peered over his spectacles at him in disbelief for several seconds, before remarking with slow gravity, 'Sometimes Denis I think you're very naïve,' which made us laugh, except Tommy, who indulged in much coughing, shook his head knowingly, and lit another cigarette.

We had three weeks in which to prepare for the semi-final and each day we trained at Iffley Road, using the new running track, mingling with the Oxford athletes, Roger Bannister, Nick Stacey, Chris Chataway and Philip Morgan who was doing a 'Dip. Ed.' with me and was in the same tutorial group.

Roger Bannister would burn his way round the track where he was eventually to achieve the four-minute mile. I tried running with him on one occasion for some fifty yards, matching his stride, and was amazed at its length. Chris Chataway on the other hand was short and stocky and we all felt that he would not get very far. We were wrong.

Nick Stacey, an Etonian with a splendidly affected voice and a delightful manner, was a most lovely runner and he'd take us in line abreast for short sprints up and down the track in front of the pavilion.

'Now we are completely relaxed,' he'd drawl gently as he ran with us, and we'd jog along letting our arms and hands flap limply at our sides. 'Now we're beginning to step out a bit faster, but still nice and relaxed,' and he'd look down our line amused at our efforts. 'Now we're really beginning to open up a bit.' And finally he'd urge us, 'come on, let's go,' and he'd surge effortlessly ahead, drawing smoothly away like a Rolls-Royce leaving behind a row of old 'bangers'.

Most of them had watched our matches and were great supporters of Pegasus. To Nick Stacey I had hired out Potts's essays for a small sum of money. Donald Carr had a carbon copy and come to think of it I'm not sure that he ever paid his fee. The essays were already becoming a sort after acquisition for those not so strong candidates about to embark upon their history Finals.

Entering the main doors of the Arsenal Football Club we climbed an impressive broad stairway of thick blue carpet, at the top of which stood the tall figure of a commissionaire, medals and all.

From the main stand we had a look at the pitch, a smooth muddy waste ironed flat, the lines broad and white, with just a vestige of green at the edges. Already a good crowd was gathering.

Vic Buckingham was talking with Jack Crayston and Tommy was deep in conversation with the Pawsons.

'You'll have to be on your toes today Ken,' Tommy warned.

'He'll go in the bag,' I assured him. I always carried my kit in an old Gladstone bag.

'I hope you're right,' he said, looking his most melancholy. 'You know Stroud's turning professional after this season.' I nodded, and was suddenly more aware than ever of the old butterflies in my stomach.

'Good luck,' said the Pawsons.

Our changing-room was spacious and first class, the tiled floors heated. While we changed Vic Buckingham wandered round and had a few words with each of us in turn. He was by far the most relaxed person there—except perhaps for Leslie Laitt who, hat upon head, was giving John Tanner some massage.

77

When we ran out the smooth wet mud bore the deep imprints of our boots. The conditions were going to be very heavy and I thought of Erith and Belvedere and hoped that we wouldn't start playing it around too short.

Denis lost the toss and right from the start Hendon showed that they intended to get on with the job. A touch from Stroud, their centre-forward, to their inside-right, Phebey, resulted in a low sweeping pass straight to Avis, the Hendon left-winger, a tall gifted player, but very left-footed. At once he took the ball up to Johnny Maughan, our right-back, teased him for a moment, then slipped past, and within seconds we were a pawn down and in dire trouble.

I stuck with Stroud who had moved into our penalty area in line with the far post and didn't go out to Avis because Jimmy Platt had come back fast and was containing this threat. John Dutchman had picked up the Hendon inside-left. Suddenly Avis accelerated on the outside of Jimmy Platt, winning space to drive a hard low centre from the by-line across the edge of our six-yard area, which Stroud met quickly. I went with him but he had the advantage of me in timing his run. Somehow I just got a leg out to block his deflection and in the ensuing scramble Ben Brown got hold of the ball and cleared our lines.

The reader may well wonder how I can recall such a detail of a match that was played over twenty-two years ago. I think most players can remember certain incidents in important games, but no more. The rest becomes only a blurr and for the complete picture of these cup-ties I have relied on the press, in particular Geoffrey Green of *The Times*.

There was one more incident in that semi-final against Hendon that stands vividly etched on my memory. This time it happened right at the end of the match and once again the threat came from Avis.

The Hendon left-winger had given Johnny Maughan a most difficult afternoon and with only two minutes remaining he was still at it. This time he had wandered inside, picked up a pass and was weaving his way through the appalling mud crossing the centre edge of our penalty area. I cannot remember where Stroud was; I think he'd dropped deep and I had let him go. At any rate I found myself confronting Avis and knowing full well that this was a tackle I could not afford to miss. He was working the ball back on to his left side, turning to set it up for a shot with that lethal left foot and I knew

78

I dared not leave it any longer. I committed myself and went into the tackle. As I did so he flicked the ball to one side and down he went, all six foot and more of him. And immediately the whistle blew and the referee was pointing to the penalty spot. 'Sorry,' he said quietly, coming across. I was standing just in front of where the kick was to be taken. 'I've no alternative.' It was a desperate moment.

I watched Dexter Adams come up and clean the ball with his hands before placing it carefully back on the spot. I saw him wipe his right boot against his stocking. He didn't hurry. He seemed quite composed. I glanced at Ben Brown, research chemist and Doctor of Philosophy and so did twenty-six thousand five hundred spectators who were strangely silent. I wondered if the Hendon and England centre-half would try and place the kick. I rather hoped he would. He went back for his run and then came in fast and true and fair blasted the ball with tremendous force high and slightly to the left of Ben who got a fist to it and sent the white ball soaring high over his cross-bar for a corner.

The following morning the press was full of it. Wrote Harry Ditton :

Wonder Save Foils Hendon. From every point of view the F.A. Amateur Cup semi-final at Arsenal Stadium was worth going a long way to see. It had everything—excitement and thrills galore, and academic skill which often left us spellbound in admiration. . .

Alan Ross was also impressed :

Pegasus and Hendon, each of whom have reached the semi-final of the F.A. Amateur Cup for the first time in their history, drew yesterday in the drizzle and mud of Highbury. Despite the conditions, however, no one who saw the game will quickly forget it, or is likely to grudge the result.

The quality of the football on a treacherous surface was remarkable, and though Hendon were the stronger, more polished team a truly magnificent display by Brown in the Pegasus goal earned his side a replay. Not only did Brown bring off nearly a dozen brilliant saves, but in the closing minutes he put a penalty from Adams, which though not far wide was going with great force, over the top. . .

Geoffrey Green had this to say :

Nowadays we have so few mysteries left to us that we cannot afford to part with them easily. That at least would seem to be the implication of this year's indecisive semi-final ties. There was yet another at Highbury on Saturday, this time in the F.A. Amateur Cup, when Hendon and Pegasus followed the prevailing fashion with a draw of one goal each in the second semi-final of the competition after a most exciting encounter. Thus they are left still jostling each other on the very threshold to Wembley, with the struggle now to be at

Selhurst Park next Saturday. And meanwhile, Bishop Auckland with arms outstretched, await the victor.

Let it be said at once, Hendon should have won. For them the afternoon was a tragedy of frustration, and, like tragedies that always are acted by artificial light in a theatre hung with black, so was the setting here in the proper mood for them. The sun put ashes on her face, heavy clouds swept low across a leaden sky, and as the battle moved inexorably towards its breathless climax rain fell sharply for the last 20 minutes upon a ground already sodden and scarred. Yet for Pegasus this was a day to remember, a day of escape, of courage, and magnificent defence, in which Brown, their goalkeeper, was the noblest hero of all.

What a climax! The afternoon must be turned upside down; the end of the story told first. With 20 minutes left and still no score, Hendon at last seemed to hold the whip hand. It was now a battle of attrition and stamina in deepening mud. But still Pegasus held on bravely in defence. At that very moment, as someone inquired about a replay, a stray pass suddenly reached Stroud some 25 yards from goal and the next second the ball lay snug in the Pegasus net, shot into the top corner past an unsighted goalkeeper with the speed of an arrow. Here, indeed, was a bolt from the blue, a stroke fit to settle any affair. Hendon had gained their just reward and Pegasus, it seemed, were out. But little did we suspect what yet lay in store.

THE FINAL DRAMA

Only four minutes of life remained when all at once Dutchman, the main-spring of the Pegasus attack, sent Tanner away on a quick burst through the middle which ended with an infringement on the centre-forward and a free kick to Pegasus some 30 yards from the Hendon goal. Dutchman took it, slashing a low shot with all his power into a packed goalmouth. As it sped by, Tanner, with outstretched foot, got a touch to divert the ball into the far top corner past the helpless Ivey, and Pegasus, amidst a bedlam of noise, by some miracle were level.

But the last drop had yet to be squeezed from the afternoon. Two minutes from the end Avis, in a quick Hendon riposte, was brought down by an un-balanced Pegasus defender as he dribbled his way across the penalty area. Penalty. Brown faced Adams across 12 yards of mud and across an ocean of silence in which the beat of one's heart was like the jangling of an alarm clock. Adams moved to the kick and suddenly there was Brown twisting to turn a fast shot to his left, head high, away and over the bar. The world seemed to shift on its axis. Umbrellas waved and hats flew in the air or were pressed down about their owner's ears. And when soon the final whistle brought blessed relief Brown and Adams were seen to shake hands and seal a moment that had been theirs alone.

Such was the ending and the boiling point of the afternoon. Yet the prologue, too, from an academic point of view was full of life and interest. The first half certainly produced the best football, with Hendon denied three clear chances in the opening half hour by the brilliant saves of Brown from Avis and Phebey. These two players were quite the best of a fast Hendon attack freely and cleverly prompted by the class and balance of Topp, and by the quick anticipation of Lynch. Avis in particular was a constant danger with his speed which too often took him past Maughan for the comfort of Pegasus. Yet by the half hour Pegasus, with Cowan and Saunders playing finely, especially in their distribution, and with Shearwood holding the dangerous Stroud, had begun to take control. Some of their sweeping attacks along the ground, based on the short diagonal pass—too short one thought—were full of promise and artistry, but two main factors, contributed against their proper completion. One, certainly, was the heavy going which demanded a pass being hit instead of pushed; the other, the blunting of their left flank by Topp and Lynch. Tanner tried all he knew against the solid Adams, and Potts, with his jinking runs, left the impression of too much attempted and too little done. But all the time Dutchman, supported by Saunders and Platt, kept the attack moving to the point of exhaustion.

At the change of ends the firm Hendon defence began to stifle the Pegasus attacks further and further away from Ivey. And now the full heat was turned on against Shearwood, Cowan and the rest at the other end. Brown saved finely in quick succession, at full graceful stretch, from Westmore, Topp and Phebey. And then suddenly a game that had been slowly coming to the boil, bubbled over to leave us limp and exhausted. The teams were:

HENDON – R. Ivey; P. Lynch, M. Lane; L. Topp, D. Adams, W. Fisher; J. Westmore, A. H. Phebey, R. Stroud, G. Hinshelwood, R. Avis.

PEGASUS – B. R. Brown; J. Maughan, R. Cowan; J. Platt, K. A. Shearwood, D. F. Saunders; H. J. Potts, J. A. Dutchman, J. D. P. Tanner, J. S. Laybourne, R. Sutcliffe.

We had a week's respite to gather our wits and consider how best we could strengthen the side to deal with Hendon in the replay the following Saturday at Selhurst Park.

The all-round ability of our opponents was abundantly clear. In attack Avis had ben a thorn in our flesh and it was thought expedient to switch Johnny Maughan to left-back and let Ralph Cowan, such an accomplished player, look after Avis. Then there was the question of whether Tony Pawson's ankle was strong enough. It was touch and go, but in the end he played. Donald Carr came in again at inside-left in place of Jack Laybourne who had been preferred when the going was heavy as at Highbury. With his accurate left foot Donald could find Tony Pawson with long cross-field passes from left to right. He wasn't as busy a player as Jack Laybourne nor as strong, but I think at the time he possessed more guile for that particular position.

And so with two new faces up front, Jimmy Potts left playing on the left and the switching of our two backs, Hendon now faced fresh problems and a different team, a fact which Tommy did not release to the press, only announcing the changes just before the kick off.

81

We left our London hotel and drove by coach to Selhurst Park accompanied by several wives, Tommy and Graham, Vic Buckingham, Harvey Chadder and Jerry, and of course our man with the sponge, Leslie Laitt. We had eaten an early lunch of boiled chicken and as we drove through the streets of London we listened on the radio to the rich voice of John Snagge recounting the 1951 Boat Race. Cambridge were in the lead and the going was very rough. Suddenly John Snagge's voice took on a new pitch of excitement 'My goodness, Oxford are in trouble, they're shipping a lot of water, I think they're sinking,' much cheering from the Cambridge contingent, 'yes, they're sinking . . . the Oxford boat is sinking, the crew are sitting up to their waists in the water.' More cheers. 'They're swimming, the whole of the Oxford crew are now swimming, this is really quite extraordinary,' and the rest of his words were drowned by the derisive laughter of our five Cambridge players.

'I reckon Tommy suspects Doug Insole's hand in all this,' said Jerry in my ear, as we drove on in high fettle towards Selhurst Park.

Unlike Highbury, the main entrance to the Crystal Palace ground in 1951 was marred by a great ugly facade of corrugated iron and a huge bank of open terrace on the far side. But, to compensate, the day was fine and the ground conditions firm, quite different from the previous week, and I thought it would suit us better. Promptly at three o'clock we began the battle all over again, this time with a strong wind at our backs.

And immediately we saw how Hendon had countered our team changes by switching Stroud to outside-right, his international berth, in an attempt to exploit Johnny Maughan, and within six minutes their move had succeeded and Stroud had scored. Ten minutes later Tony Pawson equalized and at half-time we were still level, one apiece.

It was the bitter blow that struck us two minutes after the start of the second half that I found so demoralizing. One of the Hendon forwards ran the ball a good foot and more over our goal-line and cut it back to Avis who, spotting Ben Brown already moving out of his goal—unwisely anticipating a goal kick—shot into our empty net. It seemed incredible that the referee, who was well up with the play, could fail to have seen that the ball had gone over—but perhaps he was momentarily unsighted. These things can happen.

We didn't say anything, there was no point, but we all felt plenty,

82

particularly Jimmy Platt. The ball was already back in the middle and Ralph Cowan was exhorting us, calling for the ball, and when he'd got it, coming forward into attack, committing the Hendon defence then slipping the ball to Tony Pawson. Denis too, quite unruffled, kept collecting, pushing and prompting our left flank, forcing Pat Lynch and his men to play more and more defensively. But no goal came. Two–one down and with just six minutes left we were still pressing desperately, but Geoffrey Green can tell the whole story far better than I can :

It is seldom that a game of football returns upon its footsteps so faithfully, if not in precise detail then certainly in mood and passion and timing, as did the F.A. Amateur Cup semi-final replay between Pegasus and Hendon at Selhurst Park on Saturday. If the match at Highbury the previous week had provided a breath-taking finish, the ending on Saturday positively stirred the blood. And once again it was Pegasus, on the side of the angels, who came from behind, with two goals snatched from a cloudless sky in the last six minutes, to win a great victory by 3–2 and so reach the final at Wembley for the first time in their young, exciting lives.

Thus Hendon, with the prize once more dashed from their grasp at the very end, were left to the purple dignity of their grief, and, amidst all the clamour of a finale that bordered on the hysterical, one's admiration and sympathy for them were both sincere and profound. Yet on this occasion at least the palm of victory was justly awarded. Pegasus not only were now the better footballers —the velvet pitch of Wembley will suit their style—but they proved once more that nothing can prevail against a matchless and unflinching spirit.

Again must the story be recounted in reverse. Yet how to translate into words the impressions of those fading moments that now seem so remote from reality? One must have been there to experience something of the feeling of Pegasus and of Hendon as the very aspect of the world seemed to change in a twinkling before our startled eyes. At any rate, for some 25 minutes after the interval Pegasus, 2–1 down, had hurled themselves with buoyant teamwork and skilful, closely linked approach along the ground against the firmly organised Hendon defence. With a quarter of an hour left, at last they seemed to have beaten the breath out of themselves.

Time was draining rapidly away when suddenly the spark of Pegasus flared again, kindled as much perhaps by the cool courage of Cowan as by anyone. Six minutes to go and all at once there was Pawson, gathering Platt's forward lob, to slash a centre across the Hendon goalmouth. A hurried clearance, the ball running loose at the edge of the penalty area, and the next moment Pegasus were level for the second time as Dutchman, once again showing his untold worth, hit a low shot through a crowded goalmouth past the unsighted Ivey. It was deserved, but that it had happened was beyond belief. Some no doubt were silent and still. But the impression all around was of dancing, waving figures, a solid, equable community suddenly gone wild.

Now for extra time and a fight to the finish. So it seemed. But the end was not yet, not by a mile. Attack followed attack in the last dying spasm. Blow the whistle now, for both sides' sake, one almost cried out. A minute and a half to go and suddenly there was Tanner taking a long forward pass in his stride at top speed down the left flank to force a corner off Adams. Potts placed the ball with tender care one remembers. A curling in-swinger to the near post, a backwards flick with his head by Tanner, and again there arose Dutchman, in an unguarded spot close in, to pivot quickly and slash a rising shot into the roof of the Hendon net. There was a fine quality of triumph and tragedy about that moment, but the scene now seems blurred and confused as the wave of hot excitement surged up and consumed everything. Somehow the last 60 seconds passed and soon there were the Pegasus players swamped by running figures and Saunders, the captain, and Dutchman being carried shoulder-high from the field. It was more than any nervous system should be called upon to stand on successive Saturdays.

If the plot provided a story-book ending, the match itself, too, produced a higher quality of play than the first encounter. Pegasus in particular, with a rearranged forward line which brought back Pawson and Carr, were a new combined power in attack. Pawson especially, with his quick dribbling and instinctive games sense, was a constant menace to Lane, while Potts, too, using his undoubted gifts and acceleration properly this time, now on the left, worried the redoubtable Lynch, so that there was thrust where it was most needed—down the wings. The defence, as a single unit, solidified as the game progressed, but there were moments before the interval when it was not at ease against the sudden individual thrusts of Stroud, Phebey, and Avis, though Cowan and Saunders, skilful and cultured, plugged the holes grandly.

The switching of Cowan to face the dangerous Avis was immediately answered by Hendon. Stroud took up his old position on the right wing to exploit the suspected Pegasus weak link in Maughan. After only six minutes the finesse worked, for Phebey cleverly sent Stroud past his opposing back to give Hendon the lead with a fine shot from a sharp angle. But soon, just after the quarter-hour, Pegasus were level when Tanner and Pawson, interchanging and inter-passing at speed, swept through the Hendon left flank for Pawson finally to take Tanner's short diagonal pass from the right and hit a rising shot past Ivey. This was quite the best goal of the two desperate encounters..

At the half-hour Stroud, switching with Westmore, returned to the centre, but Shearwood, watching him closely and firmly to the end, worried him out of danger. Topp, Adams, and Fisher were playing well for Hendon, but Pegasus were beginning to move on a rising concerted note in attack as half-time approached, though before it finally arrived Brown once more made a particularly fine save at Westmore's feet.

Two minutes after the change of ends Avis, dubiously retrieving the ball from the bye-line, put Hendon into the lead again with a long swirling shot into an unguarded net against a Pegasus defence that had relaxed and stopped, expecting the decision of a goal-kick. Hendon, with a sharp wind behind them, now seemed set for Wembley, and they would probably have won their place there, too, but for a great diving save by Brown to Avis, turning the winger's shot on to his post and away for a corner.

But Pegasus now arose to touch the heights. Driven on by the unhurried Saunders and by Platt, the restless terrier, Dutchman and Carr sprayed their passes into attack, left, right and centre. For half an hour they took complete control, but Hendon, with Adams outstanding, packed their defence solidly. For them the top of the hill was almost within reach when suddenly Pegasus with wings outstretched, soared past, away, and over the blue horizon. This was the stuff dreams are made of, and poor Hendon were left bowed before an intangible, irresistible force.

PEGASUS – B. R. Brown (Mexborough G.S. and Oxford); R. Cowan (Chorlton G.S. and Cambridge), J. Maughan (Stanley G.S. and Oxford); J. Platt (Hulme G.S. and Cambridge), K. A. Shearwood (Shrewsbury and Oxford), D. F. Saunders (Scarborough H.S. and Oxford); H. A. Pawson (Winchester and Oxford), J. A. Dutchman (Cockburn H.S. and Cambridge), J. D. P. Tanner (Charterhouse and Oxford), D. B. Carr (Repton and Oxford), H. J. Potts (Stand G.S. and Oxford).

HENDON – R. Ivey; P. Lynch, M. Lane; L. Topp, D. Adams, W. Fisher; J. Westmore, A. H. Phebey, R. Stroud, G. Hinshelwood, R. Avis.

10 Wembley

'Champagne for anyone who wants it back at 100 Piccadilly,' announced Bush O'Callaghan, bursting into our changing-room like some swashbuckling pirate of the Caribbean.

Bush was an Harrovian and a man of considerable wealth. His chief occupation was horse-racing and achieving his target of playing a hundred cricket matches a season. He was short, stout, had a thick moustache, a great belly of a laugh and didn't give a damn. He struck the ball ferociously, planting his left foot imperiously down the wicket and invariably opened the innings. I once had the uncomfortable experience of being driven by him at a hundred miles an hour down Piccadilly in his Bentley.

He'd been a gunner in the 49th West Riding Division, and during a break for rain whilst playing with him for a club called the Frogs at Oxford in one of his many matches, I learned from our captain, Mike Singleton, how on a certain nerve-racking occasion in Normandy he'd been shelled by Bush's battery and forced to take refuge beneath a wrecked German half-track that lay by the roadside.

However, Bush never denied his unofficial success in the liberation of the Benedictine monastery at Fécamp. And when the monks decided they'd sold just about enough bottles of Benedictine to him, he promptly rustled up a three-tonner full of sugar, a commodity the monks were very short of, and business proceeded at an even brisker pace than before.

Jim Swanton was amongst the gathering sipping a glass of champagne and I asked him if he was coming to Wembley.

'Couldn't possibly miss the opportunity of seeing you play there Ken,' he assured me.

'Give you a dover sole if you beat the Bishops,' said Ken Pitts, our fishmonger the following day back at Woodstock.

'Are you coming?' I asked.

'We'll be there,' he replied.

And so it seemed would the whole of Oxford and those who couldn't go would be watching the match on television or listening to it on the radio. Throughout the country there was an astonishing display of interest and as the Final approached the press began to make their forecasts.

Our opponents Bishop Auckland had beaten Evenwood, Shildon, Whitby Town, Walton and Hersham in a replay, and Bromley, and on the whole they were considered the favourites. David Williams considered :

Their attack is probably the best in the country. This asset plus experience should be the winning factor.

Harry Done in the *Evening Standard* also considered them to be the favourites :

Yet the majority of the 100,000 spectators will be hoping that Pegasus can spring the greatest surprise of their remarkable career. Pegasus have caught the imagination by their tremendous fighting spirit and victory for them would complete the most romantic story in amateur soccer. I expect Auckland to win, but if a replay is necessary it will take place at Middlesbrough.

Harry Ditton, under a heading, 'This Soccer Side Has a Mission', concluded :

Those with the best opportunities of judging the strength of the finalists believe the trophy will go North again. I will only suggest that it should be one of the greatest finals ever, and if Pegasus produce their top form and the 'Bishops' still prove their masters, then the North will deserve the Cup.

Rather endearingly Raymond Glendenning remarked :

Even if the Combined Universities side, Pegasus, don't beat Bishop Auckland at Wembley they will still be my football team of the year.

And under another headline, 'Proud Pegasus', someone had this to say :

Who would you name as the soccer team of the year—Spurs, Blackpool, Newcastle or Preston North End? Well, mine is Pegasus—the amateur club that has done more than your Arsenals, Aston Villas or Prestons to raise the prestige of the game.

General interest in the unexpected triumph of this three-year-old soccer baby is so great that there has been an increased rush on the tickets for the final against Bishop Auckland at Wembley on April 21st, and Stadium officials are already forecasting that the 93,000 record attendance for the Bromley–Romford clash the year before last will be broken. All seats have been sold out and only 2s. standing tickets remain. Bishop Auckland will face the battle knowing that the sympathy of the country outside of their own supporters will be behind the varsity men, because with the fading of the old Corinthians, soccer has become the poorer.

If Pegasus can lift the trophy, let us hope that there will be such a revival at Oxford and Cambridge that one day Pegasus will have a team to appear in the F.A. Cup Final.

Norman Ackland expressed a slight preference for Pegasus and I heeded in particular one of his sentences :

A lot depends on the ability of Shearwood to hold McIlvenny.

Wrote Dennis Roberts :

Two amateur footballers, Denis Saunders and Harry McIlvenny, will shake hands before 100,000 people at Wembley Stadium on Saturday; then will begin an amateur match that could not be rivalled in interest anywhere in the world.

The *Oxford Times* made no prediction.

We have a right to expect a great game with so many fine players on both sides. Probably the rivals are stronger in attack than defence, and if the forward lines function as they can do, the game should be replete with thrills. It is hinted that the Bishop Auckland right wing will need to be closely watched, while in McIlvenny they have one of the most dangerous centre-forwards in the game, a Scottish international with a string of goals to his credit. His duel with Shearwood, now at the peak of his form, should be one of the high-lights of the game, while Davidson and Nimmins, backed up by the industrious Hardisty, will find Saunders a difficult proposition. Without fuss, with quiet confidence, and with his clever anticipation and wonderful ball control the Pegasus captain will face his task with mathematical precision. Then behind him is the incomparable Brown, one of the best amateur goalkeepers in the game. We must not, of course, leave out of count the brilliant Pegasus forward line with their speed over the ground and with the ball, their strong combination and individualism so cleverly co-ordinated and their shooting. The Bishop Auckland half-backs should be tested more than they have been in any previous cup-tie this or any other season. Thus, if the rival merits of the two teams are not over-assessed, as I do not think they are, it should be a game worthy of a great occasion.

Geoffrey Green summed it all up :

The meeting of Bishop Auckland and Pegasus at Wembley Stadium this afternoon clearly promises to be the most interesting F.A. Amateur Cup final for many years. The fact that a record crowd for an amateur match of 100,000 people, among them the visiting South African cricketers, will be gathered together in the stadium to see the game—every square inch of space has already been claimed—supports this.

But beyond all the general wide interest already aroused there is an intriguing mixture of the old and the new in the occasion. Bishop Auckland, perhaps the most distinguished amateur club in the country, are making their fourteenth appearance in the final. They have taken the trophy back to their stronghold in the north-east on seven occasions and they are now in the sixty-second year of their existence. Pegasus, the combined Oxford and Cambridge Universities' club, will reach their third birthday on May 2, and it is they truly who have suddenly excited the interest and admiration of so many people. Yet in spite of the disparity between the ages of these contestants there is a fascinating link between them, for Bishop Auckland themselves were founded in 1889 by a number of Oxford and Cambridge students studying theology at the time at Auckland Castle under Bishop Lightfoot. To this day the Bishop Auckland colours are the dark and light blues (quartered) of the two universities. Here, then, is a fine historical background for a battle royal.

Bishop Auckland's feats in this great amateur competition have been outstanding. It is remarkable how they have maintained their success across the years since they first won the prize in 1896. To examine their record since the war alone will be sufficient. In six seasons they have reached the final three times and the semi-final on two other occasions. That speaks for itself and today, having disposed of the dangerous Bromley in the semi-final after a great struggle, they will take the field with six of their team that was surprisingly beaten at Wembley last year by Willington. They are a fine attacking side. There are four amateur internationals in it—Hardisty, who captained Great Britain in the Olympic Games, McIlvenny, Farrer, and Anderson. Their half-back line is particularly strong, all of whom incidentally, know Wembley— a great asset on such an occasion.

Against all this wide experience and achievement, Pegasus have little of a comparative nature to offer. However, what they do offer is something quite fresh. The formation of Pegasus in 1948 was an experiment, a crusade to win back a place once held in the sun by the universities so many years ago. In so short a time it has proved itself to be a glorious success. If a satisfactory working formula has yet to be worked out with their brothers the Corinthian-Casuals, themselves with such close ties with Oxford and Cambridge over the years, that no doubt will be achieved in time. Meanwhile Pegasus have become a symbol that has given a tremendous impetus to the game in the universities and the schools. This is a renaissance, and it is the best thing that has happened to amateur football for a very long time.

Coached by Buckingham, of Tottenham Hotspur, Pegasus play in the Spurs' style of push and run, with the ball on the ground. Like Tottenham they try to do the simple things and do them quickly. The Wembley turf, once they feel the pace of it, may suit them admirably. But besides this they possess a quality of team spirit and stamina that has brought them from behind four times in six ties. They, too, can boast four internationals in Cowan, Brown, Potts, and Tanner; Pawson and Shearwood have played in F.A. representative sides, and Saunders, their captain, has gained an amateur international trial.

Attack is their true metier and they are at their best when they are being led. Now they take their place on the national stage of Wembley without once having played on their home ground at Iffley Road, Oxford, and famous Bishop Auckland, for all their history and experience, will need to go to the final whistle no matter what the score.

We had a month to prepare for Wembley and we began by playing a reserve side, which included Jimmy Platt and Johnny Maughan, against Cambridge Town away and lost 0–1.

The following week we lost again, 2–3 to Sutton United on their ground with eight of the side that had played against Hendon. Sutton's winning goal came from a free kick hit through our badly lined-up wall, giving Colin Weir—Ben Brown was playing for England against Scotland at Hampden Park—no chance.

I had been driven to the game in Leslie Laitt's car, with Tommy sitting in the front, Denis, Donald, and myself at the back. Leslie owned a Morris Oxford, registration number FLO, which he nick-named Flossie and tended with loving pride and care. Overhead it was drizzling steadily.

'Take the next left turn Laitt ... no, left,' said Tommy. 'Never mind. Go on and take the next one.'

The traffic was heavy, cars hemming us in on either side.

'Now,' said Tommy, 'you can pull over to the left. Now. Quick man. You're too late.'

'I couldn't get in,' explained Leslie.

'You can now—look out!'

The bus in front had stopped suddenly and braking sharply we skidded along the tram lines straight into its backside.

'God,' said Leslie.

'Get over to the left and you can take this one coming up,' said Tommy, as the traffic began moving again, oblivious of the incident.

'It's a one way street,' said Leslie desperately.

'Then take the next,' said Tommy irritably. 'If you don't get a move on, Laitt, we shan't make the kick off.'

We did however—just.

'Never mind, Les,' said Denis as we surveyed the damage, 'it could have been worse.'

'A fat lot he cares,' said our man with the sponge, looking discon-solately at the back of Tommy, who was fast making tracks towards the main stand.

On the Saturday before the Final we defeated Moor Green 2–1 with what was to be the Wembley side, except that Colin Weir kept goal in place of Ben Brown, who had a damaged thumb.

Finally, with three days remaining, we played an hour's practice against the First Division leaders, Spurs, out on their training ground at Cheshunt. Once again Colin Weir had to deputize for Ben Brown, while Roy Sutcliffe came in for John Tanner and promptly scored within thirty seconds. But at the end we were 3–1 down which wasn't bad considering they had eight of their regular side playing. Observing Alf Ramsay at right-back I could see what Vic had meant. He was slow all right, but his constructive and positional sense could not be faulted.

So, barring last minute accidents, the final side was selected, the same as that which had defeated Hendon. Eight players were from Oxford, three from Cambridge. Seven came from grammar schools, four from public schools. All except two, John Tanner and Tony Pawson, were still in residence.

Looking back on it all now, I believe our strength lay in a blend of maturity, ability, intelligence and humour. Several of us had been through the war and seen active service. Most of us had done other things before going to university. Our average age was on the high side, Tony Pawson, John Tanner and myself were all on thirty. When things had gone badly and we found ourselves up against it, these extra years of experience had already proved a valuable asset.

Our ability, too, had been recognized for we could now boast four internationals, and it looked as though there would be more to come.

And with a Doctor of Philosophy in goal, a couple of near firsts on each wing, not to mention two third class Bachelors of Arts at centre-forward and centre-half, Vic Buckingham could afford his comment to the press 'I can reach their feet through their minds.'

Finally there was the humour of it all—Tommy with that perpetual bee in his bonnet that the club was being sabotaged. Leslie Laitt 'I'm not going to be spoken to like that', refusing to treat Ralph Cowan and retiring from the mud bath of Highbury in high dudgeon, all because in the heat of the battle we'd reprimanded him for examining our right-back's leg, when it was really his arm that was in question.

All this and a lot more produced a blend, sufficiently strong and resilient, upon which I always felt we could draw when the chips were down and the going tough.

On Friday afternoon we paid a visit to Wembley and looked at the pitch. It was in beautiful condition and as we wandered over the immaculate turf the Bishops arrived to do the same. We didn't make contact but I've no doubt each of us cast an appraising eye at the other. We could spot Bob Hardisty's balding head, but I wasn't sure which was Harry McIlvenny. There'd be plenty of time to make his acquaintance the following afternoon.

We spent that night, Biddie and I, at 100 Piccadilly, Bush's flat, and a strange thing happened in the morning. We were looking at our host's fine collection of bird photographs, when a barrel organ which had been playing outside suddenly broke into the Eton Boating Song. Was it an augur of things to come?

While Bush looked after four of our wives the team lunched together and then set off by coach for Wembley. Tommy, cigar in mouth, was in expansive mood, while Vic Buckingham, brown trilby set jauntily and coat flung characteristically across his shoulders, was full of relaxed confidence. When the great twin towers eventually came into view, I think it all set us thinking. But not for long, for true to form we immediately lost our way and ended up in a builder's yard at the back of the stadium, with Leslie sitting in the front directing operations and Tommy momentarily concerned lest it be some last-minute piece of sabotage. So we finally made it to Wembley, the doors opened and we drove right in.

The changing-room, with its long narrow windows spacious and light but strangely impersonal, lacked the friendly atmosphere of Highbury or White Hart Lane. We had plenty of time to change. Our kit, which Leslie had already begun to put out, was new, our white shirts carrying the bold insignia of a light blue horse flying against a dark blue background. There were hundreds of telegrams to greet us. I personally received twenty-three which included five from former colleagues in Mediterranean Landing Craft, one from the Gorran Haven Cricket Club, and one from the Mevagissey Football Club. A great wealth of goodwill seemed to surround us.

I did not feel any more nervous for this game, perhaps if anything less so. After all we had arrived and were nearly at the end of the race. It's those early matches that are so often the more nerve wracking, when drawn away on a small and hostile ground against an unfashionable but competent side that has probably fought its way through the early qualifying rounds. Then, things sometimes go wrong and Wembley can seem a thousand miles distant. But now the stage was set, the sun shining, a great crowd gathering. This was what we had been playing for, this was what Tommy had planned and hoped for. There was nothing to fear; everything to enjoy. We were prepared and ready for the final test.

'Listen now,' said Vic quietly, holding up his hands as though giving us his blessing, 'you each want the ball, every man jack of you, so be prepared to have it and take responsibility, right from the start. All right?' and he looked at us quizzically for a moment, still completely relaxed. 'Good luck then,' and we went out into the tunnel, lined up alongside Bishop Auckland and waited for Tommy and the F.A. officials to lead us out. We could hear the band playing and the crowd singing and then we were off and walking side by side with our opponents up the slight gradient of the tunnel out into the sunlit stadium—and what a sight and sound greeted us both.

There is plenty of time as one walks out and lines up yet again, to see and savour it all and I had a good look round at that vast crowd before shaking hands with Lord Wigram, the official guest. There was also time for a few last moment thoughts of what lay ahead.

We were well aware of the threat Bob Hardisty constituted and had made our plans to contain him. We decided to let him come and not bring Donald Carr back to play defensively. Then, after robbing him, we'd quickly exploit the gap he'd left behind and find Donald. Otherwise we'd continue to play just as before, with the accent on simplicity and speed, adopting Arthur Rowe's maxim 'Make it simple, make it quick', endeavouring always to give the early ball.

We knew, too, that if we supplied our forwards we had three who could take on the opposition and beat them : Tony Pawson and John Tanner by skill and sheer speed, Jimmy Potts, more by guile than speed. At inside-forward Donald Carr and John Dutchman could both open the game up. They had shooting power too. In the middle Denis would quietly take control and set things going, while Jimmy Platt, small, neat and explosive, would never be out of the game for a second. Ralph Cowan at right-back was adept at turning defence into attack, linking with Tony Pawson, often receiving the ball back, then looking up and finding John Tanner or pin-pointing a long cross. On the left Johnnie Maughan, very quick into the tackle, could match any winger for speed. Finally there was Ben, who never called, never spoke, and never got ruffled; it was just not in his nature. We both understood each other. He knew what I was going to do, though some might dispute this. I knew what he was going to do. If I could protect him from the centre-forward I would. If he could help me, he did— with quiet and graceful efficiency. I felt a great confidence in having such players around me.

But now the ball was in the centre, the clock showing three, the curtain lifting. Then the whistle blew and the game began.

Of that Final I recall little. Only the last dying moments stand out with any clarity. For Ben, in conceding a corner had collided with an upright and suffered a severe cut under his left eye.

'That needs stitching,' said Vic Buckingham who had run on and was examining Ben's eye.

'Come on Vic,' urged Arthur Ellis, who was to become such a famous referee.

'Anyone would think it was a Cup-Final,' retorted Vic, sticking a piece of plaster over Ben's eye.

'And isn't it?' said Arthur as Vic retired behind the goal to squat amongst the photographers and watch as we faced that final corner.

It was the Bishops' last chance and well they knew it, as they came swarming into our penalty area putting us under great pressure.

I stuck close to McIlvenny, but could sense the lurking menace of Hardisty lying deep outside the far post, waiting to come in over our backs, timing his run in one last desperate endeavour to head an equalizer. But Denis was there too.

And then the ball came across, a soaring out-swinger, and up we all went, the danger lifted and as we broke from the penalty area the whistle blew.

Two policemen were chasing a frantic red-faced figure who was striving to reach us, gripping an orange in each hand, waving his arms and shouting in delirious incoherence. But Chedder Wilson, most loyal of Pegasus supporters, did not on this occasion escape the arms of the law and was firmly but cheerfully deposited back from whence he'd come.

We climbed up the steps to receive the Cup and our gold medals and I was surprised at how low the ledge was that protected us from a twenty foot drop. It struck me at the time how easy it would be to topple over. And then we went down on to the pitch again and were photographed with Denis seated on somebody's shoulder. I had another good long look round at it all, savouring a moment I thought I would not see again. When eventually we left the pitch it was still a perfect afternoon.

Back in our changing-room there was a popping of corks, a lot of people and a lot of chatter with Tommy ecstatic, Jerry peering delightedly through his dark glasses, Graham and Harvey quietly going round congratulating everybody, Vic joking, Ben having his eye attended to, but not by Leslie who was busy, hat upon head, collecting up our gear.

Then into the bus, the doors of Wembley swung open and we drove through the thinning crowds with the Cup back to Paddington Hotel where we bought the *Evening News* with its heading : PEGASUS WIN TITANIC AMATEUR CUP. Then we changed into evening dress and on again with our wives and girl friends to the Mayfair Hotel for dinner and dancing.

I felt in great form—we all did. A waiter hovered in the wings. 'A drink, sir?'

'Yes,' I said, 'that would be nice. We'll have forty-eight sherries.'

'Forty-eight sherries, sir?'

'That's right.'

'Very good, sir. Sweet or dry?'

'Better make 'em half and half.'

'Very good, sir. And shall I credit them to your account?'

'I think probably not. Pegasus Football Club would be the better bet.'

'Very good sir.'

It sort of set things going.

It was Geoffrey Green who proposed the toast of the club with the Cup gleaming in the centre of the top table. Amongst the many nice things he had to say was a warning that we were about to face our most difficult time, keeping on top.

The following morning, such was my vanity, I bought every paper I could lay my hands on and revelled in the tremendous press we received. It was quite astonishing.

Great black headlines in the national papers greeted us : 'Wonderful Pegasus, I Salute Them All'—'Proud Pegasus Revive Past Glories'—'Modern Corinthians Serve Up Champagne At Wembley'—'Pegasus Showed The Spurs Touch'—'Thrilling Amateur Cup Final Victory'—'Pegasus Amateurs Made League Stars Look Lazy'—'The Best Thing That's Happened In Sport For Years', while the whole of the back page of the *Sunday Graphic* told the story in pictures. So it went on.

Geoffrey Green had this to say :

The F.A. Amateur Cup found a new resting place on Saturday when a record crowd for the final of the competition, 100,000 strong, saw Pegasus gain a great victory over famous Bishop Auckland by two goals to one at Wembley

Stadium. The trophy forthwith goes into residence, *in statu pupillari,* at the very heart of the Universities of Oxford and Cambridge, and in so doing has perhaps satisfied the desires of a sentimental majority.

Someone inquired after the match : 'What happened to the world to-day? In the Hendon semi-final at Highbury it was said to have shifted on its axis.' The world on Saturday, it can now be revealed, returned to its stately equilibrium, and the world on Saturday was left to applaud a great achievement.

The story, in fact, moved towards its finale on the sunlit and shaded stage of Wembley with a balanced and measured tread. In retrospect it would seem somehow to have been inevitable. This was but the last drawing together of the stray ends, the process of tidying up to provide a rational climax to all the emotional upheaval amidst the mud and the rain of earlier passages. Pegasus, without having to draw fully upon their resources of spirit and will, by their technical skill alone strode to a wider victory than the score will ever reflect.

For only one phase of the shining afternoon were Pegasus called upon to reach deep down within themselves. That was the opening 20 minutes, a critical spasm while they were yet attuning themselves to the ample, towering amphitheatre, to the pace of its pitch, and to the part they were yet to play upon it. It was then that their courage and mental balance led them through and away from a darkening position. If Bishop Auckland were to have won they should have won then. Within that span they had two clear chances to gain a flying start, but just as they had done against Willington in the previous year, they cast them to the four winds. Each chance, made by the accurate cross-passes of Williamson and Hardisty, fell to the left foot of Edwards and each flew narrowly wide. They found at the last that the winds are not to be mocked lightly.

IN THE CLOUDS

What may well have disturbed Bishop Auckland in their early and threatening assaults was an injury to Anderson, who was never quite himself again after a recuperative spell on the wing in place of Taylor. How great an influence this was to have on the shaping of the final pattern one cannot say. Perhaps little, for by half-time, with the score still bare and the emphasis clearly changing, Bishop Auckland as a team had largely played out their hand. They had offered up the whole wealth at their command and had gained nothing, for their seven-man attack, with Hardisty and Nimmins close up behind McIlvenny and the other forwards, made the tactical error of trying to force the issue in the clouds. Whether or not they were bemused by the symbolism of their opponents' legendary title, their passes were lofted on an undisguised central attack that might have shown—indeed, almost did—a quick profit. But once Shearwood, Maughan, and the other Pegasus defenders had recovered from the early stammerings of their testing examination Bishop Auckland showed that they had little else to produce as an alternative. Yet had those shots by Edwards found their mark there may well have been a different ending.

The man above all who led Pegasus out into the brightness of another day was Saunders, the captain. Certainly Cowan, with his cool balance, soon to be followed by Shearwood, Maughan, and Platt by their enthusiasm, lent splendid support, but it was Saunders who first pointed the way ahead. By his intelligent positional play, interceptions, and distribution of the ball he slowly turned back the tide that first ran so strongly from the north-east. By the half-hour Farrer, Marshall, and Davison, so quick and sure in the tackle previously, were being gradually unhinged by a Pegasus attack that at last had begun to find its feet and show its power down the wings. And when in the dying moments of the half Potts lost a great chance from Tanner in the very jaws of the goalmouth one sensed that there was trouble ahead for Bishop Auckland, even though they were yet to have the sun and breeze at their backs.

Trouble was not long in coming. At the change of ends Pegasus at once took wings to their heels. Almost immediately Tanner, who more and more was to have a decisive influence on affairs, made chances for Dutchman and Pawson, which Auckland somehow survived. A header by Saunders from Pawson's corner was hooked off the line brilliantly by Marshall, and then at the fifth minute Pegasus found themselves ahead. It was Dutchman, with a deep cross accurately pitched to the far edge of the goal area, who made the opening. It was Potts, moving in swiftly, who did the final damage. His header to the opposite corner of the net was thumped with a speed and precision that left White helpless. A fine goal.

FULL BLOOM

The quality of the play now took a sharp upward trend. Attack was in full bloom. The central gaps behind the Auckland seven-man attack were exploited by a series of quick ground passes between Saunders, Platt, Carr, and Dutchman, short and long, long and short, varied and intelligent. Pawson, taking the inside path of Farrer, and Potts kept the attacks rolling inwards; Tanner, unlike McIlvenny, who was in Shearwood's worrying grip, began to lose Davison by speed on the turn. Soon Pawson hit the crossbar from his square pass.

But Bishop Auckland were not done with yet. Driven on by Hardisty, who played finely and gallantly, they rearranged their forces with Nimmins, another warrior, now in the attack, Taylor at right-half and Hardisty himself on the other flank. For a spell Pegasus were again back on their heels. Brown twice needed repairs, having his face patched when he crashed against an upright; a shot by Williamson flashed only inches too high. But Pegasus regained their poise. With ten minutes left they settled matters with a second goal. Again it was well worked. Pawson, Dutchman, and Tanner split the defence with their ground passing and Tanner's shot went home low to the corner.

Their victory could have been emphasized still more in the remaining moments. All that was lacking was the finishing touch from Tanner's quick breaks. And it may have cost them dear, for Auckland, to their great credit, with one last defiant gesture brought a tense finish to the afternoon when Nimmins, with an overhead flick, lobbed Hardisty's corner kick beyond Brown three minutes from the end to narrow the gap.

But soon Saunders was being chaired by his fellows. The cup was in his hands. It caught the sun and it glistened. As the twenty-two players left the field their shadows lengthened, so that they seemed to be giants. The teams were:

97

BISHOP AUCKLAND – W. N. White; D. Marshall, L. T. Farrer; J. R. E. Hardisty, R. W. Davison, J. Nimmins; J. W. R. Taylor, W. Anderson, H. J. McIlvenny (captain), K. Williamson, B. Edwards.

PEGASUS – B. R. Brown; R. Cowan, J. Maughan; J. Platt, K. A. Shearwood, D. F. Saunders (captain); H. A. Pawson, J. A. Dutchman, J. D. P. Tanner, D. B. Carr, H. J. Potts.

Then we returned to Woodstock, where I collected my dover sole from Pitts the fishmonger.

11 End of the One-Year Rule

Our last term at Oxford began with an early cricket match in the Parks which was brought to a sudden close by a fierce hailstorm that drove all before it, whitening the ground in seconds.

A month later there was no such relief from a match of immense tedium played against Notts beneath a cloudless sky and burning sun. Oxford had made a big score in their first innings, and then Nottingham decided they'd have some batting practice for the remaining day and a half and began with an opening stand of 284. For most of that day few balls passed the bat as Simpson headed towards his double century, yet each ball had to be concentrated on and studiously covered. Eventually, his partner, Giles, misjudged his shot and got a touch. Fortunately my gloves were in the right position and I caught him standing close up.

Denis Hendren and Frank Chester umpired the game and towards the end Denis at square leg was removing his handkerchief and dabbing his eyes, at the same time glancing across at his illustrious and rather formidable colleague, Frank Chester, at the bowler's end, causing him to shake with laughter. When the last over began and the Oxford field was scattered to the far corners of the earth, the scoreboard read 578 for 7. And just to liven proceedings still further, Charlie Harris, who had scored 66, carefully took guard twice.

I suppose my real priority should have been to work hard for the examinations that were coming up for my Diploma in Education. I had a thesis to write, something about the purpose of education which I did manage to complete with the aid of Colin Weir. But I simply couldn't take the examinations seriously. Colin had also been instrumental in getting me a teaching post at Lancing College.

I had some months previously gone down to Lancing for an interview with the headmaster, Frank Doherty, and had been offered a job.

'Well,' the head had said, drawing heavily on his cigarette and

99

inhaling deeply. He always used a holder and I never saw a cigarette smoked faster. 'I've got no room for you on my staff . . . but er . . . I'm going to have you. You can teach maths? To the bottom form of course,' he added, seeing my hesitancy.

'Oh yes, I think I could manage that.'

'And you'll take over the cricket from Colin? Well then, that's settled. We shall look forward to seeing you in September.'

Our biggest problem now was to sell Laburnum House and find accommodation in Lancing, for the school could not help us over this.

So we advertised our house in the *Oxford Mail* and *Oxford Times*, and eventually, having shown round an assortment of people, on each occasion hurriedly stuffing everything out of sight yet suffering such comments as, 'how nice it could look', we sold the little house for what we had given for it and with much regret.

One June day I set off for Sussex with Jerry Weinstein to see if we could find a house. I had arranged to pick Jerry up at seven in the morning.

'Don't be late,' I warned.

'Am I ever late?' he replied.

The following morning, on the dot of seven, I called for him and found him still in bed.

'Bloody hell, Jerry, I thought you were never late.'

'Go and get me a *Times* and wait in the car,' he retorted and I did as I was bid.

Now a 1936 Ford Eight was never a particularly spacious vehicle and by the time Jerry opened his *Times* and begun reading, half covering me and the steering wheel in the process, there wasn't much room for driving. And when eventually he emerged from behind his paper some twenty minutes later, I saw that he had not shaved and quickly resolved that it would be better not to show him the school this time, a resolution which was promptly scotched by his next observation, 'a small public school of ecclesiastical temper on the South Downs. Evelyn Waugh describes it in *Decline and Fall*. Well, I'm very much looking forward to seeing it.'

'I doubt if we'll have time, Jerry.'

'We'll bloody well make time, mate.'

To which I made no reply, but smiled and drove on towards Lancing and the sea.

It was this fact—that we would be once more living by the sea—which made the prospect of my teaching at Lancing such a pleasant one for us both. I was also acquainted with the school, for the Royal Navy had taken it over in the war to train their officers. As one of a group of matelots I had been driven up the winding drive in a bus one bleak winter's day in 1942 and off-loaded alongside the soaring unfinished chapel, the last great gothic structure to be built in England. It was raining and the grey flint buildings had looked cold and uninviting. For six weeks we had been instructed in navigation, gunnery, signalling, and taught the meaning of O.L.Q., short for that awful phrase, 'officer-like qualities'. Finally, as each division passed out, before going on to King Alfred, in Hove, to complete their commissions, we all had to take part in an entertainment which the C.O. and his officers attended. I was cast in the role of the Archangel Gabriel and had to flap my way on and off the stage with a pair of huge and ridiculous wings fastened to my arms, knowing that upon my performance could well hinge the success of my commission.

As we came now to the old toll bridge and saw the great chapel and school silhouetted against the skyline those memories came flooding back.

We visited an estate agent in Lancing, who arranged for us to see several properties.

Eventually we found a pleasant little bungalow, high up, close to the Downs, fairly close to the school, and with a view of the sea. It cost three thousand pounds.

'This is the one Jerry,' and we went back to the agent where I paid a deposit.

'Now we'll go and have a look at the school and your future employers,' said my friend, and I knew there was no way out.

We were both hot and tired; it was almost four o'clock.

'Could do with a cup of tea,' Jerry said, as we parked the car beneath the chapel, and walked towards the broad flight of steps that lay at the side of the headmaster's study.

And just at that precise moment he chose to appear.

'The head,' I warned Jerry, devoutly but unsuccessfully hoping he would not see us.

'Hello,' I said, as he caught sight of us, 'we've come down to find somewhere to live ... may I introduce my legal adviser, Jerry Weinstein?'

'How d'you do,' said Frank Doherty, a little curiously, as Jerry shifted his stick to his left hand and with a fearful unshaven leer peered lop-sidedly at the headmaster through his dark glasses, then shook his hand.

We found Colin Weir and had a cup of tea in the common room. Opposite me someone was reading *The Times*. Suddenly I was aware of being watched, and looking up caught a glimpse of pale blue eyes before the paper shifted sideways again.

Colin came and saw us off.

'Who was that behind the paper?' I asked him.

'Henry Thorold, the assistant chaplain.'

'Ah,' I said, 'he seems inquisitive.'

'Henry doesn't miss much.'

On the 16th of June an important meeting was held at St. John's College, Oxford, to discuss matters affecting the future policy of Pegasus, at which the following were present: A. H. Chadder, the president, A. G. Doggart, the treasurer, Dr. H. W. Thompson, the secretary, and Messrs. Shearwood, Heritage, Saunders, Cowan, Platt, Hall, Brown, Maughan, Tanner, Potts, Robinson. Apologies for absence had been received from Messrs. May, Vowels, P. Jones (Falcons' representative), Pawson, Carr, Dutchman.

After the president had expressed his pleasure at the great success achieved by the club, he explained that this meeting had been called on a wider basis than a formal committee in order that the views of a larger number could be obtained on matters of general policy which would affect the whole future welfare of the club. These would later be considered by the committee itself and appropriate recommendations made.

It was decided to recommend that Vic Buckingham receive a dispatch case (I hope it was leather) as a token of gratitude for all his help, and Leslie Laitt an honorarium of ten guineas. We were an amateur club all right!

Then, as secretary, Tommy gave a brief report on the affairs of Pegasus. He explained that an enormous number of letters had been received congratulating the club on its Amateur Cup victory, and expressing the hope that it would go on with even greater strength. These had come from amateur and professional clubs, from schools and masters, from past Oxford and Cambridge men, and very many others. There was no doubt that the public interest everywhere had been astonishing. It was a special pleasure to receive kind messages from sister clubs such as Leander and Achilles. He outlined the consequence of the club's success, such as the formation of Peritus, a North Wales university club, and an all-university team in the Manchester area, the naming of a school house in Liverpool, requests for matches by French clubs, requests for coaching, the institution of a new trophy by the *Tatler*, and so on. There had been many requests for Festival of Britain matches, for cricket matches, and for games next season. The club had incurred a great responsibility, but fortunately it should now possess a substantial bank balance to meet some of the expenses which might be required.

Finally we came to the crux of the whole matter, the future policy of the club, and Tommy launched into a long account of how he viewed the present situation and the future. I caught Denis's eye and couldn't help grinning as that slow deliberate voice, analytically broke it all down, almost spelt it out to us as if we were at one of his lectures on infra-red spectroscopy in structural diagnosis. In fact he was putting his cards firmly on the table for all to see and I quote in full the recorded minutes of that meeting.

He began with three statements of why there was a need for this discussion.

1. Present circumstances demanded special consideration.

2. The dates of the Amateur Cup had now been altered, the first round being on 15 December next.

3. Some players had expressed a definite wish to have more games before Christmas.

He felt that it was abundantly clear that substantially the whole country was behind the club and asked us to do more to continue our good work. In his opinion, this could not be done by playing a few games against relatively poor quality opposition and schools, but as events had shown only by raising the strongest possible side to command publicity. We had been presented, providentially, with the means to do this.

He explained that the first round of the Amateur Cup would be on 15 December, the varsity match being only one week earlier, on 8 December. No one could really believe that we would ever succeed by fielding a half-baked team one week after the varsity match when most players had had a hard term playing for their university, were rather stale, and had not had a chance to play together. This argument would apply quite apart from the question of whether the younger undergraduates were good enough. He felt that if anyone denied this view, there could only remain a fundamental and irreconcilable difference of judgment between them and him.

He felt that the wish of some players to have more regular games before

103

Christmas was natural, and should be encouraged in every way possible, having regard to our resources. Otherwise, players would certainly become dispersed or lost altogether to the game. If we refused to have such matches, we should be acting very foolishly.

The secretary said that he felt that our main difficulties and problems had come from our relationship with the Corinthian-Casuals club, and differences of opinion within our own club about the one-year rule. He explained that he could not visualize a continuation of the Pegasus club successfully, or even at all, if the state of affairs which had existed during the past two years were to persist. He illustrated his meaning by the following points:

(a) The treasurer, he said, had repeatedly tried to limit our success by opposing the playing of a few senior players. The treasurer had proposed formally in the committee that they should be excluded both from the tour and subsequently, and had written letters to him (the secretary) about it at intervals during 1950–51.

(b) He knew that there had been a good deal of lobbying and gossip in London along the same lines. There had been propaganda against us by word and deed. Most disheartening of all—he had received recently a letter from Mr. D. J. Insole stating that he, Insole, had got the approval of some members of the Pegasus committee for his article in a Cambridge magazine early this year attacking the Pegasus club.

(c) There had been deliberate attempts to unsettle our players, to coerce them, to say unpleasant things about them because they were loyal to us, and so on.

The secretary felt that this could not be allowed to continue. He had therefore recently met Mr. W. H. Webster, chairman of the Corinthian-Casuals club, on two occasions. The meetings took place on 16 May and 24 May, 1951, and were entirely amicable. Both parties had agreed that no good could come of raking up past grievances, and that we should try to act wisely for the future. The secretary explained that he had analysed the whole position with Mr. Webster in great detail, and had given logical reasons why he felt certain essential steps should be taken for the good of all concerned. A memorandum on this talk had been prepared and would be included in the club files. The main point was that he, the secretary, had made the suggestion that the two clubs should agree to make the following joint statement:

After considering all the circumstances, and with a common wish to promote the best interests of Amateur Football in the schools, universities and elsewhere, the Pegasus F.C. and the Corinthian-Casuals F.C. wish to make the following joint declaration of policy:

1. Every effort should be made to enable Pegasus F.C. to raise its strongest possible XI, and whilst the individual player must always decide his own policy, this view is made clear so that players need have no anxiety about divided loyalty.

2. Pegasus F.C. will confine its membership to past and present Oxford and Cambridge men.

3. Corinthian-Casuals' players, who by reason of past connections during seasons before 1951, have an established position with the Corinthian-

104

Casuals club should not be expected to forsake that club in favour of Pegasus.

4. Pegasus F.C. will encourage its leading players to support, and when available, to play for the Corinthian-Casuals if required.

5. Pegasus F.C. will encourage other university players at Oxford and Cambridge to play for Corinthian-Casuals' teams, some more satisfactory agencies being established to this end.

Pegasus F.C. to state that it appreciates the public-spirited attitude of the Corinthian-Casuals and will co-operate to the full in the above respects, that it will not act unreasonably in asking for players to be held back for the cup-ties, and also in less important matches after the cup-ties have been concluded or at appropriately other times, will make senior players available to the Corinthian-Casuals if required, and thereby give a chance to more junior players to play for the Pegasus club.

The secretary felt that if these proposals had been acceptable to the Casuals club, real success for all in the future would be assured, but without some directive to players he felt that the same impossible situation would continue and both clubs would suffer.

Mr. Webster had promised to consider these proposals, although he stated that he did not think that his committee would accept them. He stated that his committee would be meeting on the evening of the day of the second discussion.

Unfortunately, some time later Mr. Webster had written saying that his committee had not considered the proposals, and that he did not think that they could do so before the meeting of the Pegasus club on 16 June. The secretary expressed his disappointment at the apparent unwillingness of certain members of the Casuals club to see the whole position realistically and without being influenced by personal factors.

He then raised the question of the treasurer's (Doggart's) position as an active member of both clubs. He understood that Mr. Doggart had just been elected president of the Casuals club and that he thereby hoped to benefit both clubs. He, the secretary, could not see how this could work out satisfactorily, and had already written to the treasurer several times pointing out that it might have the opposite effect. He felt that if the proposals which he had made to Mr. Webster had been accepted, the link which Mr. Doggart hoped to be might indeed be good, but since they had been refused this did not apply.

The secretary explained that in spite of the risk of losing good games, he had deliberately not arranged any matches for next season until it had been clearly agreed what the players as a whole wished. It would obviously be disastrous to take on strong games if there was a danger of our not being able to field a reasonably strong team.

He therefore made his position clear as follows:

1. He felt that the club would fail in its responsibility to the country and to the game if it did not try its utmost to maintain the high standard which it had set, and to hold the esteem which it had created for itself. This would require a maximum effort in every way, apart from very careful organisation, and particularly during next season.

2. He could not personally undertake to continue any longer in a position

where there was permanent uncertainty and unsettled policy, undermining of his own actions by a small section of the committee, and when letters written by him to outside bodies were copied by them and circulated secretly to certain members of the committee, and so on.

The secretary felt that it was for the players themselves to settle the future, but he earnestly asked them to realize the permanent influences which their decisions would have.

The treasurer replied and stated that he was not in any sense acting against the club's interests and disliked the suggestion of sabotage. He could not imagine the club without the present secretary. Pegasus could now claim to be regarded as the premier amateur club, and he thought that any suggestion that it should wind up its affairs was nonsense. He had raised in committee the question of players who were beyond the one-year rule, but had not pressed it. He now felt that players would have to decide for themselves for which club they wanted to play. He had felt that after last January our relations with the Casuals club had deteriorated, and he deplored this and hoped that in his new position he might bring the clubs together. He felt that the members of the Casuals club had wished Pegasus well and had shown it by coming without invitation to the Pegasus team at lunch before the semi-final game.

The secretary replied that he must point out that the treasurer had in fact written to him about the playing of senior players some time after raising the point in committee. Also on the question of allegations of sabotage, it was only fair also to ask that Pegasus players should not be stigmatised for showing loyalty. If the player were left to make a free choice, without any guidance, there would be the same coercive methods going on in London as hitherto. He thought too that Mr. Doggart was unaware of the remarks made to some Pegasus players by members of the Casuals club. Mr. Doggart had also referred to the Insole article. The secretary wondered whether he intended to take players from Pegasus to the Casuals or vice versa, or whether the real aim of Mr. Webster and Mr. Doggart was to re-form the Corinthians at a later date from Pegasus players. He wondered whether the alleged deterioration of our relations with the Casuals since last January had any connection with our success since that time.

Messrs. Potts, Saunders, Tanner, Shearwood, Platt, Hall and Brown expressed their views on the points already raised. There was a strong feeling that with great regret it seemed impossible to allow the natural development of Pegasus to be restricted by the interference and attitude of some members of the Corinthian-Casuals club. After much discussion of details, the rules of the club were considered, and a revised version was drawn up for submission to the committee and through the latter to an Extraordinary General Meeting of the club, to be held if possible in October next.

The following day the Cup side played a cricket match against Cowley Works on their ground. I was batting in a net when Graham approached : 'How easily you play games, Ken,' he said, quietly, standing at the side of the net, a remark that gave me much pleasure.

'By the way,' he went on, smiling, 'there's a small item of forty-eight sherries that seems to be unaccounted for.'

'Ah,' I said, 'I do remember.' We arrived at a very fair compromise. Before the match began the committee held a meeting at which recommendations of the previous day were duly agreed upon. Vic Buckingham was to have his dispatch case, Lesley Laitt his cheque for ten guineas, Denis was to be captain for the next year and Jerry Weinstein was elected an Honorary Member in recognition of his great support and help during the past season.

Over the vexed question of the one-year rule it was agreed that the new version discussed and drawn up the previous evening—that 'all members shall be eligible to play for the club'—should be submitted to an Extraordinary General Meeting, to be held sometime when convenient in October. Meanwhile the secretary was instructed to proceed with arrangements for next season on the assumption that all members of the club would be eligible to play.

In fact, that Extraordinary General Meeting never took place. At a committee meeting held at Iffley Road ground on Saturday 3 November 1951 we heard some very sad news. Graham Doggart had suffered a serious illness and was no longer able to continue as our treasurer. It was decided to ask Mr. W. V. Cavill, M.C., M.A., to take over these duties until the Annual General Meeting to be held at the Public Schools Club on 8 December.

And it was there, with thirty-two members present, in addition to the officers, that the revised rules of the club were presented for ratification, the honorary secretary explaining that these had been carefully considered during the summer and that the committee had authorized him to act upon them during the autumn pending accep-tance by the A.G.M. After some discussion the revised rules were accepted, twenty-nine members voting for and none against.

In future all members were now eligible to play for the club. The one-year rule no longer existed.

So the summer term wound down and our time at Oxford came to a close. I took my examination for a Diploma in Education but never went to see whether I passed. Later I received an impressive looking document that seemed to signify something.

Finally, we said goodbye to all our friends in Woodstock, and closing the front door of Laburnum House for the last time, set off for Lancing.

12 Lancing

I believe in Providence, I always have, though it would sometimes appear an irrational conviction.

I had never been cut out to be a fisherman and I was certainly never cut out to be a schoolmaster, nor ever had any particular intention of becoming one; yet here I was back once more at Lancing.

Throughout my schooldays I had been little more than a cheerful nuisance—my last lesson at Shrewsbury I spent sitting at the back of the form dressed as a parson—until the master could stand it no longer and drove me from the room. Always occupying humble positions in lowly forms—the mark system ensured that all failures and successes be well labelled and known to all—it gave me perhaps one advantage, an instinctive sympathy for the academic underdog and an awareness that encouragement was a schoolmaster's most precious gift, something that never seemed to come my way, though I've no doubt that was largely my own fault.

I was down to teach history, english and maths. The first two subjects I could cope with, but maths was going to prove a problem, particularly geometry. So I rang Blackwells in Oxford to enquire whether by any chance they had a key to all the geometrical riders in Durell, the book I was to use.

They hadn't, a voice said, but they could get me one.

'Would you do that, please, and get it off to me as soon as possible? I'm in dire need of it.'

'Who shall we send it to?'

'Ken Shearwood, Lancing College, Sussex.'

'The Pegasus centre-half?'

'Yes.'

'I watched all your matches, sir.'

'You did?'

'I certainly did. Great they were. Are you going to continue playing?'

'I hope to—if the headmaster will allow it.'

'You must persuade him sir. At any rate I'll get this sent off to you as soon as possible,' and I thanked him.

I managed to postpone the teaching of geometry for three whole weeks, concentrating on arithmetic and algebra, often getting stuck, but learning much on the way.

Now right in the middle of the front row sat a 'know-all', who was in due course to become a doctor.

'When are we going to start and do some geometry sir?' he would ask with the utmost regularity.

'All in good time,' I'd reply, for the book with the answers had still not arrived.

But at last it came and we embarked on a week of geometry, starting at the beginning, and for a while know-all seemed satisfied. And then he suddenly fired a broadside at me.

'Can you do any question in this book sir?'

'I wouldn't be teaching you if I couldn't,' I replied in my most patronizing manner, hoping this would shut him up.

'Can you do this one on page 360, number 10?'

'Of course, but you wouldn't understand it. You'll probably none of you ever get as far as that all the time you're here.' I was quite certain I wouldn't.

They waited expectantly.

My desk was well above their heads so they couldn't see my little flat book, which held the key to all my troubles.

For a few seconds I put on my most studious frown whilst discreetly turning up the answer to this wretched problem on page 360. Then with as much nonchalance as I could muster I turned towards the blackboard and began to write it out. It was as meaningless to me as it was to them, but 'know-all' seemed satisfied, at least for the time being.

But gradually I grew a little too confident, with that small book tucked up my sleeve so to speak, and would take a problem which I hadn't prepared beforehand, and looking up the answer begin to write it out on the blackboard. I did this on one occasion and when asked to explain why AB equalled CD, found I was quite unable to understand the solution myself.

'You can't understand it?' I said, turning the tables and looking at them with feigned amazement.

'No sir,' said 'know-all' of the front row, grinning delightedly, 'we can't, sir. Can you?'

'Yes, of course I can,' I laughed rather hollowly, and then pulling myself together. 'Look here, I'm not going to do everything for you. I've written the blasted solution out on the blackboard. It's crystal clear. You've got some preparation for me tonight, haven't you? (at Lancing it's called Evening School). You can jolly well use your brains for a change and work it out for yourselves. It'll do you good.'

Later that night, over several glasses of sherry down at the Sussex Pad, the late Parnell Smith explained to me exactly why AB equalled CD. I was to have many such sherries with Parnell, a Cambridge mathematician and a veteran of schoolmastering in his late sixties. He wore stout black boots, was very small, and once commanded the Corps at Lancing, stood as a Liberal candidate, saving his deposit, and played a more than shrewd hand of bridge. He smoked innumerable cigarettes using a holder, and his hand shook so badly that his straight line drawn between two points on the blackboard was famous. He had kindness, a fine command of the English language and despite experiencing more than his fair share of sadness, possessed a splendid sense of humour.

He told me many things about the school, particularly of his time under the late headmaster, Cuthbert Blackeston who had been forced to leave. The latter was a huge scholarly man who'd once been a housemaster at Eton and was known as the 'Blacker'.

'He'd break wind a lot,' Parnell would reminisce, 'and I remember once passing him in the lower quad carrying a number of toilet rolls in his cassock which he held before him as though it were an apron. "Parnell," he said, "this is a damnable disgrace." '

Apparently he had that morning received a letter from a parent complaining that their son's bottom had been burnt. Promptly flying into one of his fearful and uncontrollable rages he had begun a searching investigation which soon revealed the source of the complaint. In the old 'groves' (lavatories) at Lancing, there was no individual flushing system, but disposal was by means of a flowing trough beneath each pan. A group of boys indulging in a prank had lit some paper boats—miniature fire-ships—and set them on course to float down the trough, their flames wreaking havoc upon the many unsuspecting ones seated about their morning business.

On another occasion the 'Blacker' had assembled the whole school and staff and, with much sideways shaking of head and quivering of jowls, had glared at the assembled company before thundering forth

'Your private parts are sacred. I will not have you meddling with them.'

Parnell's close colleague 'Putt', short for Puttock, another Cambridge mathematician, also well turned sixty, would often come to my help. He'd been a boy at the school and only had the use of one arm. Apart from his time at Cambridge, he had spent most of his life at Lancing, and despite his disability rolled his own cigarettes, played a good game of tennis and had represented the school at cricket. He would polish off *The Times* crossword by the end of the break and was a stickler for punctuality. The pair of them saved my bacon on more than one occasion.

The school was peculiar in that it had its own resident doctor—Gordon Crisp—who lived on the premises and was dedicated to the place. He had to be for he was paid a pittance. He was a big, warm-hearted man with an ugly rather jaundiced face who hated all cant and was something of an authority on ancient civilizations. He once gave Patrick Halsey, housemaster of Fields, an injection which took such effect that by the middle of the morning he was almost blind.

'Well Patrick,' said Gordon, studying the stricken housemaster. He had a loud emphatic way of speaking. 'It's quite clear what's happened; we've given you too damned much of the stuff. We'll know better next time,' and the following day Patrick recovered. Gordon's patients always did. In one term he managed to remove a spate of boys' appendices, as well as the headmaster's, his wife's and daughters', and of course Patrick Halsey's. The operation was carried out in the school sanatorium, which had a proper operating theatre.

'The last thing I remember seeing as I went under,' said Patrick, 'was Gordon bending over my stomach, pipe in mouth, stray ends of tobacco falling untidily over the bowl, which I was certain would drop into my stomach. Worse still I had a horrible feeling that Gordon himself was about to perform the operation.'

It was an elderly common room and a friendly one and I liked my introduction to Lancing. The school had a relaxed atmosphere and the headmaster the respect and liking of his staff. Common room meetings were blessedly short, and the headmaster would address everyone as Mr. so and so, though on informal and private occasions he would always use their christian names.

We didn't see a great deal of him. He was usually in bed by ten. He'd had a difficult stewardship, for the school had been evacuated during the war to Ludlow, and not unnaturally numbers had fallen.

111

His immediate task had been to get the place back on its feet again and he was succeeding. But it had taken its toll of him and he was tired now and ready for retirement.

Yet to see him about, one had little doubt that he was the headmaster, for he walked with a measured and erect authority, his handsome face serious beneath a full head of iron-grey hair. In short, he was impressive, a man you would look at twice.

Tommy had written a detailed and informative letter to him about the purpose of Pegasus, ending with a request for me to be allowed to play for the club during the coming season. When I went to see the headmaster about the matter he could not have been nicer. 'Provided you make up the work you can certainly play.' I noticed the ash on his cigarette lengthen as he drew heavily through the holder, inhaling deeply, 'How's it all going?' he asked, looking at me steadily, his face rather too grey and heavily lined.

'Fine,' I assured him.

And just as at the Woodstock school, when things became a trifle tedious in form, we'd get on to football and Pegasus.

'Did you win, sir?' they'd ask on Monday morning, and off we'd go. And towards the end of the week it would be a question of, 'Who are you playing on Saturday, sir?' and we'd be off again. But in the interim we did some work, and I never had another peep out of 'know-all'.

Just as Geoffrey Green had predicted, it wasn't going to be easy keeping on top. We lost our first game of the season 4–5 playing with a certain frivolous ease. 'Shall I take it with my left foot or right?' I enquired of Denis before doing something about a free kick awarded to us just outside our penalty area.

'Oh get on with it,' said Denis, 'and kick the bloody thing.'

So I took it with my swinger. My left foot miscued abysmally and the ball found its way to a much surprised Leyton centre-forward who promptly shot and scored.

Ben Brown patiently retrieved the thing with an imperturbable smile, taking it all in his stride, as was his wont. Denis gave a wry grin, John Tanner looked, I thought, a trifle tight-lipped, while Tony Pawson chuckled his head off on the right wing. Fortunately I couldn't see Tommy.

But we pulled ourselves together the following week against Cambridge City where we drew one–all. And we were still in the 1950–51 A.F.A. Cup which had been held over from the previous season and had yet to be played off. In the semi-final of that cup we defeated Ilford convincingly, 4–1 at Oxford, but lost the final a month later to Cambridge City 1–2.

We defeated the Welsh Amateur Cup winners 2–1, and successfully negotiated the opening round of the 1951–2 A.F.A. Cup against St. Albans, winning 5–3 on their ground. By the time the first round of the Amateur Cup was upon us we had played some thirteen matches including one against Lancing College.

We had been drawn away against Kingstonian, a London side, and the match was to be televised.

That our opponents should have won this cup-tie in the first twenty minutes there was no doubt, least of all in the minds of the Kingstonian players, in particular their centre-forward Whing, who was to play for England. They hit the upright, they smacked the cross-bar, they had us going all ways. We seemed to have no time to start things going. And then, right against the run of events, Peter May scored with his head, and then John Tanner scored, and scored again, and yet again and they were finished. Throughout most of the second half we were on top. But the breaks had been ours and frustrated Kingstonian lost their confidence and became desperate.

Towards the end I was covering one of their forwards closely, concentrating on the play that was going on around the Kingstonian goalmouth, when I received a sudden back-heeled hack on the shins which fortunately struck my guard. I felt sorry for him and not in the least bit angry for I could understand his feelings.

It was the same player—and on this occasion I did feel angry—who gave me a sharp shove in the back as I went up for a corner early on in the game, when Kingstonian were putting us through the mill, causing me to miss a ball that was clearly mine. They scored, but fortunately the referee (helped no doubt by my whoop of indignation) had spotted the incident. The television commentator I learnt afterwards had spotted it too.

So we got through that first round by four clear goals, a score that did not reflect how fortune had favoured us. We'd been forced to make three changes from the side that had played in the Cup Final. Miles Robinson, who had played cricket once for Sussex and claimed the wicket of Cyril Washbrook, had taken over the left-back position from Johnny Maughan, who was in the process of becoming ordained.

113

Peter May had filled the inside-right berth, since John Dutchman wished to play for the Casuals, and Roy Sutcliffe had taken Donald Carr's place at inside-left. The latter was vice-captain of the M.C.C. which was touring in India and Pakistan.

Of the newcomers Peter May, tall and gangly, took up intelligent positions and was good in the air. Roy Sutcliffe, who had played before of course, was a direct runner, more suited to the flanks where he had some freedom and a measure of protection from the touchline. But I thought we missed the guile of Donald Carr and the all-round ability of John Dutchman.

Before we travelled north to play our next opponents, redoubtable Crook Town, we flew to Switzerland, taking with us our wives and new coach, Reg Flewin, captain of Portsmouth. We stayed at Lausanne and played two matches, against Schaffhausen and Malley.

Against the former—having first viewed the Falls of the Rhine—we lost 4–1 on a pitch that was ice-bound, a veritable skating rink. It was impossible for defenders to turn, and Schaffhausen, with their forwards moving early on to balls that were held judiciously before being laid in behind our defence, beat us comfortably.

After seeing the New Year in, followed by some training next morning and a tactical discussion in the evening, we defeated Malley 5–0 and with a splendid headline tucked under our belts—'Brillante demonstration des champions d'Angleterre amateurs'—flew back to England and promptly gave a very far from 'brillante demonstration' against Wealdstone the week before the second round of the Amateur Cup.

We met Friday afternoon on King's Cross station. Seats had been reserved for us. We all knew this was to be a hard one and for the last few days my mind had been full of it. Crook Town were of the same calibre as Bishop Auckland and Willington, competent, and hard to beat—doubly so on their own ground. I caught sight of Guy and Helen Pawson, who were travelling up with us and went across to talk to them. Jerry was leaning on his stick talking to Denis. Tommy of course was looking worried. He had some cause to be. He caught our eyes and came towards us, his overcoat turned up, his shoulders hunched, a faded Blue's scarf round his neck, brown trilby tilted, a cigarette in the corner of his mouth. 'They're going to miss this train if they leave it much longer,' he announced with grim certainty,

114

shaking his head and coughing. The Cambridge contingent, Ralph Cowan, Peter May, Roy Sutcliffe and Jimmy Platt had failed to arrive. 'They were told to be here . . .'

'It's all right, they're coming,' said John Tanner as Roy Sutcliffe came bursting through the ticket barrier slightly ahead of the others. 'Got held up, Tommy,' he explained bluntly, puffing and grinning.

'Well . . .' Tommy began, but there was no time to hear his further comment for the whistle was blowing, doors were banging and we climbed aboard. Very shortly the train began to move.

'Bridge?' enquired John.

'I'm not partnering Shearwood,' announced Jerry.

'I suppose I'd better,' said Tony.

And we got the cards out and began to play.

I always enjoyed travelling to an away match. It tends to bind a side closer together. It certainly did in our case, because unless on tour, we were never together as a unit. The Oxford and Cambridge contingents trained separately, while Tony Pawson, John Tanner, Denis Saunders and myself had to do our own training. We met once a week in the changing-room, and perhaps for a brief moment after the match. A long journey such as the present one gave us an opportunity to get to know each other better. We'd discuss everything under the sun, from the one-year rule to the splitting of the atom, for hadn't we two scientists in our midst, a legal mind, undergraduates past and present, even a couple of schoolmasters to toss ideas around? It was amusing and stimulating.

'Four hearts,' called Tony.

'Double,' said John.

'Redouble,' said I.

'Bloody ridiculous,' said Jerry.

Whereupon Tony made his call, which gave us the rubber, much to Jerry's annoyance.

'Who'll take penalties?' enquired Reg Flewin just before we went out.

'I'll take 'em,' said Roy, 'I've never missed one.'

So it was decreed.

Ten thousand watched us draw one–all with Crook Town on a ground that was wet and treacherous. They were a good side and got on with it right from the start, cutting out the frills, making direct

115

sorties upon our goal, hitting the ball about, attacking us on the flanks, coming at us from all quarters. They scored their goal from an out-swinging well-met corner, fairly early on in the first half. John Tanner, who played very well indeed, got our equalizer. And then we were awarded a penalty well on in the second half, which Roy Sutcliffe took and hit—if he will forgive my saying so—unforgivably high over the cross-bar.

'Thought you'd never missed a penalty, Roy,' remarked Reg Flewin when we were once more back in the changing-room, the match over.

'That's right,' said Roy, 'I haven't. I've never taken one before.'

It could be said to have cost us the match, for in the replay at Oxford—Jack Laybourne replaced Peter May—we got knocked out on the university rugby ground before another ten thousand spectators by the only goal of the match, and I for one felt very low.

'Sorry you lost sir,' they said on the Monday morning. 'What went wrong?'

'Should have clinched it the first time,' I suggested, and told them about the penalty incident.

But there were still plenty of matches to play, including one against Tottenham Hotspur Reserves which we won 3–1, and another for charity against Charlton Athletic which we lost 1–4. And we were still in the A.F.A. Cup and met Kingstonian for the second time that season in the final, on 5 May, at Griffin Park, home of Brentford Football Club. There we won by the only goal of the match.

The surface was bone hard, it was the back-end of the season and Kingstonian sought their revenge. They didn't get it, though at times they did 'play most foully for it'.

The season was over, and cricket was upon us. Though we had not distinguished ourselves in the Amateur Cup this time, we'd won another, the Amateur Football Alliance Cup.

Reading through the minutes of a committee meeting held at St. John's College, Oxford, on 29 March 1952, I discovered how much difficulty Tommy was having in raising suitable teams, since it had been stated at Cambridge that in the Hilary term (in addition to the Michaelmas term) the claims of university matches should be placed before those of the Pegasus club. Before any commitments for 1952 were undertaken he wanted to know what our playing resources were likely to be. He mentioned that only two Falcons had joined the club during the present season.

116

At a later meeting of the committee in June, he pointed out that only one member of Cambridge University was present, Jimmy Platt. The committee recommended that Jerry Weinstein be made an assistant honorary secretary, Leslie Laitt be given his grant of ten guineas, and Reg Flewin an honorarium of twenty-one pounds.

Some of the minutes of those committee meetings highlight the innate difficulties Tommy faced in running Pegasus. Cambridge, by nature of the fact that the seat of control remained in Oxford, may have felt isolated, but without their co-operation the club would never achieve its potential. Many clubs had invited us to play them and Tommy was rightly loath to put out weak sides. It was a very real problem, and behind it all there lurked a feeling at Oxford that the Cambridge players were going to abide by the one-year rule. We had no concrete evidence, but already we had lost John Dutchman from the cup-winning side and earlier Guy Shuttleworth, Hubert Doggart, Doug Insole and others. There seemed every likelihood that more would follow.

And these problems apart Tommy had his work to do. He was here, there and everywhere, lecturing, preparing lectures, popping over to America or Europe, attending meetings then coming back and working in the laboratories till late into the night. Yet still he found time to cope with the running of the club.

He was immensely gifted, hard working and efficient. And being Tommy he did not try and conceal the burden he carried on our behalf.

'You know Denis,' he once said dolefully when travelling to an away match, 'I think Pegasus is ruining my marriage.'

'Oh, I don't know Tommy,' said Denis reassuringly.

'Well ... I don't think any of you fully appreciate the work that is involved.'

But had we tried to lighten his burden at this stage—not that we were ever really in a position to do so—he would not have wished it, for in his heart he believed we were potentially the best amateur club in the country.

So he held on, calculating each step, informing us discreetly and sometimes not so discreetly, that there was more sabotage afoot from you know who, that he was not feeling very well and that he didn't know how he was ever going to carry on.

That he did of course was due entirely to one person, his wife Penelope, who shared all his worries, intelligently putting them into

117

perspective—she had a first class mind—laughing off trivialities, welcoming us all. She kept him going, still does, and she was as much a part of Pegasus as anyone.

My first summer term at Lancing I found delightful. The school, with the Downs rolling away westwards towards Chanctonbury at the back, and the channel a ribbon of light glittering in the sunshine a mile distant on its southern flank, is magnificent. And it has the best of all worlds too, quick access to civilization—Brighton, London, Worthing, Shoreham—yet stands solitary in its own flint kingdom up on a hill. No boy need wander far to house, form-room, library, chapel or playing field. The school bell summoned us and the motor mowers cut green swathes down the quads, while master and boys went about their business. Saints' Days were frequent and welcome occurrences, for they meant a 'lie-in' for those who did not attend early communion, and no first periods of teaching for the staff. And for the more important Saints, and there seemed an abundance of these that first summer at Lancing, we'd have a holiday from mid-morning.

Cricket was still the major game and school matches were watched by the masters sitting in deck chairs within the privacy of their own sheltered garden, a natural little grassy amphitheatre surrounded by rhododendrons up on the bank. As master in charge of cricket I spent a lot of time up there watching the boys make fools or heroes of themselves, and listening to the comments of my colleagues. On one flank we were protected by the white wooden side of the school shop up which red and yellow roses rambled towards low, thatched eaves. Through the only window tea would be passed out to us. And while we drank and chatted, wickets tumbled, batsmen came and went, until the chapel bell began to ring, evening shadows stole once more across the square, and stumps were drawn with the match resolved one way or the other, to the satisfaction of at least one of the masters in charge.

I played in two cricket matches for Pegasus that summer term, the first against Morris Motors, who did us proud though we beat them, the second against a Kent side at Penshurst Place, the home of the De Lyles, where the Pawsons lived in the King's Wing. There, Biddie and I spent the night with them, and very gracious it all was too. I seem to recollect we won the match; we certainly didn't lose it.

Right: Pegasus defeat Brentwood and Warley 2–1 in the second round of the Amateur Cup of 1949. Pawson on the left, Iffley Road pavilion in the background.

Right: Sir Stanley Rous and the Rev. K.R.G. Hunt (first president of Pegasus) watching from the balcony of Iffley Road.

Below: 22 February 1949. Oxford fans queue for tickets for the Bromley 4th round cuptie at Iffley Road.

Above left: 1949: Bromley 4 Pegasus 3. Author clears his lines in 4th round cup-tie.

Above right: 1st round replay Amateur Cup 1950 at White House City ground. Pawson watched by Heritage shoots despite close attention by two Erith and Belvedere defenders.

Below: George Brown of Bromley scoring his second goal.

Above: Amateur Cup semi-final 1951. Pegasus 1 Hendon 1 played at Highbury. Avis the Hendon outside-left is brought down by the author.

Below: Ben Brown memorably saving Dexter Adams' penalty kick in the very last stages of the above semi-final.

Above: Dutchman beats the Hendon goalkeeper, Ivey, to score the winning goal in the closing minutes of the 1951 semi-final replay at Selhurst Park.

Left: Three goalkeepers. Ditchburn of Spurs watched by Brown and Weir.

Below left: Saunders talking to Billy Nicholson and Arthur Rowe to Pawson and Walters.

Below right: Alf Ramsey at Cheshunt talking to Ralph Cowan.

Above: Buckingham explains a point. Left to right: Burgess, Carr, Buckingham, Walters, Dutchman.

Below left: Tommy at work.

Below right: 'Bush' O'Callaghan escorting Biddie to Wembley.

Above: Bishop Auckland coming out at Wembley.

Left: Denis Saunders, Arthur Ellis and Harry McIlvenny.

Above: Potts scoring the first goal for Pegasus with a spectacular diving header.

Below: Tanner taking on Farrer.

Left: Nimmins takes a dive over Brown.

Below: Saunders watched by Hardisty heads the ball out of the hands of White, the Bishop Auckland goalkeeper.

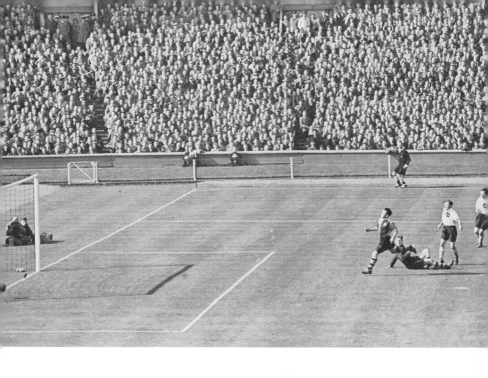

Above: Tanner scoring the winning goal against Bishop Auckland.

Right: Amateur Cup winners. 1951

Above left: Tommy prepares to celebrate.

Above right: Geoffrey Green and Dick Blundell.

Below: New Year Tour 1953. Playing a 'friendly' against Bishop Auckland on their ground in wintry conditions. The Bishops won 2-1.

Above: 'Up the Pegs!' A section of the 12,000 crowd at the Oval to watch the Pegasus Corinthian-Casuals 4th round cup-tie of 1953.

Below left: Brown saves from Doggart watched by McKinna.

Below right: Denis Saunders shaking hands with Doug Insole watched by W. Ling.

Above: Ben Brown and the Pegasus defence under pressure during a Southall attack in the 1953 semi-final at Highbury.

Below: 1953 players and officials outside the Iffley Road pavilion.

BACK ROW: Dr. H. W. Thompson, A. H. Chadder, G. Ainsley, R. Sutcliffe, G. H. McKinna, B. R. Brown, R. G. Lunn, J. S. Laybourne, W. V. Cavill, L. Laitt, J. L. Weinstein.

FRONT ROW: K. A. Shearwood, J. D. P. Tanner, H. A. Pawson, D. F. Saunders, F. C. M. Alexander, R. C. Vowels, D. B. Carr.

Above: Setting out for Wembley from Paddington.

Below: The Bishop of Willesden shakes hands with Bob Lunn. Wembley 1953.

Above left: Davis, the Harwich centre-forward challenging strongly in the air.

Above right: Saunders takes the ball from Pearson.

Below: Harwich inside-left Cooper shoots as he is tackled by Vowels the Pegasus right-half.

Above: Shadows. Sutcliffe beats Nightingale for possession watched by Laybourne and Saunders.

Below left: Denis Saunders heads Pegasus's first goal from a corner.

Below right: Laybourne the Pegasus centre-forward challenging King.

Above: 'That's it!' Carr scores his second and Pegasus's sixth and last goal of the 1953 Amateur Cup Final.

Left: Denis coming down with the cup for the second time in three years.

Below: A summer's day.

BACK ROW: Doggart, Crisp, Dutchman, Carr, Platt, Brown, Clegg, Tommy.

FRONT ROW: Laitt, Tanner, Shearwood, Saunders, Cowan, Maughan, Potts.

Indeed I never remember us ever being beaten at cricket, for after all we could, if need be put out a side of county strength.

Abruptly the summer term came to a halt and the boys disappeared like a swarm of locusts and some of the life went out of the place.

Just before the term ended Frank Doherty offered us school accommodation which we really had to accept, though at the time neither of us relished being too close to the school. Consequently the first part of the holiday was spent moving into our new abode with rather mixed feelings for we'd grown to like our bungalow and we hadn't yet paid for the curtains. However we got on with the job and then set off once again for our old haunts in the West.

13 Was it Luck?

There were two new faces in the side that lost the opening match of the 1952–3 season against St. Albans City 0–1, necessitated by the fact that Ralph Cowan and Jimmy Platt, abiding by the one-year rule, had decided to join the Casuals. Their positions were taken by two Cambridge players, Jerry Alexander and Reg Vowels. Neither Jimmy Potts nor John Tanner were available for selection at the start, so the Oxford forward, Bob Lunn, who'd already played for us the previous season, came in at outside-left. Ernest Tweddle, who had also previously played in a number of games, including that final of the A.F.A. Cup against Kingstonian, came in at inside-right, Roy Sutcliffe moving to centre-forward.

A week later, watched by our new coach, George Ainsley of Leeds and England, we defeated Welwyn Garden City. Jack Laybourne replaced Ernest Tweddle, and Mike Pinner, a young cat-like goalkeeper from Cambridge with tremendous potential (he was to play more amateur internationals than any other goalkeeper in the country and eventually turn professional) deputized for Ben Brown. Pinner apart—and heaven knows he was good enough—and with a switching of the forwards, these eleven players were to prove our most successful combination.

Our new coach, George Ainsley, was a big, tall, fair-haired extrovert. We didn't attempt any new style of play, but continued as before to bring our wingers right back. And were they not present to collect a ball from defence, we'd soon let them know it. Indeed we'd been doing so from Vic Buckingham's days, sometimes so vociferously that our flank men had formed their own exclusive 'wingers' union' of which Jerry had been made an honorary member.

Of course we had a good knowledge of what we were trying to do, a number of us had now played together for some time. We knew each other's strengths and weaknesses. We practised no set piece moves and didn't worry about them much. In retrospect our training was unimaginative compared with today, but we gave the game a great deal of thought and would discuss our problems in depth, gradually ironing out the difficulties. In that way we developed faith in the pattern of our play, which remained basically 'push and run' but which never at any time discounted the individual's freedom of expression.

By the first round of the 1952–3 Amateur Cup we'd played ten matches, won five, drawn two, lost three and tried out thirty-three players, old and new.

And we'd had one real set-to in November with the Chelsea reserves in a so-called 'friendly' at Oxford. We had a strong side out and were 4–2 up at half-time. Towards the end of the first half the Chelsea captain, Joe Willemse, marking Tony Pawson, who had already scored twice, got, as they say, well and truly stuck in.

I was marking Bobby Smith, who was to play at centre-forward for Spurs and England. He was physically immensely strong and for high balls down the middle, held me off with a back as broad as a barn door, so that by half-time I had not won a single ball in the air.

'Lie off him a bit,' advised George Ainsley, 'and come in with a run.'

I did so, soon after the start of the second half, and sailing in high through the air won the ball, but caught Bobby Smith in the small of the back and down he went, all thirteen and a half stone of him.

'Sorry,' I said, and he gave me an old-fashioned look as he got to his feet.

'There's too much bloody sorry in this game mate, I'm getting stuck in from now on.'

'Not into me I hope,' a plea that bore little fruit, for true to his word the Chelsea centre-forward joined Willemse in what I can only describe as a battle, more bloody and infamous than any I ever experienced. Throughout the game the referee ran nervously to and fro, a fixed smile upon his face, seemingly oblivious of the outrageous fouls being perpetrated, not only now by Chelsea I hasten to add. Eventually, and in near desperation, he finally blew his whistle and both sides withdrew, scarred but unvanquished, with the score standing at four apiece.

'I hear some of our lads had a bit of a set-to with yours the other day,' Joe Meers, the Chelsea chairman, mentioned to Tommy the following week.

'Well . . . I suppose you might call it something like that,' replied Tommy laconically.

Two days after our 'friendly' with Chelsea, Tommy sent out a circular which gave us all food for thought :

Our members already know that our opponents in the Amateur Cup on 13 December are Hayes, on their ground, kick off 2.15 p.m. A short time ago a circular was issued asking all probable players to regard the next three weeks as a period of intensive preparation. Our matches on 29 November and 6 December are against relatively weak opposition, and in themselves will be little use for getting the team really fit and able to last a strong game for the full ninety minutes.

Our coach has asked me to make another appeal to all those who may be called upon to play at Hayes, and to draw their attention to several points brought out in our match against Chelsea yesterday. Many of our players seemed to have no stamina in the second half, and were slow off the mark. Slow steady lapping is useful but what may be more needed is a good deal of sprints from a standing start, in ten yard runs. It is not easy for non-resident players to fit in two evenings a week for training, but all should be able to arrange this if they make the effort. We must regain the reputation we have usually held, namely that we can fight harder during the second half of a game than at the start.

Our success at Hayes will put us into an extremely strong position, assure the success of our tour both as regards enjoyment and finance, whereas failure in the Cup would prejudice the whole future.

I am sometimes accused of taking a too realistic view of the position; may I therefore for the last time draw your attention to some facts about Hayes. On the past three Saturdays they have

won 6–0 against Redhill

won 5–0 against Clapton

(away. Amateur Cup)

won 6–0 against Cambridge University.

They are stated never to have been beaten in the Cup at Hayes, and during the past seven years have in every season finished near the top of the Athenian League. They have frequently won the Middlesex Senior Cup and other trophies. It needs no more to make it clear that we shall have to play as well as we have ever done to win. I think that if every man plays his part, marks his man, and concentrates upon the cause at stake, we can win, but I am sure that anything short of that will prove disastrous. I do not intend therefore to refer to this match again other than in making the appropriate arrangements. In order to avoid unnecessary fatigue due to long travelling, the players can, if necessary, come to London on Friday, 12 December, but this will be discussed later. We are at a disadvantage in having to play this match a week after the varsity match as everyone knows, but we cannot help that and must conquer the handicap.

Please therefore get yourself ready, before it is too late. This is only fair to the coach, and to all members of the club who have helped to make its name what it is.

24 November, 1952.   H. W. Thompson.

The circular did not mention one other ominous fact, that Hayes had convincingly defeated us the previous season on their own ground by four goals to one.

On 8 December the side had been finally selected and it was decided to play Jerry Alexander, the Cambridge international, at right-back, where he had played for Pegasus on four occasions earlier in the season. But there was some risk inherent as he had last played in that position back in a floodlit match against the Wiltshire F.A. one night early in October. Since then he had been playing regularly at centre-half for Cambridge.

The forward line contained those same players who had played earlier against Welwyn Garden City, but it had been radically rearranged, Jack Laybourne moving to centre-forward, Roy Sutcliffe to outside-left and Bob Lunn to inside-right. Donald Carr and Tony Pawson retained their old positions at inside-left and right-wing. Ben Brown was in goal of course, Gordon McKinna at left-back, and Denis, myself and Reg Vowels made up the half-back line. Our reserves were Jimmy Crisp of Oxford, and Cyril Tyson of Cambridge.

The Times made this brief comment :

Unlike their brothers, the Corinthian-Casuals, the Pegasus formation, which contains internationals in Brown, Saunders, Alexander, and Pawson, will be playing together for the first time this season. They will in effect be playing for time to develop an effective understanding.

We met for dinner at the Great Northern Hotel on Friday evening and later had a long tactics talk with George Ainsley, at which there was the usual constant flow of side comment with nobody appearing to pay any attention at all. In fact nothing that was being said was missed by anyone. It was all part of our make up, a light-hearted euphoria which prevailed during those rather tense hours before a match, which drew us closer together, concealing the seriousness of our intent, often deceiving our coaches, even Tommy at times.

It was raining the following morning, a miserable overcast day, befitting the 13 December, when we set off for Church Road, the Hayes ground in Middlesex, to begin our fifth quest for the F.A. Amateur Cup.

'Can't think why we ever play games seriously,' I confided to Tony as we bent putting on our boots. I noticed his were far from clean. He took a perverse pride in their not being so and would show them to me with relish.

In a little over ninety minutes, always excepting a draw, one of us

123

would have gone under. It needed only an early slip, an error of judgement, a missed open goal, a moment of panic to send us on our way. In the other changing-room Hayes would be experiencing all that we were going through. They'd be just as keyed up, just as keen to win, just as determined, just as fit and well prepared. What then would prove the ultimate factor in deciding our fate? Skill, style of play, strength—we had a big, powerful defence—speed, intelligence, captaincy, experience, character? All would play their part. But where would the edge lie?

I'm tempted to suggest that the key to the final solution lay somewhere amid the last two factors. I felt sure, during those remaining nerve-wracking moments before going out, that we possessed sufficient character, blend of experience, determination and confidence in our corporate ability, which would overcome the inevitable moments of crisis we'd run up against, and see us through in the end. At any rate our supporters seemed to think something of this kind, for when we emerged they gave us a great welcome, dressed in their gowns and mortar-boards, waving many a home-made banner of the Flying Horse. And then we were once more in the thick of it and the battle was on.

It was apparent immediately that everything Tommy had predicted about Hayes was correct. Right from the start we had our backs to the wall and in the twenty-first minute were a goal down. Twelve minutes later Hayes scored their second goal, a perfect header from a free kick, and almost immediately Gordon McKinna cleared off our goal-line with Ben well beaten.

Two goals down in an away cup-tie is not a particularly happy predicament for any side to find itself in at half-time. And there wasn't an awful lot we could do about it, apart from continuing to play football, do the things we believed in, and keep going to the end. I have no recollection of anything in particular being said when Denis took us out for the second half. As in that first match against Enfield everything would depend upon what we could produce in the next forty-five minutes. It was up to us.

The light was very poor when we kicked off again, using a new white ball. Within a minute Jack Laybourne had been put away down the left wing and from his cross Bob Lunn drove the ball into their net. From that moment on we pushed them back and their defence had a sore time of it trying to keep us out. But they did and the minutes ticked away alarmingly until there were only three of them left. And all the while the light had been failing until it was difficult to see the length of the pitch.

I caught a glimpse of Tommy sitting on the touchline next to George Ainsley. He was leaning forward, hatless, elbows on knees, his fair head bent, looking dejectedly at the ground. In contrast big George Ainsley was sitting bolt upright, staring intently at the play. A great noise was coming from the many hundreds of spectators. Our own supporters were doing their best, but the brave strains of their version of the Eton Boating Song were being swamped.

We were attacking again. The referee had already glanced at his watch twice and I wondered if the match would be abandoned. I hoped it would, it seemed our only chance. And still we pressed. I watched isolated from the halfway-line, a helpless spectator as Roy Sutcliffe raced down the left wing and cut into the penalty area. He was going at top speed, right on target, when the ball and his feet were swept from under him and the whistle shrilled piercingly above the clamour. Vainly and desperately Hayes protested, gesticulating against the referee, who remained a grim, statuesque figure, pointing at the penalty spot. Twice Donald Carr had to replace the ball on the spot and wait, for the Hayes' players had now turned their full attention on him, and great was the pressure he was under. But Donald had a cool head for such occasions. Not for nothing had he played against the Australians in a Victory Test at Lords and walked out to face the bowling of Keith Miller. When eventually he took the kick, he did so with an easy rhythmic swing of his left foot, timing it to perfection, hitting the ball as though he were driving another four through the covers, giving the Hayes goalkeeper no chance whatsoever.

They were shocked, and before they had time to recover, Roy Sutcliffe had scored again. Now, mortally stricken, and as though paralysed, they watched as Jack Laybourne took advantage of an unbelievably bad defensive error and popped in our fourth. As the ball was brought back and Hayes kicked off in those last dying seconds, Jack Rawlings, their veteran international, who had so nearly sunk us in that first ever cup-tie against Enfield, turned his back on it all in bitter disgust and had already reached the touchline when the final whistle blew.

Was it luck then that had been the deciding factor of this match— good for us, bad for them? I think it would be difficult to deny that we had not been lucky. And yet nobody could say that it had been exactly a bed of roses for us at half-time.

It is often remarked, and I'm inclined to agree, that barring injuries and the fallibility of referees, a team makes its own luck. There was certainly nothing lucky about the manner in which we had kept Hayes subjected to constant pressure throughout most of the second half, the product of which had been that last despairing tackle from behind.

Our good fortune lay in the fact that the referee had chosen not to award Hayes a penalty for a similar incident committed by one of our players in the first half.

There is a cruelty about such moments. Hayes had vanished. The air was now filled with shouts of 'Up the Pegs!' 'Good old Pegasus!' as our delighted supporters swarmed around us, oblivious of the home crowd filtering slowly away, turning its back upon a scene which, for them, had suddenly become as distasteful and sombre as the gloom of that bleak winter's evening.

Very shortly after Christmas we set off on a tour of the North, starting with a match against a Sheffield representative side at Bramall Lane, winning 8–1, six of the goals coming in the second half. Then on to Elland Road where we put paid to the Leeds and District F.A. 4–3, finally ending up losing 1–3 in a match against our old foe, Bishop Auckland, their pitch covered in a thick carpet of snow. It had been an excellent tour and our stay at the Royal Hotel, Scarborough, could not have been more pleasant. Tommy always saw to it that we did ourselves well on these occasions.

Before we took on Cockfield in the second round of the Amateur Cup, at Iffley Road on 24 January, we first disposed of the Royal Navy Air Command and the Northern Nomads.

We knew little about our next opponents, except that they played in the Durham Central League and their centre-forward had been given a trial with Burnley. On the day, however, we knocked them out by five clear goals, conceding none. At the last moment John Clegg, the Oxford University outside-right, came into the side in place of Jack Laybourne, who had suddenly gone down with influenza. John Tanner was also unfit. And for the third time in five seasons we became one of the last sixteen clubs left in the F.A. Amateur Cup.

On Monday morning a half-column report of our match appeared in *The Times* alongside Geoffrey Green's full-length column of the

Corinthian-Casuals fine win against Finchley, and I quote his opening two paragraphs for they are pertinent to the story :

All good things have an end and Saturday saw the end of Finchley's great record. They had stood supreme since the season's beginning against all amateur opposition. But now for the first time in this sphere they met their masters in the Corinthian-Casuals, who gained a magnificent victory by four goals to one, before a record crowd of 10,000 people at the Oval and so reached the third round of the Amateur Cup.

The Corinthian-Casuals are now clearly a force to be reckoned with. Displaying all the fine qualities of attack and defence inherent in their illustrious hyphenated name, they held a distinct advantage in speed, determination in the tackle, and resilient spirit. Furthermore, by their clever blend of short and long passing, in which the point of attack was switched, they were the tactical masters who took their chances splendidly with the long game—much in the Arsenal manner. It was this ability to turn defence into counter-attack in economical moves that completely confounded a Finchley defence often caught on the wrong foot. With eight former Cambridge Blues in the Casuals' side, the shining occasion merely served to underline the revival of university football since the war.

'Well . . .' Tommy confided to some of us over the weekend, looking his most gloomy, 'they're now very much in the reckoning. I believe it would be utterly disastrous if we were to draw them in the next round,' a pronouncement we thought perhaps a little excessive, though I've no doubt the Casuals were sharing similar presentiments.

And of course as fate would have it we did draw them, slap bang out of the hat, and immediately I heard the news I got the shivers and the more I pondered it, the more shivers I got. In the middle of the week I received a cryptic type-written post-card from Jerry, who was now at Corpus Christi, Cambridge, where he was to obtain a Diploma of International Law :

You had better get a heavy lock for the Gladstone on the 7th. The bag will never need to be as tightly closed again as on that day. See you Saturday. Love to Biddie, Paul, and Kim.

Jerry was right. I'd be marking Hubert Doggart, a big, awkward and very determined customer. He'd not be easy to get into the bag. And because I knew most of their players, I at once began to play the match in mental anticipation, the more so as the occasion drew nearer.

Surprisingly the Bishops had been knocked out by Southall. But the North had retaliated, for Willington defeated Bromley, and Hallam had beaten Dulwich Hamlet. Hendon too were out, defeated at home by Hounslow; and Carshalton, another fancied club, lost

127

their home-tie against Romford. But Walthamstow Avenue, the holders, were still there, having been held to a draw by the Athenian League champions, Wealdstone. On form Walthamstow looked to be the most dangerous club left in the competition, for they were having a great run in the F.A. Cup. Drawn away against Manchester United in the fourth round, they drew one–all at Old Trafford and were the toast of the amateur game. But then the wheel of fortune turned full circle for them and they lost both their cup replays.

Generally, the London press seemed partial to the Corinthian-Casuals. Leslie Nichol of the *Express* concluded :

One question the match will settle: Who are the present mid-century Corinthians—Pegasus or Corinthian-Casuals?

Already the game was a sell-out. The gate had been limited to 12,000 to protect Surrey's cricketing interests, otherwise the Oval would have been filled.

Before the encounter we received a nasty jolt, losing 5–1 away against Wycombe Wanderers. And the following Monday morning we received a further rather ominous reminder of what lay ahead, in the form of another of Tommy's circulars :

There is no need for me to tell you how much our cup-tie against the Corinthian-Casuals next week is exciting the general public. The demand for tickets here is similar to that at the time of the Amateur Cup Final two years ago, and in my own opinion this may well prove to be this year's effective Final. I have received a few kind messages from some of our friends this week, but as you will all have seen the Press in general has tended to line up against us, and it seems that many of them regard our chances as poor.

It is my own regret, and yours too, that we have to try to defeat the Casuals in this game, for in spite of all the ill-informed remarks against our own club, we have certainly assisted them—and the game incidentally—more than they have assisted us. Yet it was my hope to avoid any such clash which might lead to disappointment on either side.

But we have to do everything in our power to win this match. I am confident that this is within our powers, if every man is properly fit and can reach his best form. Certainly, the Casuals have older players of experience gained indeed from our nursery, but none the less a firm defence can overcome their powerful attack and our own attack is capable of big things. I therefore appeal to all those likely to be called upon for this game to regard it as the really important match of their career which it well may be. Reputations can be made on this day which will last long, our high prestige can be maintained and success in many ways can be assured.

It was strange running out and seeing at the end furthest from the great gasometer all those familiar faces. There was Johnny Dutchman moving about in that rolling professional gait, and Jimmy Platt rubbing his hands and glancing curiously in our direction. Ralph Cowan looked as classy and confident as ever. And there were all the others who had played for us : Doug Insole, Guy Shuttleworth, Hubert Doggart, Norman Kerruish, and Lionel Boardman, who was a registered player but had not played. All eight of them hailed from Cambridge; seven of us came from Oxford. It was almost another varsity match, except so much more was now at stake.

Tommy had earlier remarked with characteristic bluntness to the Press : 'This match should have been reserved for Wembley. The winners must play in the final.'

Insole had been quoted as saying that Pegasus relied on the old men to ride the Flying Horse.

But there was no time for joking now. The gates had long been closed; the whistle had blown, and our task lay ahead; mine, to ensure that Hubert Doggart never received a ball without my closest and most destructive attention.

It proved a dire, uncompromising battle. Perhaps there was too many good players on both sides for any liberties to be taken. Perhaps we knew each other's play too well. Whatever it was, the game never quite reached the excellence that had been anticipated. I did not envy Tommy having to sit and sweat it out on the touchline for those ninety long minutes.

Afterwards, when the final whistle had blown and Hubert had gone into the bag for keeps, we sat weary and delighted in the dressing-room, while the poor old Casuals faced a weekend and more of gloom.

'He played a blinder,' Tommy was saying, 'I thought Reg Vowels played an absolute blinder', and he shook his head in bewilderment, coughed loud and long and disappeared in the direction of the Casuals' camp.

He was right of course. Reg Vowels had played well, very well indeed. But my man of the match was Denis, so cool and resourceful—and so thought Geoffrey Green when he wrote in *The Times* :

There was only one really positive emotion that attended the clash of the Corinthian-Casuals and Pegasus in the third round of the F.A. Amateur Cup at the Oval on Saturday. It was that one of these brothers had to be left behind by the wayside. That Pegasus, the younger of them finally emerged victorious by one goal to none to reach the last eight of the competition for the third time in five years, was perhaps just about correct on the balance of chances. But all through a cold, sunlit afternoon one could sense the feeling of divided loyalties in a record crowd, nearly twelve thousand strong, that lined the ancient enclosure.

It was sad, too, that the occasion did not live itself out in a blaze of glory. Higher artistry was missing and there was a strange absence of a stinging sharpness about the exchanges. Instead, there was offered a somewhat prosaic hard-fought struggle of uneven quality, and if this was punishment for imaginations that had perhaps roamed too freely in the waiting hours before, it was well to remember one thing. These sides played first to win, and not necessarily to give artistic satisfaction.

Pegasus on this occasion found themselves playing a role it has not often been their lot to fill. Instead of having to come from behind they now held on firmly to a lead snatched early in the proceedings by a volley from Pawson, always a man to reckon with at any time. Any doubts that they might find themselves out of character, however, were finally set at rest. For in the last twenty minutes of the match they produced their usual strong finish that might well have brought them two more goals from Laybourne—a more than adequate deputy for the absent Tanner—after they had withstood a couple of rallying periods by their opponents.

In retrospect a number of things were evident. First, that just as Pegasus helped to gain themselves the victory by their cool and measured start, together with its vital goal, so the Casuals, in spite of seven corners, helped to beat themselves in the twenty-five minutes before the interval. The crux of the battle really was contained within this spasm, which saw the tide suddenly turn against Pegasus. Within it there came an open chance to Dutchman close in from Insole's square pass, two or three narrow shaves in the air from deep centres, and a really magnificent full length save by Brown to his right as Insole fairly crashed Boardman's cross with his head to the far corner.

But for all the threat for this critical period the one positive effect it had was to help consolidate the Pegasus defence. It came out of the fire as tempered steel. And the Casuals beat themselves at this point because they failed to realise that their persistent long, high crosses into the Pegasus goal area became less and less the way to penetrate tall, strong defenders like McKinna, Shearwood, and Alexander. So the Casuals played into the Pegasus heads and paid for it. Indeed, looking back, one cannot recall Brown, whose judgment and handling in the air were above reproach, being once tested by a shot worthy of the name.

Pegasus, on the other hand, having planned a long game to match their opponents—quick, deep passes out of defence to Pawson and Sutcliffe, with Laybourne also moving to the wings—created their openings on the ground. To begin with, in their thrusting, controlled start it was only Cowan's outstretched leg that kept Laybourne's low shot out of the Casual's net. But out of this, at the twelfth minute, came Sutcliffe's corner, Carr's headed flick sideways, and Pawson's instant right-foot volley from an angle which dipped past everyone just inside the far post.

From then on it was largely a war of attrition, a battle for the midfield spaces. There followed next, of course, the Casuals' up-surge in which Dutchman and Insole for the one time really gained some space for Boardman and Kerruish down the flanks. But the Pegasus centre held firm in the air and

130

the challenge in effect brought nothing except a promise for the future. Yet the second half in its turn brought still another change. Saunders at left-half, all through the coolest, most resourceful player, was now finely supported by the firm tackling of Vowels on his flank. Together they won bit by bit the midfield authority to blanket Dutchman and Insole, and this finally helped to make Pawson's goal decisive.

The second half, indeed, apart from one desperate spurt by the Casuals which saw Shuttleworth and Boardman head wide narrowly, largely belonged to Pegasus. They fought seven corners to none and had Cowan, Eastland, and others more often in trouble with the switches of their more direct attacks. Sutcliffe in particular was a danger, but Pawson suffered through Carr's inaccurate service, though the inside—always ready with a shot—covered much ground with Lunn in those vital central areas.

That Pegasus almost added to their lead through a flashing header by Vowels to Sutcliffe's corner and when Laybourne, breaking clean through, was robbed only by Bunyan's daring dive at his feet, merely showed where the stronger pulse now beat. In the dying moments, too, Laybourne hit the cross bar from point blank range, but it mattered little, for by then the pale sun had already gone down on the Casuals, and on all those who would wish to serve two masters.

CORINTHIAN-CASUALS – D. J. Bunyan; R. Cowan, D. W. Newton; G. M. Shuttleworth, D. H. Eastland, J. F. Platt; N. Kerruish, D. J. Insole, G. H. G. Doggart, J. A. Dutchman, L. J. Boardman.

PEGASUS – B. R. Brown; F. C. M. Alexander, G. H. McKinna; R. C. Vowels, K. A. Shearwood, D. F. Saunders; H. A. Pawson, D. B. Carr, J. S. Laybourne, R. Lunn, R. Sutcliffe.

14 Wembley again

Roy Sutcliffe and John Tanner saw us through into the Amateur Cup semi-final of 1953 with a goal each in the second half, when we defeated Slough Town once again on their ground, the Dolphin Stadium, before a capacity crowd of 9,000. We had the same side out that had played against the Casuals, with the exception of John Tanner who displaced Jack Laybourne, the Cambridge player, a controversial decision and one only taken after a great deal of thought.

The selection of our sides—particularly the cup ones—had never proved easy right from the start, for however unbiassed the selectors tried to be, they had always to contend with a natural and understandable dichotomy within our ranks, brought about by the very nature of our make up, and irrespective of the one-year rule.

Our selection committee consisted of the president, three representatives from each university, one of whom was to be the captain of the university at the start of the current season, and two others to be elected annually together with the captain of the club. The secretary was always to be in attendance, and the coach—though surprisingly this was not written into the rules—was naturally consulted. Had the coach been able to attend all our matches I for one would have liked him to have always had the final say in selection. As it was he could only attend a limited number of our games and so had to rely on the opinion of the selection committee.

After our defeat of the Casuals there were those who considered that Jack Laybourne should have played against Slough, for John was injury prone and his explosive speed on which he relied so much, seemed now at times to be deserting him. Jack Laybourne, a Bevin boy during the war who had spent four years underground as a miner, was a different type of centre-forward, very capable on the ball, bandy-legged, neat, stylish, incisive, and though not tall, well built and determined. He was soon to play for England and once for Tottenham Hotspur. It was a difficult decision and in the end the selectors had plumped for John and he'd played well and come up with a goal. He had in fact, from the club's inception, scored more goals for us than any other player. So he was chosen to play against Southall, our opponents in the semi-final, the match to be played at Highbury.

The afternoon was bright and sunny, the ground bone hard, when we emerged from the tunnel just before three o'clock and ran out on to the Arsenal pitch to see what we could make of Southall. I had taken a measure of comfort in recalling what *The Times* had said in concluding the report of our previous cup-tie with Slough :

Since being two goals down at half-time at Hayes in the first round, the Pegasus defence has not been penetrated in five and a quarter hours of football, while their forwards have scored 12 times. There is a warning here to the rest of the field.

Glancing across at the other end where Southall in their red and white striped shirts were warming up, I wondered whether they had taken any heed of this warning.

Their progress so far had been impressive. In the first round they'd travelled the long distance down to Saltash and won the replay. In the second round they'd disposed of Bishop Auckland, in the third Wealdstone, who had just defeated the cup-holders Walthamstow, and in the fourth Romford in a replay at Romford.

A ball came over and bounced awkwardly before me. I didn't like the look of the pitch or the feel of it underfoot. It was altogether too nobbly and sparse of grass. A day for mistakes I thought and thereupon made up my mind to get in fast and win the ball if possible before it bounced. I glanced at the main stand speculating where Biddie was sitting, watching along with 30,000 others. Then the whistle blew and I closed up on Parker their centre-forward whom I recognized from the portrait and pen pictures of their side which was in the Arsenal's official programme.

And at once the bounce was most treacherous, and a moment extra dwelling on the ball was to court immediate pressure from Southall's eager and hungry forwards. I felt vulnerable as the reporter from the *Guardian* made abundantly clear :

Southall started with a smooth competence which forced the Pegasus defence to kick wide and wildly. Shearwood as near as makes no difference, scored through his own goal and a few moments later made an appalling back pass which should have cost a goal had not Parker stumbled over the ball and Brown thus been able to clear.

133

And I wasn't at all sure what to make of another of his comments :

Shearwood is an extraordinary centre-half and his display varied sharply between the heroic and the comic. He was completely lacking in polish or constructive ability and yet innumerable times in desperate situations a long leg would dart like a chameleon's tongue or a leaping head appear when all seemed lost.

But it was obvious that the man from the *Guardian* had enjoyed the match for he wrote in his opening paragraph :

During the last few days one has travelled more than a thousand miles to watch Association football matches. The last of these journeys was infinitely the most worthwhile because not for a long time has one seen such a virile, exciting and wholly entertaining game as the F.A. Amateur Cup semi-final in which Pegasus drew 1–1 against Southall here today. This was a game of rare contrasts, particularly in the football of Pegasus, which varied from moments of high adventure to ones of incipient brilliance.

As for that back pass, I remember it very clearly. It was one of those tight situations, the ball bobbling before me needing but the most delicate of touches to Ben who had left his line. I tried to stroke it to him, conscious of the drumming footsteps of Parker hard on my heels as I screened him from the ball. Very gently I touched it—too gently—and Parker following through was on to the thing in a flash. Incredibly he failed to score, somehow tripping over the ball which Ben gathered calmly and without a flicker of emotion.

Fast and desperate was the encounter and with only seven minutes remaining, Southall got the equalizer. When we left the field shortly after to do battle another day the score was still one apiece. Geoffrey Green had this to say :

There was a duel in the sun at Arsenal Stadium on Saturday, where a gathering 30,000 strong saw Pegasus and Southall leave the battlefield at the end still locked in deadly combat with one goal each in their semi-final tie of the F.A. Amateur Cup. In truth, it was not so much a subtle duel as a resounding clash of arms with no quarter asked, and it is to be continued at Craven Cottage, Fulham, next Saturday.

Whether the character of the struggle will alter now depends on a number of things. Certainly it was abundantly apparent at this first meeting that the hard, rather sparse Highbury surface ran much in favour of Southall's robust, first time game, with the lively ball given plenty of air. Backed by a strong tackling defence and a slight edge in physique, they cleverly off-set the Pegasus artistry by making their opponents play the match where they least wanted to play it —off the ground.

Clearly then the struggle has become one of contrasting methods. Southall have had the conditions to their liking once; now Pegasus will pray in the meanwhile for a drop of soothing rain to increase the holding properties of Fulham's richer surface. Whether they will be able to assert their style on the floor must remain one of the unanswered questions. Whether, too, they have learned more than Southall from this opening bout remains another query. Perhaps they have. Certainly by already deciding to bring in J. S. Laybourne for Carr at inside-right they recognise the need for a bit more 'devil' in attack.

If the real quality of Saturday came largely from Pegasus—and that merely in fleeting spasms—it was nevertheless a gripping occasion, full of escape and movement. As someone remarked afterwards, it was an afternoon for the edge of one's seat. And let there be no question about it, Southall fully deserved, on a territorial basis, their right to fight again, even though their equalising goal came only seven minutes from the end.

Southall's high, long passing approach was not entirely lacking in method, and it so flustered one or two Pegasus defenders at the beginning—unhappy with the lofted, high-bounding ball—that Southall might well have settled things in the opening half-hour. The chances, in fact, were offered to them. No doubt they had hoped for just this very thing, but it did not quite come off. Twice, indeed, in the first twenty minutes Shearwood, who later emerged successfully from a disturbing start, nearly sent Southall on their way to Wembley. First, as close as a touch, he all but diverted a cross from Reynolds into his own net, and then badly misjudged a back pass to his goalkeeper. How Parker failed to score from the closest range after a simple interception was incredible. In his surprise and anxiety he first trod on the ball, then lost complete sight of it, allowing Brown to bring off a cool clearance.

Brown, indeed, with the rest of the Pegasus defence, all through the afternoon was frequently under pressure in the air, but his work was faultless. Once, too, at the half-hour he parried a swift rising shot by Blizzard finely. But generally, after that struggling opening, Alexander, McKinna, and Shearwood settled down to give him strong protection from the thrusting bursts of the dangerous Blizzard and Reynolds down the wings. If Alexander perhaps distributed the ball the more intelligently on the ground, it was McKinna who more than once saved awkward-looking situations with his head.

Yet for all Southall's lofted pressure it was Pegasus who carved out the scoring chances in their moments of low, flowing attack. Only in short bursts—particularly at the end of the first half and during the opening twenty minutes after the interval—did the attack really move as it can, a concerted unit. When it did move like this, largely through the impulse of its left-wing triangle, there was always the chance of a goal. Here Lunn especially, supported by the cool Saunders, showed his strong, thrusting qualities and quick distribution.

Unlike Southall's, these chances were self-created and one of them brought Pegasus a fine goal against the run of the play two minutes before the interval. An exchange of passes between Lunn and Sutcliffe down the left, sending Prior and Merry the wrong way, saw Lunn's curling centre partially touched away, but Pawson, quick to seize this particular offering, worked the ball round from right to left into an open central space before hitting the net with a low, left-foot shot. That was one of the few effective things Pawson did. Too often he dribbled quickly inwards in a detached sort of way straight into the quick

135

tackling of Hardy, Sloane, and Mears, who had a splendid game in the centre of the Southall defence. Still, Pawson now did his part and Pegasus held on to that goal until the last stages.

In the first twenty minutes of the second half they should have settled matters when first Sutcliffe and then Tanner swept close up to goal from lovely passes by Carr only to miss by inches, Tanner's in particular being a dashing effort in full sail. Those intelligent moves by Carr might have done the trick, but generally his approach was rather too frail for a battle of this sort. And now, Southall, still with hopes and passes running high, mounted their last assault, with Mears coming up the middle to add weight. With seven minutes left Blizzard, taking McKinna with him, suddenly appeared on the left, and as Brown punched out his cross Wenlock shot home the rebound from some twelve yards to the great joy of his colleagues. Either side still might have won in the last seconds but the struggle was best left where it was.

PEGASUS – B. Brown (Oxford); F. C. M. Alexander (Cambridge), G. H. McKinna (Oxford); R. C. Vowels (Cambridge), K. A. Shearwood (Oxford), D. Saunders (Oxford); H. A. Pawson (Oxford), D. B. Carr (Oxford), J. D. P. Tanner (Oxford), R. G. Lunn (Oxford), R. Sutcliffe (Cambridge).

SOUTHALL – E. Bennett; T. Prior, E. Hardy; A. Merry, C. Mears, R. Sloane; J. Blizzard, J. Way, E. Parker, W. Wenlock, M. Reynolds.

The replay took place the following week on Fulham's ground, Craven Cottage, in conditions much the same as at Highbury. We'd made one change in the side, bringing in Jack Laybourne at inside-right in place of Donald Carr.

Barely fifteen minutes had elapsed when I received a severe kick on my ankle, at the same time wrenching it badly. There was no question of there being a foul. I had raced Parker for a through ball and stuck out my leg to block his shot, taking the full impact of his kick on the inside of my ankle which I then somehow twisted. I knew the injury was serious; I know also that it was something that I either had to ignore or go off. So I tried to pretend it was not there and got on with the game. At half-time the ankle was thick and shapeless and rather than remove my boot—I don't think I would ever have got it on again—I eased the laces while Leslie pressed a cold wet sponge against my sock and George Ainsley poured lead opium around the bruising.

I'm not sure how I got through that second half. It helped a lot that Parker stuck to the middle and did not work the wings allowing me to stick with him by hook or by crook. But the pain when I ran and tried to turn was intense. It was the longest forty-five minutes of

136

football I ever experienced. Surprisingly Southall seemed totally unaware of the fact that I was injured and so missed a chance of putting
me under the kind of pressure which would have exposed my physical
handicap. Equally surprising, though there were mentions of the
injuries sustained by John Tanner and Mears, the Southall centre-
half, there was no mention of mine in the press reports, apart from one
in the *News of the World*, which more than made amends with a
spectacular and personal headline that did something to restore my
morale, but little to improve the condition of my ankle. However,
much to my great relief the X-ray showed no broken bones.

The match we won—and rightly so according to Denis Compton
who wrote :

Pegasus fully deserved the right to yet another visit to Wembley. And their
performance was even more remarkable, in that for well over half the game
Tanner was virtually a passenger on the right wing.

The entire team played superbly. Pawson though not among the goalscorers,
was responsible to a great extent for this brilliant display. He was the outstanding forward on the field.

He was very capably supported by the hard-working and hard-tackling Lunn,
and Laybourne, their inside-right, was always dangerous near goal. Once in the
first half he shot on the turn from 18 yards and the ball hit the post a
tremendous crack,

Southall's performance was creditable. Had it not been the score would have
been much heavier. But they lacked the cohesion and method of their opponents
and their finishing was weak.

They suffered a great blow when Mears, their centre-half, was injured midway through the second half, but I am convinced this would not have altered
the ultimate result.

Pegasus took the lead after thirty minutes with a Tanner header.

Immediately after the resumption Sutcliffe shot over the bar from one yard
out. But he atoned soon afterwards by scoring.

Southall's goal was the best of the match. Reynolds got the ball well out and
took it on and loosed a terrific shot from about 25 yards. It left Brown helpless.

The Times wrote :

By their defeat of Southall by two goals to one in the replayed semi-final tie of
the F.A. Amateur Cup at Craven Cottage on Saturday, Pegasus have qualified
to appear at Wembley for the second time in three years—a remarkable performance for a club of five years' standing—where they will meet Harwich and
Parkeston.

By the manner of their victory Pegasus must be regarded as favourites, a
rank to which they will do full justice if they can reproduce their present form.
They are a finely balanced side. To pick out individuals in a team victory is
perhaps invidious but mention must be made of Laybourne and Vowels, who

137

played above themselves, and lent an added thrust to an attack which threatened at one time to swamp the strong Southall defence.

That Southall were able to contain their opponents for so long was proof enough of their worth but in truth their attack lacked the imagination and rhythm to out-manoeuvre the solid Pegasus defence. An injury to Tanner and the consequent switching of Pawson to centre-forward probably deprived Pegasus of a greater margin of victory, but this was later offset by injury to Mears, an outstanding centre-half, midway through the second half when Pegasus were two goals in the lead. Paradoxically enough this was the signal for a spirited Southall revival during which they reduced the margin and came near to saving the match. But Pegasus were not caught and proved themselves worthy finalists.

Conditions favoured a fast open game and soon there were escapes at both ends. First, Wenlock intercepted a Pegasus back-pass from a goal kick only to waste a good opportunity, and then Laybourne nearly opened the scoring with a glorious shot, taken left-footed from outside the penalty area, which crashed against the Southall upright. A minute later it was Southall's turn once more when Parker shot just wide, again from an intercepted Pegasus back-pass. At this stage Pegasus were distinctly uncertain in defence, but at the half-hour their confidence was restored with a well-taken goal. A corner taken by Sutcliffe was partially cleared to Pawson, whose lob into the goalmouth was headed by Tanner past Bennett.

Two minutes later Lunn nearly converted another centre from Pawson and again Laybourne went close after a brilliant coup by Pawson, who was running riot on the right-wing. Then came Tanner's injury—a pulled leg muscle—and at half-time Pegasus were worth rather more than their lead of one goal, for their defence had only been in trouble of their own making.

Within a minute of the restart Pegasus should have increased their lead when Pawson, now at centre-forward, worked the ball along the bye-line from a throw-in, only for Sutcliffe unaccountably to shoot over from almost under the bar. Ten minutes later a brilliant move by Lunn and Pawson ended with Bennett making a fine save from Sutcliffe's shot. But such pressure was bound to bring results and with half-an-hour left Pegasus went further ahead. Another fine move by Sutcliffe, Lunn, and Pawson was finally converted by Sutcliffe after Bennett had parried his initial shot at close range.

Shortly afterwards Mears was injured in a tackle and Southall in desperation, were spurred to their counter-attack. First, McKinna headed out from under the bar, then Brown saved magnificently from Blizzard, and with twenty minutes remaining Southall's fortunes were revived when Reynolds picked up a loose ball outside the penalty area and scored with a glorious shot from fully 30 yards' range. Now Southall for the first time really began to fight and Pegasus were pinned in their own half. But in spite of sustained pressure at the last their defence held firm to make Wembley a reality once more.

SOUTHALL – E. Bennett; T. Prior, E. Hardy; A. Merry, C. Mears, R. Sloane; J. Blizzard, J. Way, E. Parker, W. Wenlock, M. Reynolds.

PEGASUS – B. R. Brown (Oxford); F. C. M. Alexander (Cambridge), G. H.

138

McKinna (Oxford); R. C. Vowels (Cambridge), K. A. Shearwood (Oxford), D. F. Saunders (Oxford); H A.. Pawson (Oxford), J. Laybourne (Cambridge), J. D. P. Tanner (Oxford), R. G. Lunn (Oxford), R. Sutcliffe (Cambridge).

So there it was; once more we were back at Wembley and if selected I had exactly three weeks to get fit for the Final. It took a week of treatment to get rid of the swelling and because of the bruising, Biddie could only begin light massage at the end of it. In the middle of the second week I began to do some running and light work with a ball. Finally with a well-strapped ankle and in some trepidation I played at Iffley Road in the first round of the A.F.A. Cup against Histon United, a match we won 4–1. Donald Carr came back into the side and Jack Laybourne took over John Tanner's position at centre-forward. My ankle pained me considerably and thickened again, but it had survived the test and there was still another week before the Final.

It now seemed likely that this would be the team that would play at Wembley and John would have to miss the Final. It was hard for him, but Jack was a very good player and fit. And no doubt recalling how John had broken down in the 1949 quarter-final cup-tie against Bromley, the selectors settled on this side that had just played against Histon.

The spring days were drawing out and each afternoon of that last week I'd jog across the field known at Lancing as the 'sixteen acre', and practise with a ball on the first XI pitch. A number from the college and the surrounding district were coming up to Wembley, and those who were not would be watching on television. I received many requests for tickets, but there were none to be had; the match was a sell-out.

And suddenly it was all happening again and we were up in London together trying to get a sound last night's sleep without interruption —not always easy on such occasions. But when the following morning we set off from the Great Western Hotel, Paddington, we did this time manage to avoid ending up in a builder's yard at the back of Wembley, making our way with unerring accuracy towards the great stadium whose doors once more swung wide to swallow us up, bus and all.

We changed in the same changing-room that we'd used two years ago. My ankle had been strapped up on Friday by the Brighton and Hove trainer, the reason being, I'd played once for their reserves

139

against Luton, a fact rather astonishingly mentioned in that now extinct 'National Humorous Weekly', *Blighty*. I still had twinges of pain, but I knew I could get through. And then it was time to go and we were in the tunnel again, and after waiting awhile, walking up the slight slope and out into that vast arena side by side with our opponents, the sun as brilliant, the sky just as blue and cloudless as it had been in 1951.

And there, on that sunny April afternoon at Wembley we murdered and buried Harwich and Parkeston by six clear goals to nothing. They had previously defeated Whitton United, Harrogate, Clevedon, Leytonstone, and in the semi-final, Walton and Hersham. But that afternoon they simply had no answer and it proved our easiest cup-tie of that year. Denis got our first goal, climbing typically and inimitably high above everyone to head home a corner from Roy Sutcliffe. Davies, the Harwich and Parkestone centre-forward, was suffering from a knee injury which broke down early in the first half. A player they were relying on, he'd been given a pain-killing injection before the match in the hope that it would see him through. But a knee injury is a very different kettle of fish from an ankle injury and he should not have played.

The *Guardian* summed it all up with a headline : 'Pegasus Overwhelm Harwich' and I quote two paragraphs from the report written by an Old International :

The marked disparity in height and weight between the two teams, not to mention the finer points of the game, removed from the start all hope of a balanced contest. Those tall and leggy Pegasus half-backs, Saunders, Shearwood, and Vowels, all spent a pleasant afternoon out-jumping their smaller opponents and in nothing was their advantage more clearly shown than in the compelling weight of their tackles. Behind their protective screen the two backs, Alexander and McKinna, had long spells of agreeable exercise; while Brown in goal had to wait till very late in the game before he got any but the most sparse and fleeting opportunities to display his skill.

Apart from the fundamental beauty of the Pegasus method, based as it is on accurate ground passing and intelligent positional play, there were two features of their cup-winning performance, especially in the first half, which must have left a profound impression on the minds of the Harwich defenders. One was the lusty, beefy swing which that square, stocky Lancastrian, Sutcliffe imparted to all his shots, centres, and corner kicks, and the other was the ball control and, above all, the neat, precise passing of that most artistic inside-forward, Lunn. Forward skill, in the modern sense, no longer consists in holding the ball, however prettily, but in diverting it smoothly, and with the minimum loss of time, to the point of maximum potential pressure. In this,

140

until he tired, Lunn stood head and shoulders above everyone; after which his burden was taken up by Vowels, a powerful right wing half-back, who rounded off a polished display with remarkable vim and freshness.

Wrote Geoffrey Green :

Wembley in spring time is to Pegasus what Headingley and Worcester in summer once used to be to Sir Donald Bradman. The rich emerald surface now sparkling once again under the proverbial Wembley sunshine, and the steep packed curve of this amphitheatre seem to act as a stimulus on them. So it was on Saturday when an all-ticket crowd of some 100,000 saw them carry off the F.A. Amateur Cup for the second time in three seasons. Theirs was a mature exhibition of pure football that cut poor Harwich and Parkeston to ribbons to the tune of six goals to none and reduced them to the status of a selling plater that has strayed by mischance into classic company.

After the first quarter of an hour it was never really a match. Two well taken goals within that opening span, rather against the run of the early play, left the rest of the proceedings with a mere academic interest. Yet it was an interest that offered much aesthetic satisfaction, no matter where one's sympathies really lay. For now Pegasus proceeded to unfold themselves majestically, calling up the heights of their creative instinct as they brought a variety of designs to the attacking picture.

Harwich in spite of their gallant and tireless efforts, had a heartbreaking experience. To make matters worse, Davies their centre-forward, suffering all week from a damaged knee quickly showed that he should never have played, and for all his subterfuge in bandaging both legs to confuse the opposition, it was really his own side who were quickly confounded. They were scarcely in a position to face Pegasus in such a mood with only ten men. Not that it made any effective difference one way or the other. Pegasus, once they had settled down after a lethargic opening, seemed to have 22 players on the field; their positional play and imaginative passing, long and short cut along the ground to the last refined inch magnified the Wembley pitch, so much space did they win for themselves. They seemed to have the ball on a string, tantalising opponents who were a yard behind the pass for most of the afternoon.

Harwich came from the edge of the cruel sea and know adversity. The most one can now say for them is that they went down bravely with all their colours flying in a stiff breeze, with Pearson at inside-right and Christie behind him at wing-half, playing themselves into the ground. Once, just after the second Pegasus goal—around the quarter-hour—Pearson worked his way through cleverly on the right, only to see his low cross pass go begging in front of an open enough target, and soon after the interval Pearson again opened the way for Cooper to hit Brown's crossbar. Those two fragile moments apart, Harwich never looked like scoring. Beaten in the tackle, outpaced and out-thought, their close passing seldom disturbed a strong Pegasus defence that moved smoothly into position and used the ball with precision.

Pegasus, in fact, were a team, a single unit. To see them on this sunlit day

141

was to admire the inner workings of some Swiss watch. Everything and everyone hung together. The mechanism worked perfectly. Yet, if it was a team victory, one must pick out especially the great foraging and constructive work of Lunn at inside-left, who inspired Carr to act as the perfect foil in keeping a swift attack flowing through the centre and down the flanks. In defence, too, Vowels—one of the most improved of players—and Alexander in particular took a page out of Saunders's tidy book in their cultured use of the ball.

Yet how did the ending match the opening ten minutes, when Harwich began so full of life and hope. There were the seeds of a surprise in that beginning, but a quick Pegasus counter at the eleventh minute destroyed the flower that might have been. A searing shot by Sutcliffe was turned past the bar by King at full stretch, and from the left-winger's measured corner kick Saunders glided unseen into the goalmouth to head past a goal-keeper going the wrong way. Three minutes later a glorious pass by Lunn sent Pawson tearing past Tyrrell, and from his low centre Sutcliffe forced the ball over the line with the support of Laybourne.

In a trice really the match was over. And shortly before half-time another fine move, one of many, but this time, as a contrast, conducted from head to head between Saunders, Lunn, and Laybourne, saw Carr take the final nod in his stride and find the corner of the net with an angled left-foot shot.

For a moment at the change of ends the support of a swirling wind seemed to revive Harwich, but Cooper's shot on the bar killed their last hope. Pegasus went smoothly on their way, with Sutcliffe and Pawson, the latter making light of a temperature, indulging in clever scissor movements with Lunn, Carr, and Laybourne. Soon Laybourne unleashed a left foot rocket into the roof of the net from Carr's pass to make it four up, then King fumbled a swift low cross from Carr on the right—part of another scissors movement—leaving Sutcliffe to pick his spot in an empty net.

The final touch came five minutes from the end. Pawson suddenly turned up on the left; Laybourne nodded down his centre and Carr stroked home the final goal to bring the widest victory ever achieved (war-time apart) by any side at Wembley. Looking back, how much history was held at the end in those last fateful minutes at Hayes last December! And now, if certain conditions are overcome, Pegasus will be seen in the F.A. Cup itself next year, for better or for worse.

It was a eulogistic account by any standards, bettered only on that score by what Denzil Batchelor had to say in his autobiography *Babbled Of Green Fields*, published eight years later. But he was referring to our earlier Cup-Final when he wrote:

The best football ever seen in a Wembley Final wasn't shown by Blackpool and Bolton in 1953; that must take second place to the Amateur Cup Final won in 1951 by Pegasus against Bishop Auckland.

Astonishingly he continued:

If Pegasus could have been given three seasons' full-scale training as an in-

142

tegral combination they would have been good enough to win the World Cup in 1954.

He had, of course, now gone much too far, but it nevertheless makes very nice reading! And a fitting end to the first part of this story.

15 Hong Kong

That summer of 1953 was to be Frank Doherty's last at Lancing and I for one was sorry. The headmaster elect, John Dancy, was a Wyke-hamist aged thirty-three, who had taught classics for five years at his old school.

I met him first one hot afternoon in the middle of the summer term. He'd walked across the sixteen acres with John Handford, one of the senior housemasters, and arrived on our doorstep, shirt-sleeves rolled up, his jacket over an arm. As he limped across our threshold to be welcomed by Biddie, I saw the extent of his legacy from the polio he had suffered in 1949. Then for an hour we talked and I found myself, as I invariably do on such occasions, speculating more about the person than concentrating on what was being said.

The man sitting opposite me was tall and thin, tufted above the ears, otherwise nearly bald, apart from a few wisps of fair hair span-ning his considerable cranium. He had a youthful and engaging enthusiasm and when he smiled his eyes would brighten, and his expressive, highly intelligent face would light up. It was also a smile which I guessed could be switched on and off with all the significance and warning of a flashing light at sea. I noticed he had long sensitive hands.

'Well?' I asked Biddie when he had gone.

'I liked him,' she replied. 'He seems a nice and friendly person.'

'Yes, I thought so too,' and we left it at that.

The next time I saw John Dancy was at the common room meeting at the beginning of the September term when naturally we were all intrigued to see the professional cut of his jib. Nor did we have long to wait.

'I won't beat about the bush gentlemen,' he began, 'when I tell you that I have been appointed to Lancing to raise the academic standard.' And before many of us had fully digested this important piece of information, he continued, spelling it out in clear economic terms, 'Life is competitive and we're going to have it competitive at Lancing.'

But what really did grate on that first official occasion was his habit of referring to the staff, a number of whom were much older and considerably more experienced than he, by their surnames.

And then we were off, the term got under way, the new broom began to sweep and some dust arose.

To stress the competitive side of life he began by intensifying the mark system. There were fortnightly orders, first half-term orders, second half-term orders, full-term orders. There were set marks, raw marks, scaled marks, cooked marks, examination marks, combined marks, until come the end of term, swamped by lists of names, bemused by graphs, slide rules and God knows what, we finally arrived at some preposterous total simply to establish who should be first and who last. It was time-wasting, educationally meaningless and psychologically disastrous—serving only to point another accusatory finger at the wretched failures and encourage the habit of cheating.

From the start Dancy decided to do some teaching at every level in the school to get an educational 'feel of the place'. He got it all right, and to his credit stuck to it. But he was a true scholar and found it hard going at the bottom end. In a different way he found it not so easy at the top end when he took over the classical sixth from John Handford. Despite his unquestioned intellectual capacity he had not the teaching experience of the older man nor yet the wisdom that comes of years.

An incident illustrates the latter clearly. I was going into chapel one Friday evening, the day's work over, when Dancy accosted me at the west door.

'Who was that singing upstairs in the New Block at the end of last period?' He was aware that I taught up there; he'd been teaching below.

I told him who I thought it was and gave the matter no further consideration.

The following morning the master was sent for, and after being well and truly admonished for singing a hymn in Latin at the end of a period, told to write an apology to his colleagues for the inconvenience he had caused them and pin it to the common room notice board.

It was an extraordinary thing to do, explained only perhaps by the fact that he'd been teaching a lower form at the time—a task that was probably driving him to near distraction—and the sound of singing had been the last straw. The master, Donald Bancroft, was a forthright and respected Yorkshireman, a first in classics from Corpus, Oxford. He was a valuable man on any staff, who knew exactly what he was doing—a fact which Dancy later recognized when he made him his personal assistant.

Our new head preached his first sermon, a lecture really, based on the teleological approach, and delightedly I recognized what he was talking about. A chance here I thought to do myself a bit of good. But try as I might I never quite found the right opportunity or phrase to convey the fact that I, too, was aware of Aristotle.

But the man's enthusiasm was infectious and though he did some things which were hurtful and unnecessary, it was largely the result of impatience, inexperience and bad briefing. Given time there was much that he could and would do for Lancing and vice versa. Particularly I was grateful to him for he allowed me to continue playing for Pegasus, never expecting me to go cap in hand to beg permission each time.

Leslie Compton, centre-half for Arsenal and England, was our new coach for the coming season in which the club played thirty matches. I played in twenty-seven of these, eleven thanks to John Dancy in that September term when we brought a side down and popped in nine goals against the boys by half-time. We split up after that.

Prior to our first-round Amateur Cup-tie with Clevedon at the end of 1953 we played two flood-lit matches against Portsmouth and Watford. At Fratton Park a large crowd saw us—a goal down at half-time—lose 3–1 to their full First Division League side which included five internationals : Stephen of Scotland, Dickenson, Frog-gatt, Philips, and Harris of England. Against Watford in another excellent game we lost 1–2 before some 12,000 spectators.

Before the Portsmouth game I had gone into our opponents' dressing room to get some strapping, as Leslie Laitt had slipped up with our medical equipment.

'Can I help?' asked one of their players who was sitting on a medical couch swinging his legs.

'I'm looking for some elastoplast to strap my ankle.'

The man regarded me for a moment with amusement.

'Get your sock off and I'll do it for you,' and he sprang lightly off the couch. 'What's your job?'

'I'm teaching at Lancing.'

'Any chance of coming over and doing some coaching?'

'Of course.'

'Tuesday any good?' He had deftly completed the strapping.

I nodded. 'Why not come and have some lunch first?'

'Fine,' said the player, 'I'll see you after the game then—that's if you haven't kicked us all to death,' he added grinning at me as I left the room.

It was the beginning of a long friendship and Jack Mansell taught me how to coach and a lot more about football. His son, Nick, is now in my house at Lancing and playing for the school.

On 19 December we put paid to Clevedon in the first round of the Amateur Cup by three clear goals. That Christmas we spent at Evesham with Biddie's mother, who had moved to Oxstalls, an old farm house on a bend of the river Avon.

The day after Boxing Day I bade farewell to my family and set off to join the rest of the Pegasus side in London to begin our New Year Tour.

We flew from Heathrow to Hong Kong in a noisy Argonaut, putting down at Zurich, Rome, Cairo, Basra, Karachi, Delhi, Calcutta, Rangoon, and Bangkok on what proved a long and tiring journey.

Disembarking at Cairo and inhaling deeply I was suddenly acutely aware once more of all those familiar smells of the war and a host of memories assailed me. I wondered where my old Mark Four Landing Craft which we'd paid off in the Bitter Lakes now was. Where too was the tall dignified Arab who would greet Peter Bull (then C.O. of the 21st L.C.T. Flotilla, now actor, author) and myself each morning as we emerged from the Continental Hotel? Was he still accosting the residents in that impeccable English. 'Would you like me to show you round the bazaar today sir?'

We flew on, playing bridge most of the while—once being requested and with some urgency—to evacuate the round part in the after section of the aircraft as the wretched thing was flying tail-heavy. We talked a great deal and tried to sleep, ate unwisely at Calcutta and spent one restless hot night at Rangoon where I shared a room with Jimmy Potts.

Jimmy did things his own way—as he usually did—on this occasion insisting that there was no need to get under a mosquito net. The result was no sleep for either of us, since my companion spent what short time we had at our disposal doing battle with the mosquitoes, successfully swatting them against the wall with the palm of his hand, producing a series of cracks as explosive and deadly as a German 88 millimetre. Eventually, just when all seemed quiet, a dreadful row broke forth outside. Poor Denis had been one of those who had taken food at Calcutta, and feeling dreadfully ill had staggered out into the courtyard and vomited over a sleeping Burmese. But by then it was three o'clock and time to get up; we were flying at four.

'I don't like the look of Saunders,' pronounced Tommy from out of the darkness as Denis was assisted aboard the bus. 'We'll be lucky to get him home, let alone on to a football pitch.'

And then we were motoring towards the airstrip outside Rangoon, the lights by the wayside flickering wanly across each dark threshold of the humble Burmese abodes.

Dawn broke and we soared up into a magical sky for the last lap which required a special pilot to negotiate Hong Kong's short landing strip.

'Fasten your safety belts, please,' we were politely requested for the umpteenth time, and then after a few hair-raising moments threading our way down the hillside, we landed safely to face a battery of cameras.

Playing-wise the tour was a disaster. We lost all three of our football matches and were completely outclassed in a golf contest in which I partnered Leslie Compton against the Hong Kong champion and another who appeared almost as good. I spent most of the day on my own for I seldom if ever reached the green which, if nothing else, served to amuse my bare-footed young caddie who each time insisted that I used the club of his choice and then proceeded to shake with silent uncontrollable mirth as I struck, or rather attempted to strike the ball. His innumerable excursions into the deep undergrowth—the ball once almost disappeared into communist territory—never failed to produce a result.

However, we did a little better in a cricket match and I felt privileged to captain our side. Our opponents, the Hong Kong Cricket Club, were captained by T. A. Pearce, well known in English cricket. The honorary secretary, Mr. Owen-Hughes was an Old Salopian who had already entertained us royally in his beautiful home on the summit of the island. We drew the match, declaring at 228 for 8. Poor John

Tanner, who was handicapped by an injury, insisted vehemently that Jimmy Platt should not be his runner—in his opinion he considered the latter did not sufficiently understand the game—and was promptly run out by him for nought, which didn't please him at all. However, Jimmy Potts then hit a very good century and I got what was described as a lively sixty-seven.

None of us slept much that first night, for the rooms were excessively hot and all night long fireworks were going off in celebration of New Year's Eve. I was still sharing a room with Jimmy Potts who, much to my astonishment suddenly announced late one night that he was going out to find a doctor to remove his big toe-nail which was giving him trouble. He returned in the early hours of the morning full of gory details and minus his big toe-nail—which didn't prevent him from playing later that same evening.

We were lavishly entertained and no one was more solicitous of our welfare than a certain Tak Sing who would arrive early each morning and invite us, not unsuccessfully, to visit his shop and buy his garments. He sold us silk kimonos and black, gold-embroidered slippers, and swell-looking white pyjamas with red dragons, which, once worn never quite looked the same, splitting along the seams at the slightest provocation and fraying dreadfully.

Eventually, after a final banquet in Kowloon we assembled wearily at the Kai Tak airfield and climbed aboard another Argonaut—no mass of cameras and reporters this time to see us off—only one solitary well-wisher, our friend Tak Sing, who greeted us with unfeigned delight and stood waving his arms frantically as we tore along the runway and soared low out over the sea.

It had been an exhausting tour. Several of us had suffered the usual stomach complaints and we'd had no time to acclimatize ourselves. We were not only physically below par but not at full club strength, having left behind Tony Pawson, Donald Carr and Gordon McKinna. We were also ill-prepared for the conditions we had met. It was extremely hot and the grounds bone hard. Most of us had used boots suitable only for the heavy conditions of an English winter. We should have worn rubbers. The Chinese, skilful and sharp, mastered the lively ball much better than we had done and were well worth their three victories.

'Well...' Tommy had said, at the first post mortem after we'd lost the initial match 1–4 before a crowd of 15,000, 'you've got to win the next one.' And when we'd lost it by the only goal of the match three minutes from time he began the second post-mortem in tones even more serious. 'It's absolutely vital you win this last match.' Later that evening he had confided in several of us, 'I sat with His Excellency the Governor yesterday and I didn't find the man at all forthcoming. The trouble is they're expecting us to win all our matches and they feel we're letting them down.' It didn't much help matters when we promptly went and lost the last match of the tour 1–4 and this despite playing seven internationals.

The plane banked steeply and began to climb. We unfastened our safety belts and sitting back got out the cards. Two days later, on 9 January, we arrived back in London, thirteen days after having set forth.

A fortnight later, this time in icy conditions, we met Gedling Colliery on their ground, Plains Road, Mapperley, in the second round of the Amateur Cup.

Our supporters, many of them wearing mortar boards and gowns and holding aloft on poles their flat wooden replicas of the Flying Horse, lined the roads to the ground long before the kick off.

Gedling Colliery had played their way right through from the first round of the qualifying competition—five long months of cup-battling. Champions of Nottingham Alliance, they had only been beaten once in fourteen months. They had everything to gain and little to lose.

As for ourselves, cup-holders, fielding ten of the side that had won at Wembley, six of whom were internationals, it was a match fraught with danger, one that seemed to have all the ingredients of the cup-tie that goes wrong—and very aware of it we all were—Tommy had made certain of that.

And in the opening period it did feel very much as though things might go wrong, for Gedling, whose training had been supervised by the Nottingham Forest Manager, Billy Walker, played with tremendous competitive spirit, meeting the ball early and tackling in deadly fashion, roared on by a crowd of 6,000. But in the end we had scored 6 and they 1. Alan Hoby wrote:

It was 'massacre', but for fifteen glorious minutes the miner's grit matched the skill of amateur soccer's top team.

The Times wrote:

Gedling Colliery, after a fine run in the F.A. Amateur Cup, were beaten on

150

their own ground on Saturday by the holders, Pegasus, in the second round by six goals to one.

Although the score gives the false impression of a totally one-sided game—play was much more evenly balanced territorially in the first half—it serves to underline a recreated punch in the Pegasus forward line and must stand as a warning sign to those who have thought that the combined Oxford and Cambridge team was in temporary decline.

The quality of some of the goals emphasised the splendid right-wing triangle of Vowels, Pawson, and Carr, while the intelligent skill of Lunn, who scored three times from his new position, suggests that Pegasus have now solved their centre-forward problem.

But how different the story might have been if Riley's shot had scored instead of hitting the bar with Brown beaten just before the interval! By then, though Pegasus were two goals ahead, they had not been really in command. The first goal was indeed a scrambled affair. A bad clearance turned into a high centre which Salvin dropped and Carr pushed the ball into the net through a crowd of legs. The second was headed in by Lunn after Saunders had headed Sutcliffe's corner kick over Harper.

For a long period after this Gedling pressed and seemed likely to score. Relying on their wingers—Martin caused Alexander anxious moments and McKinna took a long time to settle down—Gedling mounted their attacks. Twice defenders blocked shots from Martin and Riley while Brown saved two drives by Nutt and a dangerous cross by O'Dowd. Shearwood, however, kept a tight hold on Kay, and the half ended with Pegasus two up.

In the tenth minute after the interval, however, Gedling scored. O'Dowd—who switched well with Nutt—moved down the right wing and Martin volleyed his cross to Kay who headed past Brown from close range. This inspiration for Gedling, was, alas, short-lived. Within two minutes Lunn ran through and although Salvin parried his shot, Pawson was at hand to shoot into the net.

This was the beginning of the end. Six minutes later a classic movement brought the first of three goals in quick succession for Pegasus. Vowels set Carr off and he chipped the ball to Pawson who beat two defenders before crossing to Lunn who headed down for Carr to score from a good position. Another Pawson dribble and centre followed and Lunn scored. Finally Blythe and Carr sent Lunn down the middle and he shot past Salvin after emerging from two strong tackles.

Kirk, the gallant Gedling captain, who had a balanced struggle with Sutcliffe, in a last manoeuvre switched himself to cope with Pawson, but by now the Flying Horse had well and truly bolted.

Teams:

GEDLING COLLIERY – R. Salvin; W. Kirk, G. Wileman; P. Stainwright, J. Harper, E. Lawrence; A. Nutt, G. O'Dowd, J. Kay, J. B. Riley, E. J. Martin. PEGASUS – B. R. Brown; F. C. M. Alexander, G. H. McKinna; R. C. Vowels, K. A. Shearwood, D. F. Saunders; H. A. Pawson, D. B. Carr, R. G. Lunn, J. H. Blythe, R. Sutcliffe.

At the beginning of the Easter Term of 1954, John Dancy

151

announced to the common room that since he wasn't sure what went on in certain areas of the school he intended to come round and listen to us teaching. 'I will,' he added, 'try and give masters as much warning beforehand as I can,' a proposal that did little to alleviate the unpleasantness of such a prospect.

'You'll be all right, Henry,' I remarked, 'at least you'll be able to see him coming.'

For the Reverend Henry Thorold always taught with his door thrown wide open so, he would explain, 'I can always make a quick getaway if need be.'

I wondered what John Dancy would make of his blackboard work, which remained unaltered—most of it at any rate—not for the term, but for the whole year. Written in his beautiful handwriting at the top was a bald statement, 'Only sixty more lazy days till the end of the term', the number naturally decreasing each day. Beneath lay a coloured and carefully drawn coat of arms with the ancestral name, 'Sir Marmaduke Strickland Constable, Bart'. At the bottom right-hand corner was the only reference to work, 'Remove Classics Evening School, Prose 23'—which also would remain to the end of the year.

Henry Thorold was a scholar of Eton, had not taken a degree at Oxford (we never discovered why), was the proud owner of a vintage fabric-covered Rolls-Royce, loved good food, and resided at Marston Hall, Grantham, Lincs. He taught classics his own way, interspersed with odd irrelevant questions from the form.

'What car have you got sir?'

'I have no car sir. I have a Rolls-Royce. Keeler sir, construe.'

'I'm not quite sure what you mean sir.'

'Keeler sir, you are an ignoramus.'

'Can we have the door shut, sir?'

'There is no door, sir. Triptree, construe.'

But behind this eccentricity lay a very shrewd mind and a prodigious memory. An outrageous snob, he unashamedly loved the good things of life and left those he disapproved of to go their way with a cool indifference that was without rancour or judgement. I saw him always as a medieval priest more fitting to pre-Reformation times than the twentieth century. In many ways he was good for Lancing, for he debunked much that needs debunking in the educational world.

'Flying horses, my foot, more like dumb geese, if you ask me,' began the *Guardian*'s report, quoting an ebullient red-faced northerner's loudly proclaimed comment on our performance in the third round F.A. Amateur Cup-tie against Willington, played at Oxford, on 6 February 1954. Exactly five years ago and, in the identical round we had defeated the same team 3–2 at Oxford in that first ever venture.

Now, beneath a headline—'Willington's Tactics More Impressive'— *The Times* found us lucky to survive :

The North has got a firm grip, or so it seems, on the Amateur Cup this year, and Willington clearly showed their intention of trying to keep up with their neighbours from Co. Durham when they drew at one goal each with Pegasus at Iffley Road Running Ground, Oxford, on Saturday.

Indeed, it would not have been unjust if Willington had joined their neighbours in the next round at the first attempt, for they were the better side, and though Pegasus had their chances to score in the second half Willington ought by then to have been well in the lead.

Pegasus opened with a flourish before anybody had a chance to see how players and ball would react on the hard turf, which here and there still had little patches of frozen snow. Vowels began it with a magnificent drive from over 20 yards, which Hazelton finely pushed round for a corner. From Pawson's kick the ball was headed against the bar and from the scrimmage Potts lobbed it across for Carr to shoot into the net. Apart from a header by Lunn which sizzled past the post and a splendid chance created by Pawson for Blythe, who shot weakly wide, the rest of the first half was fought out in and around the Pegasus danger zone.

M. T. Robinson found difficulty in turning to combat the speed of his namesake, and Alexander disdained close contact with Rutherford. The result was an onslaught by Willington down the wings which brought the very best out of Shearwood and out of Brown, who made one truly memorable save from Rutherford. Lewthwaite, who advanced unmolested for much of the afternoon and Marks a promising young player, supported the attacks relentlessly, and it was astonishing that only one goal—headed by Taylor five minutes before the interval from a cross by Rutherford—emerged from the continual mêlées.

In the second half Pegasus began seriously to exert themselves. Potts, when well-placed by Saunders's pass for a careful shot or a push back, blazed the ball over the goal, but Blythe nearly scored with a swerving shot on the turn which Hazelton pushed on to a post. But Willington employed the more impressive tactics throughout; their defenders, though occasionally miskicking, cleared their lines quickly and in mid-field they moved the ball about and tackled quickly as the conditions demanded. Pegasus, in defence and in attack, insisted on keeping the ball too close. Only Carr showed punch among the forwards and they must hope that Sutcliffe will be fit for the replay and bring some direct method back to the attack.

PEGASUS – B. R. Brown; F. C. M. Alexander, M. T. Robinson; R. C. Vowels, K. A. Shearwood, D. F. Saunders; H. A. Pawson, D. B. Carr, R. G. Lunn, J. H. Blythe, H. J. Potts.

WILLINGTON – R. A. Hazelton; D. Conley, W. Craggs; J. J. Lewthwaite, A.

Beech, A. Marks; J. Robinson, E. Taylor, B. Smith, M. R. Armstrong, S. Rutherford.

Seven days later we made the long journey north for the replay only to find that the ground had been declared unfit by the referee and the match postponed.

The following week, amidst another mining community and on a wet treacherous pitch, we took them on again before a small partisan crowd of 3,500.

Our start could not have been more hysterical. In the opening seconds a beautiful low-angled cross ball laid deep behind Gordon McKinna at right-back—Alexander was unfit—found Armstrong, the inter-changing Willington inside-left, cutting in at tremendous speed to blast a glorious shot which gave Ben no chance whatsoever. At that precise moment it felt very bad. The slippery surface was making it difficult for defenders to turn, and we were stretched to our uttermost limits. Nor did it help, though it made me laugh slightly hysterically, when a minute later Ben Brown drop-kicked a ball straight at the back of Gordon McKinna's head. For a split second Ben stood, staring at Gordon's massive frame stretched motionless in the mud. The danger was imminent, for the ball had run loose to the edge of our penalty area and Ben was still out of his goal. But Denis was on hand. Racing back, he just beat the Willington forwards, only to chip the ball high and wide of Ben's reach smack against our crossbar, the rebound falling dramatically into our goalkeeper's grateful arms.

'Keep your head down next time Gordon,' I suggested as he got shakily to his feet, whilst Ben, who had cleared his lines properly this time, was once more back in goal, surveying the scene with all his customary composure. Wrote *The Times*:

In confident and thrustful mood Pegasus reached the last eight of the F.A. Amateur Cup for the fourth time of their meteoric career when they overcame Willington by four goals to two in Saturday's third round replay.

For this they summoned up strength from the brief but distinct tradition that they have only once lost to opponents who scored first during those six years, and after Willington had taken a first-minute lead they settled down to play football which, for long spells, was of the high standard to which they have always aspired.

Played in heavy mud, the match had a stern quality in the resolute tackling of both teams. Willington brought in their regular centre-half and captain, G. Brown at centre-forward, while Pegasus switched Blythe to the middle, moving Lunn to his normal position to partner Sutcliffe.

Willington opened the afternoon with the best goal of the match. Marks sent Rutherford away and from his perfect pass Armstrong slipped by McKinna —moved to right-back in the absence of Alexander, who was unfit—to score with a fine angled shot as Brown came out. A few moments later Armstrong headed past the post. Thereafter Vowels shadowed him relentlessly and in the face of the steadiness of Shearwood and Brown, Willington, in spite of second-half switches, had few chances to look really dangerous.

Although once McKinna, attempting a vast clearance, sliced the ball with a thump on to his own cross-bar and was later felled by a drop kick from Brown, Pegasus were by then into their stride and in the lead. After a quarter of an hour Pawson lobbed the ball for Carr to hook past Hazelton, and then Sutcliffe, with a tremendous drive, hit the post and Blythe shot home the difficult rebound. Five minutes after the interval Blythe, who showed sharp perception in his positional play, rounded off a fine sweeping movement between Lunn, Carr, and Sutcliffe, and five minutes from the end the centre-forward flicked the ball on to Sutcliffe who scored the fourth.

In between these goals Willington at first threatened to collapse as the Pegasus forwards moved in patterned precision, and then for a brief period revived. But even when Rutherford scored from the penalty spot Willington had not the resources to challenge further.

WILLINGTON – R. A. Hazelton; D. Conley, W. Craggs; J. J. Lewthwaite, A. Beech, A. Marks; J. Robinson, E. Taylor, G. Brown, M. R. Armstrong, S. Rutherford.

PEGASUS – B. R. Brown; G. H. McKinna, M. T. Robinson; R. C. Vowels, K. A. Shearwood, D. F. Saunders; H. A. Pawson, D. B. Carr, J. H. Blythe, R. G. Lunn, R. Sutcliffe.

We were all delighted and over dinner on the train home discussed the prospects of our fourth round cup-tie with Briggs Sports the following Saturday.

'I hope to goodness,' Tommy warned, 'that we don't take them for granted. They're obviously a good side with an excellent record.' And for added emphasis he sent round a circular that week warning us of complacency, as did Leslie Compton.

On the Monday (the fourth round had already been played) the draw for the semi-final was made and we heard on the radio that either Briggs or ourselves were to meet Bishop Auckland up at St. James's Park, Newcastle. But first Briggs Sports had to be dealt with. And once more it began to feel very much as though it could all be happening again.

Unbeaten on their own ground in the Spartan League that season, Briggs Sports were coached by Jim Paviour, the old England amateur centre-half, and had at centre-forward a young sixteen-year-old, Les Allen, who was to turn professional and play for Spurs and England.

We lunched together, that last Saturday in February 1954, and then left central London by car for Dagenham and that was the start of a lot of our troubles. We had left ourselves insufficient time. Frustrated by the traffic, we eventually arrived at Victoria Road only to find ourselves further delayed in our efforts to discover somewhere to park, for the immediate vicinity around the ground was jammed with cars and people. It was quite the wrong way to approach any match, let alone a cup-tie, and we had to change at great speed in cramped conditions. There was no time to muster our thoughts, no time for Leslie Compton to say anything more than a few hurried words. When we left the dressing-room we were in the wrong frame of mind, mentally too casual and unstimulated. And we paid for it. Right from the start Briggs Sports showed a sharpness we never matched. There was an apathy about our play that simply could not be shaken off. Towards the end when they had scored their third goal a Briggs' supporter sitting behind Biddie bellowed down her ear, 'The bloody old Flying Horse is a gonna this time!' and he was right.

But what I remember most about that cup-tie, which was watched by a record crowd of 6,500, and which turned out for us such a sad occasion, was the difficulty I had in getting to grips with Les Allen. He was always on the move, darting about as slippery as an eel, playing slightly off centre, dropping away and flicking first time, or when possible holding and turning whilst another went hunting down the middle for his through pass—which was what happened in the first few minutes.

Moving deep into his own defence and feeling he had time and room to hold the ball (I had failed to go all the way with him and so was not on his back) the young centre-forward turned and sizing up the situation in a flash, hit the ball down the centre to find Keen, the Briggs' outside-right racing inside Miles Robinson to score their first goal. After that we were never really in the game.

When the final whistle blew I shook hands with Les Allen, wished him luck in the semi-final against the Bishops—they had been watching the match—and left the field wondering once more why anyone ever plays games which are remotely serious.

Eighteen years later I met Les Allen again when, as manager of Queens Park Rangers, he brought them to Lancing—Rodney Marsh and all—to do some training on the school grounds. But by then the stinging memory of that cup-tie was only something of the dim and distant past.

156

The Times summed it up :

Before a record crowd inside their closed gates at Dagenham on Saturday Briggs Sports decisively beat the holders, Pegasus, by three goals to none and so reached the semi-final of the F.A. Amateur Cup for the first time in their history.

Indeed Briggs Sports are the only team from the Spartan League to have progressed so far for many many years, and with victories against two Isthmian clubs, including the champions Bromley, behind them, on the evidence of Saturday's match they can face Bishop Auckland with confidence.

On the bumpy ground, with the ball bobbing and bouncing at all heights, Briggs, clearly used to the conditions, drew early blood with a fine goal. Allen, whose astute roaming and passing belied his young age, sent a through pass down the middle to Keen, who swept past a tackle and crashed the ball into the net before Brown moved out. The speed and force of execution of this movement set the pattern for Briggs. They swung the ball about and tackled with great vigour and swift intent.

The central battle which one had expected between the strong Briggs defence—which has so far conceded only two goals in five cup matches—and the Pegasus attack, with 14 goals in four games to its credit, was delayed until midway through the second half, by which time Briggs were two goals in the lead. Instead of this, the Pegasus defence was kept at full stretch and was in constant difficulties in spite of an excellent display by Shearwood.

Indeed the Briggs forwards might have scored more than three times. A great drive by Goddard, whose support for his forwards was too much for Saunders, again from a good pass by Allen, struck the post and rebounded off Brown; while twice the ball was cleared off the line with the goalkeeper beaten. Allen, too, late in the game had a fine effort brilliantly saved by Brown. Pegasus, though combining poorly, nonetheless had their chances. Lunn missed an open goal when Sutcliffe lobbed the ball to him with Garrard out of position and Carr once shot high over the bar and later missed a headed pass from Saunders by the goalpost.

In the eighth minute of the second half Briggs scored again with a fine header by Allen over Brown, who seemed unsighted or distracted perhaps by the vigorous flagging of a linesman. Then for the only time in the match Pegasus got into their stride with a series of attacks which yet in the final analysis lacked incisiveness.

Their wingers were completely subdued and the rearrangement of the forward line, with Lunn at inside-left and later Pawson at centre-forward, could not break down a splendid Briggs defence, well-grounded in their primary responsibilities of clearing their lines.

Thus when the Pegasus attacks did break down the long clearances of the Briggs defenders were always dangerous. The last word was certainly with Briggs. In the final minute Goddard scored their third goal with a finely taken direct free kick from some twenty yards while the Pegasus defensive wall took up a curiously miscalculated position.

BRIGGS SPORTS – J. Garrard; R. Bumpstead, J. Morgan; G. Goddard, C. Bradford, C. Guiver; J. Keen, A. Herbert, L. Allen, D. Kempster, W. Green.

157

PEGASUS – B. R. Brown; G. H. McKinna, M. T. Robinson; R. C. Vowels, K. A. Shearwood, D. F. Saunders; H. A. Pawson, D. B. Carr, R. G. Lunn, J. Pearson, R. Sutcliffe.

16 Two Quarter-Finals

At a committee meeting held at the East India and Sports Club on 9 May 1954, Tommy announced with regret that he was no longer able to continue as secretary of Pegasus, a statement that was to mark a turning-point in the club's short history, though perhaps not appreciated by many at the time.

And at that same meeting a discussion took place about the organization for 1954–5, in which three decisions were taken. Two were obvious and sensible ones : that a second eleven be formed, and a booklet be prepared about the club for distribution to members. But it was the first decision that caught the eye—a bald statement— 'that the club should continue'. I could find no record as to who suggested the possibility that the club might not continue, but that such a prospect be even contemplated as early as May 1954, cast the first real shadow of doubt over our future, a shadow that was to grow darker and more ominous as each year passed.

Five months later at the A.G.M., Tommy was unanimously appointed the first chairman of the club while Ben Brown became the new secretary, with John Tanner and John Blythe of Cambridge acting as assistant secretaries for their respective universities. W. V. Cavill continued as treasurer, with W. J. Sartain as assistant treasurer at Cambridge and Jerry Weinstein at Oxford—the latter was also on the selection committee. Harvey Chadder remained the club's president, sympathetic and gentle as ever.

Finally Denis was re-elected captain for the coming season and Joe Mercer became our new coach.

The summer term of 1954 at Lancing passed quickly. In June, Pegasus played their annual cricket match with Morris Motors, Jimmy Potts made his usual century, Tony Pawson craftily bowled his off-spinners, while I kept wicket, aided and abetted by John Tanner at first slip who had also kept wicket for Oxford.

With the key to Durell by my side and Parnell Smith down at the Sussex Pad should that fail, I no longer feared the geometry periods and had become quite blasé about the teaching of mathematics.

159

The highlight of the term was Founder's Day, when the staff sat on the dais in Great School, while the parents gathered to listen to the speeches. The Chairman of the Governors, Admiral Sir William Whitforth, K.C.B., D.S.O. of Narvik distinction began with an introductory few words.

I was sitting at the back between my two sexagenarian colleagues, Parnell and Puttock, both already nodding away peacefully, when the Admiral suddenly wheeled round and addressed us all as though he were once more back on the quarterdeck of Warspite (I saw her receive a direct hit by a guided missile at Salerno) and we were his ship's company : 'I would ask the staff to do one thing,' and he fixed us with a fierce eye, 'maintain the object.'

'What was that?' said Parnell Smith with a start.

'We've got to maintain the object,' I whispered.

'Oh,' said Parnell, and promptly closed his eyes.

The Bishop of Peterborough, Spencer Leeson, spoke next and informed the parents that, as headmaster of Winchester, he'd known John Dancy well. 'And I can assure you he's a very good chap. You're lucky to have him.'

Finally Dancy (it was his first Founder's Day) made his contribution which included a jocular reference to the Lancing staff that perhaps he might be able to show a few of the old dogs some new tricks.

But by then Parnell and Puttock were fast asleep.

We played thirty-four matches in the 1954–5 season, won twenty, drew five and lost nine—losing the first match of all against Walthamstow Avenue away 0–4.

I met Joe Mercer for the first time at the Royal Military Academy, Sandhurst. We were waiting to go out and Joe had said his piece. 'How's your leg?' I asked him. He'd broken it very badly in a collision with his team-mate, Joe Wade, when captaining Arsenal against Liverpool in the last league match of the 1953 season.

'I don't want the lads to see it,' he confided as we began to move out, his face wrinkling in good humour. As the last man left the dressing-room he quickly drew up his trouser leg and I saw as nasty a looking leg injury as I'd ever seen.

We won the match 2–1 and then took two scratch sides down to play against Collyer's School, Horsham, and Lancing College, winning 10–1 and 12–0.

In the second week of October we played the Northern Nomads in the final of the 1953–4 A.F.A. Cup, a match which I did not forget in a hurry, for I woke that day with a severe headache which I could not shake off.

'You'll be all right,' Leslie assured me over lunch at Oriel, arranged by our new secretary, Ben Brown, who was a fellow of the college.

'It's imperative we win this one,' urged Tommy who promptly produced a spasm of intense coughing.

'Just push it around and get control of the middle,' said Joe. He'd already gone round and had a few words with some of us. 'And enjoy yourselves,' he added as an afterthought, 'because that's what it's really all about.'

My head was buzzing and I fervently prayed that I would enjoy myself and not have too much to do in the air; still more important that the game would not go to extra time. But my prayers were unanswered for I soon found I had a great deal to do in the air. To make matters worse, just before full time our opponents equalized. So we were forced to battle on into extra time until finally, after two hours of it, we defeated the Northern Nomads 3–2 winning the A.F.A. Cup for the third time.

The following week we lost under floodlights to Portsmouth at Fratton Park 1–4, after holding them 1–1 at half-time. Three weeks later at the Dell we drew with Southampton 3–3 having led 2–0 at half-time. In the New Year Tour of 1955 after being two up against a Brighton and Hove Albion side, we again drew 3–3. Although these were friendly matches and the professionals were under no pressure, we could nevertheless often hold them for a half until our physical fitness began to tell and the professionals, urged on by the possibility that they might lose, stepped up their game. We lost heavily to Poole Town on that tour but rounded it off by knocking Worthing out of the A.F.A. Cup.

Before playing Dagenham in the first round of the Amateur Cup of 1954 we defeated both universities, Cambridge 4–2 and Oxford 7–0.

I took Graham Collier with me, our new director of art at Lancing, to watch the latter match. We drove to Oxford by car, talking ceaselessly. Graham had found his way to Lancing in rather peculiar circumstances. He had been teaching at Giggleswick and had come down to visit relatives at Lancing. Wandering round the chapel after having had a look at the school, he'd bumped into John Dancy and they'd started to talk. By the time Graham had said his piece about

161

extra-sensory perception, the compass points of consciousness, the purpose of life and a good deal else, he was in and the current art master was out. Perpetually broke, he would put half a gallon a time into his ancient and thirsty Ford V8, free-wheeling whenever he could to make it last as long as possible. Long, well-groomed hair swept back over his ears, tall and lean to the extent of being cadaverous, with an inquisitive moustache whose ends antennae-like twitched as mischievously as his eyes shone bright, he had a distinction that could not be denied. He was impatient with colleagues, had rows galore and at regular intervals handed in his resignation which John Dancy would calmly accept, but with tongue in cheek, for Graham, above everything else, was first-class at his job.

On the way back we stopped at Guildford and had a drink. By the time we reached Lancing it was very late and blowing one gale of a wind.

'Biddie's in hospital,' her mother greeted me as I opened the door. 'The sea road's blocked,' she explained, 'so Mr. Tydd very kindly ran her in by car.' Bill Tydd was the school Bursar who lived next door.

I rang the hospital at once but there was no news. I went to bed and thought about Woodstock and all the troubles she'd encountered when Paul had been born and I prayed that everything would be well this time.

Immediately I awoke I telephoned again and learnt with delight that Biddie was fine and we had a daughter, born in the very early hours of that last Sunday of November 1954. She was to be called Vanessa. My prayers had been answered.

We had no particular difficulty in disposing of Dagenham, despite the fact that they had knocked Sutton United out of the London Senior Cup and won eleven out of the fourteen league matches they had so far played. We won 4–0, scoring two goals in each half, a couple by George Scanlan, a compact and competent inside-forward from Cambridge, and one apiece by John Tanner and Tony Pawson. Of our second goal *The Times* commented :

. . then Tanner reminded one of his past greatness with a glorious goal. A push pass from Heritage, a hook over the centre-half by Tanner, who sped to meet the dropping ball and flash a volley, swift and lethal as a thunderbolt, into the Dagenham net, and it was all over.

The following played : B. Wakefield; J. P. C. Newell, G. H.

McKinna; S. G. Heritage, K. A. Shearwood, D. F. Saunders; H. A. Pawson, G. Scanlan, J. D. P. Tanner, R. G. Lunn, R. Sutcliffe.

That cup-tie was Bob Lunn's last game for Pegasus as he was leaving the country to work overseas. It was a serious blow and we were to miss this tall, graceful, and exceptionally gifted player.

His place was taken by John Blythe and apart from this one change, the side that had defeated Dagenham journeyed to Stevenage and knocked the Delphian League club out of the competition, 5–2, Tanner and Pawson each scoring two goals, and Scanlan, who again played with impressive control, one. It was a good result, three of the goals being scored within seven devastating minutes and as *The Times* observed : 'Pegasus took ample revenge indeed for the defeat of their brothers, the Corinthian-Casuals on this same ground a month ago.'

In the third round we were drawn at home, this time against West Auckland, who had played right through from the preliminary round and won their last eight matches to get as far. Except that Mike Pinner took over from Brian Wakefield in goal, the side was the same and won convincingly 4–1, two goals by Roy Sutcliffe, one each from John Blythe and John Tanner.

So for the third successive year we reached the quarter-finals of the Amateur Cup and went into the hat along with Bishop Auckland, who were drawn to play against Finchley, Wimbledon against Hendon, Alton Town or Carshalton Athletic against Hounslow Town, and Wycombe Wanderers against . . . you know who.

'It will be our first real cup test of the season,' remarked Joe Mercer to the press. 'If we win we can talk of Wembley with confidence.'

Unchanged, we went to Loakes Park on 26 February 1955, and on their notorious sloping ground (it slopes eleven feet from one side line to the other) with our backs well and truly against the wall, fought desperately in the mud to hang on to a goalless draw. It was one of those matches at the end of which every muscle is an ache, every step an effort. Mike Pinner was magnificent in goal, catching an unending stream of dangerous high crosses which Wycombe floated down that wicked slope, an advantage they knew exactly how to exploit. Wrote *The Times* :

WYCOMBE WANDERERS 0, PEGASUS 0

Wycombe Wanderers and Pegasus stand poised to face Bishop Auckland, the favourites, in the semi-final round of the F.A. Amateur Cup. There may have been no goals in their postponed fourth round tie at Loakes Park, High Wycombe, on Saturday, but there was sufficient excitement one way and another to cause some repairs at the weekend to nibbled hats and gloves. Iffley Road, Oxford, definitely is to be the scene of the next stage of the argument next Saturday. The suggestion was thrown out that since the Oxford ground holds no more than 6,500—half the 14,000 attendance that crammed into Loakes Park, a crowd larger than at most of the Second and Third Division games of Saturday—the replay should be transferred to Reading. But Pegasus have allowed no considerations of finance to interfere. Oxford it remains.

Yet how lucky are Pegasus to be allowed a second nibble. But for a generous ration of luck and some fine defensive covering—especially by an inspired Pinner under his crossbar and by the powerful McKinna at right-back— Wycombe Wanderers would now be preparing for their third semi-final in history. This is not to say that their chance is gone by any means, for they are a clean, strong, and dangerous side. But with a shift of scene there must also be a slight shift of odds, nor are the Pegasus forwards, as a co-ordinate line, likely to be so mute again.

With another instalment to follow, both sides have now had a good look at each other. They should know which delicate spots to put their fingers on next time. Pegasus, switching McKinna from left to right-back before the start to watch the dangerous Bates, in the end found Worley's footwork a greater thorn at outside-right and it is on that flank that Wycombe may again look for the victory that eluded them. Truett, too, at centre-forward, backed by the strength of his wing halves, Wicks and Moring, was an incessant threat with powerful shooting, and this in spite of Shearwood's heroic spoiling work with head and feet at the heart of the Pegasus defence.

But the conditions should be different next time. On Saturday the ground was a severe task-master indeed. Slanting giddily downwards from one flank to the other—a drop of some four yards along each goal line—it nevertheless lay there at the start like some pleasant, green and well rolled oasis amid the surrounding heights of snow. What a deceptive creature it turned out to be! By half-time it was a muddy glue pot throughout its middle in which the frail trio of Pegasus inside forwards, after a promising opening, were finally all but sunk as they chafed against the collar. Only Pawson—supported by Heritage, who shuttled back and forth gamely—brought occasional relief in attack as he shot like some lonely meteor across the afternoon.

For the rest it was largely Wycombe hungry for a goal and Pegasus existing on a slender margin. Pinner was a jack-in-the-box diving to shots by Truett and others; once before half-time McKinna saved Trott's point blank header on the line dramatically and somewhere near the end brought off a tremendous saving tackle when Trott was put clean through by Truett. Trott also hit Pinner's cross-bar with only ten minutes left and the fading seconds of all brought a mass of sprawling figures in the Pegasus goalmouth as the ball somehow or other squirmed just outside the post. Oh, one's fingernails!

WYCOMBE WANDERERS – D. Syrett; F. Lawson, F. Westley; M. Wicks, B. Darvill, J. Moring; L. Worley, C. Trott, G. Truett, J. Tomlin, P. Bates.

PEGASUS – M. J. Pinner; G. H. McKinna, J. P. C. Newell; S. G. Heritage, K. A. Shearwood, D. F. Saunders; H. A. Pawson, G. Scanlan, J. D. P. Tanner, J. H. Blythe, R. Sutcliffe.

164

We'd got away with it all right at Loakes Park. But I knew that although our chances of success would be better at Oxford, only our very best form would do. For Wycombe were a very good side; they didn't stand on ceremony but beavered away at it content to take the quickest and most direct path to goal.

'Will you win the replay?' asked the boys.

'It's not going to be easy,' I told them guardedly.

Nor was it, and we lost the cup-tie 1–2. *The Times* beneath a headline 'Pegasus Given a Taste of Their Own Medicine' told the story :

Wycombe Wanderers, winning their fourth-round replay at Iffley Road, Oxford, are now in their third semi-final of the F.A. Amateur Cup and about to face those northern giants Bishop Auckland, whom most people fancy will be first up the steps to the Royal Box at Wembley Stadium on 16 April. But much can happen meanwhile. And certainly Bishop Auckland can take nothing for granted against a determined Wycombe side that did to Pegasus on Saturday what Pegasus themselves have so often done to others in the past.

It needs a team of character to pull a game out of the fire, and that is exactly what Wycombe achieved. Coming from behind they scored their two goals in the last twenty minutes and timed their finishing thrust perfectly in the process. There is nothing like a winning goal as the fading moments unwind themselves. There is seldom any answer to it. The referee, already beginning to consult his watch, takes on the role of an executioner. Thus when Tomlin swept Bates's pass beyond Pinner with only some ninety seconds to go all that was finally left to Pegasus was a dignified retreat from a game they might have won at the opening of the second half.

But really it proved an undistinguishing afternoon. Its attacking thread had little continuity or design and both forward lines, expending considerable energy, seemed to achieve little against well-organised defences. The deciding factor in the end perhaps was the strength of the Wycombe half-back line. Here Wicks and Moring—except for a period on either side of half-time—effectively blanketed the close passing of Scanlan and Blythe at inside-forward, an infection that sapped Pegasus and which should have been thrown off earlier.

Here was one of those tussles that leave behind no particularly sharp picture. It was touch and go, but with little quality to light the way and in the end it went to Wycombe because of their stamina and spirit. But if it was they who pricked the bubble at the end Pegasus for a short spell just before and after half-time did air some of their football after a stammering start which found Pinner, on tip-toe under his crossbar, carrying on where he had left off the week before.

For those central twenty-five minutes or so indeed Pegasus for the one and only time really got on top because Scanlan and Blythe freed themselves. But because they are not the team they were they failed to settle matters. In the end it was clear that they face a problem at centre-forward, for hard though Williamson worked in Tanner's old place, this is not his position. Nor was there

165

the former penetration and balance on the wings. Sutcliffe, mixing the bad with the good, certainly worried Lawson sufficiently on occasion to gain a number of free kicks for unethical tackles, but Pawson on the other flank this time amounted to nothing, merely running himself time after time into a cul-de-sac.

So it was that the Pegasus defenders for much of the afternoon had little respite against the straightforward open approaches of Truett, Worley, and Bates. The defeat cannot be laid at their door, for McKinna, Saunders, and Newell, now shadowing the tricky Worley with coolness, did all that was asked of them. But Wycombe, driving hard and goaded on by their half-backs to the end, took two of the three real chances that came their way, and because of that just about deserved to get home.

There were three important moments in the opening half. First Tomlin shook Pinner's crossbar for Trott somehow or other to hit the sky from the rebound. That was a reprieve indeed, but it seemed to awaken Pegasus. At the half-hour they began to find something of their old stature with smooth, quick attacks. Williamson, hitting a Wycombe post, saw Blythe shoot home, but an offside decision—it seemed against Sutcliffe, a bystander—brought it to nothing. In the next moment, however, Scanlan glided Saunder's free kick against the bar and Williamson at close range sent Pegasus in at half-time one up and with one foot in the semi-final.

Yet that was as far as they reached. Had Blythe, following a Sutcliffe run, and Williamson found the target at the start of the second half it could have been over. As it was, Wycombe, with Wicks, Darvill, and Moring the heroes, closed their ranks, found a new stamina, and in the end played leapfrog over their opponents.

With twenty minutes left Trott sent in Tomlin's free kick to see Wycombe level. And as the last seconds drained away Tomlin hit Pinner's net from Bates' diagonal pass, leaving Pegasus with a disagreeable taste of their own medicine.

PEGASUS – M. J. Pinner; G. H. McKinna, J. P. C. Newell; S. R. Heritage, K. A. Shearwood, D. F. Saunders; H. A. Pawson, G. Scanlan, L. J. Williamson, J. H. Blythe, R. Sutcliffe.

WYCOMBE WANDERERS – D. Syrett; F. Lawson, F. Wesley; M. Wicks, B. Darvill, J. Moring; L. Worley, C. Trott, G. Truett, J. Tomlin, P. Bates.

We felt thoroughly punctured sitting in the Iffley Road changing-room. Jerry, clad in his excessively long officer's airforce coat leant on his stick and lifting his head and rolling his eyes, kept muttering, 'Bloody hell, bloody hell'.

'Never mind lads, you did your best,' Chedder Wilson quavered with tears in his eyes, his hand shaking dreadfully as his knife, more lethal than ever, hacked chunks of orange for us, 'there's always another season.'

In front of the fire stood Tommy, his shoulders hunched, peering over his spectacles, a cigarette in his mouth, God knows what was

166

going on in his head. John Tanner looked very serious. Harvey Chadder, our president, was quietly going round commiserating with each of us, and Joe Mercer, as upset as anyone, was doing his best not to show it. Only Leslie Laitt appeared unperturbed as, with hat upon head, he got on with the business of collecting up our dirty gear.

Teas for the losers never quite taste right and when I got upstairs most of the talking was coming from Wycombe.

'Bad luck, Ken,' said Helen Pawson gently, touching my arm.

'So near,' said Guy Pawson smiling wistfully and peering sideways at me.

'Unfortunately not near enough,' said Tony joining us.

And then Wycombe were suddenly leaving and we wished them luck. Presently we too broke up and went our different ways home.

I felt very tired and dispirited as I drove back alone in my old and rather sedate black Rover saloon. Mentally I went over and over the match. They'd shown more fight than we had and I wondered if my contribution had been good enough. I didn't feel that it had. I nearly dozed off and had to put the window down and breathe deeply the fresh cold air. Eventually, because I couldn't keep awake any longer, I pulled off the road and slept for a while.

Biddie had long gone to bed when I got back, so I undressed in the dark.

'What bad luck,' she murmured sleepily, 'we heard it on the wireless.'

'They were better than we were.'

'Were they? I expect you played well.'

'No, I don't think I did. Children all right?'

'They're fine.'

I peered briefly through a gap in the curtains. The moon was well up and I could see its light upon the sea. Then I climbed wearily into bed.

Three days later I went down with a bad attack of mumps. Jerry kept me supplied with books and news and gradually I got better only to go down with 'flu. However, by 23 April I was fit once more and able to play in a friendly at Oxford against Leytonstone, a match we lost 0–3.

The following week, again at Oxford, we met St. Albans City in the semi-final of the A.F.A. Cup and won 2–1. It was the last match of the season.

17 Arthur Rowe

I began my last full season with Pegasus on 25 August 1955, by playing for a Southern Amateur XI against Schaffhausen at Ilford. The game was billed as an international representative match and included players from Woking, Wycombe Wanderers and ourselves. We had met the Swiss side, Schaffhausen, on tour back in December 1951 and lost 1–4. In 1954 Schaffhausen had drawn with Queen's Park (Glasgow) and as part of their training for the World Cup, England had played them, winning 4–2. We did well to beat them 3–1, that hot August afternoon, John Tanner scoring twice, G. Hamm of Woking once.

In September, at Earls Court, in a B.B.C. five-a-side television tournament, Pinner, Saunders, Pawson, Scanlan and Tanner defeated Scotland 2–1, but lost to Wales 0–1. Four years earlier I had played in a similar competition at Wembley Pool when we'd ended up with the wooden spoon.

How fortunate we were that season to secure the help of Arthur Rowe to advise and coach us. He had managed Tottenham when they had won successive Second and First Division Championships in 1950 and 1951 and sent us that memorable telegram at our first Wembley Cup Final 'Make it simple, make it quick'. 'For football,' he'd often repeat, 'is basically simple. It's we who make it difficult.'

In 1954 he'd appointed Billy Nicholson as coach after his partnership with Vic Buckingham had broken up when the latter went to manage Bradford. Then, his plan that Alf Ramsey should become his assistant came to nothing, for Alf left to manage Ipswich Town. In the end, opposition from certain quarters in the boardroom and a serious illness finally drove him from High Road, Tottenham.

In his autobiography *The Double and Before* Danny Blanchflower wrote of Arthur Rowe 'His push and run philosophy and the manner in which he guided the great Tottenham team of the late forties and early fifties to such soccer delights had been a great source of inspiration to many of the young hopeful players that I knew.' And Alf Ramsey, in *Talking Football*, wrote about Arthur's profound and constructive approach to the game and its problems.

Now, to occupy himself temporarily after convalescence, he was promoting the sale of his own soccer boot, the Arthur Rowe Streamline, forerunner of the flexible soft boots of today. Utterly direct and honest in all his views and dealings, humorous and sympathetic, he was still vulnerable and far from fit when he came to us in 1955.

At every opportunity we'd discuss and analyse the game with him and he would put us wise and tell us stories about the Spurs.

'I never saw a sadder-looking bunch sitting in a dressing-room than after our semi-final F.A. Cup-tie with Blackpool in 1953. I felt so sorry for them, because most of that side would never get another chance to play at Wembley, they were too old,' and he ran through the team : Ditchburn, Ramsey, Withers, Nicholson, Clarke, Burgess, Walters, Bennett, Duquemin, Bailey, Medley.

'We'd played so well. It was right on time. Alf Ramsey had run a ball down the line and struck it back outside the box to Ditchburn and then gone wide to collect the return. Unfortunately the ball stuck in the mud. Little Mudie, chasing hard, nipped round and just beat Ditchburn to it. After that there was only time to kick off before the whistle blew. What can you say to them? To make matters worse one of the directors railed on and on at me about Ramsey. In the end I told him to shut his mouth.'

'Leeds were the first team to deal successfully with our deep lying wingers. We were up at Elland Road and their backs—both hard men—had been told to come all the way with Walters and Medley however deep they dropped. We lost that one, the first in nineteen games. We also learnt a lesson. From then onwards we got Duquemin to exploit the gaps behind any opposing backs that marked our deep-lying wingers tightly. If the opposing centre-half went wide with Duquemin, then Bennett, a natural front runner, would go hunting through the middle. Similarly when Duquemin moved out to the right, Bailey or Medley would do the bit down the middle, with Burgess and Nicholson feeding from behind.'

'You must bear in mind that every player, of necessity, and however great, spends nineteen-twentieths of a match without the ball, so how he spends those eighty-seven minutes is critical. And while this may seem a devastating fact, that a player's possession period rarely exceeds three minutes in a whole match, and if we assess possession time for any particular player as three to five seconds, then possession in a match can be looked forward to on average thirty to forty times, which is not so discouraging.' He would stop and smile as we digested this piece of analysis and then continue. 'It's an inescapable fact, whether it's junior football, school, university, or international level.'

'Marvellous kicker of a dead ball, Ramsey. He could drop it on a sixpence.'

'Walters at outside-right scored fourteen goals one season for us, all from set-piece movements. He'd hang ten yards deep and time his run as Willis the left-back was running up to take the kick, while the other forwards would come short, bringing their opponents out with them. Walters would keep running and the ball would either arrive at his feet, or it wouldn't. If it did, he had a good chance of scoring. If it didn't, it didn't matter. We got 14 that way.'

'So much of this game is just plain commonsense. Never stop thinking when you haven't the ball, and when you've got it, make sure you pass to the same shirt as your own. Have plenty of movement; supporting movement from behind, attacking movement in front. And limit your passes to thirty yards. If you're inaccurate over that distance then you can't play.'

'Which just about bloody well scuppers you, Shearwood,' said Jerry maliciously.

The Michaelmas term of 1955 was spoilt for most of us, certainly for me, by the arrival of Her Majesty's Inspectors. Their task was to inspect the school from top to bottom, and then, after a full week of it, depart and write their report, which would be sent to the headmaster and published. Immediately every head of department began to prepare lengthy screeds about the intentions and purpose of his department with all sorts of educational theory which was never put into practice but would, it was hoped create a good impression on the inspectors. An inspection is also a very convenient way for headmasters to get rid of any members of their staff whom they wish to see the back of. It has as well, I suppose, some value in ensuring that a bad school is exposed, though even then I doubt whether it is entirely successful in achieving this.

What an inspection really does successfully is to disturb the natural routine, put the common room on edge and produce a good deal of toadying. The boys, of course, take it all in their stride and enjoy it.

'Ready for the inspection, sir?'

'Oh, of course, I'd forgotten all about it. When are they coming?' They might have been taken in.

'D'you mind being inspected sir?'

170

'Mind? Good heavens no. They're usually failed schoolmasters.'

'We'll not let you down sir!'

Fortunately, 'know all' had moved on and in any case I was no longer teaching maths, which was just as well. An alarming experience the previous term had been instrumental in my ceasing to be a member of the Lancing maths' department.

John Dancy had invited a number of preparatory school headmasters to meet the Lancing heads of departments and have an exchange of views in the school library.

'I'd like you to be there, Ken,' he said, 'since you teach the new men maths and your views might be helpful,'—an invitation that promptly sent a cold shiver up and down my spine. No key to Durell's geometry could possibly get me out of this one.

On the appointed afternoon, twenty or so preparatory school headmasters sat facing us across the floor of the library and exchanges began. I kept very quiet indeed and everyone seemed to have a great deal to say. After well over an hour I began to think I would be all right. But not a bit of it. Somebody fired off about a certain method and asked whether we used it in teaching maths at Lancing.

Dancy leant forward and looked down the line at me. 'I think that Ken Shearwood is the man to answer this one as he teaches the new men.'

I'd never heard of the method and promptly went off on a slightly hysterical tack about the general untidiness of new boys on paper and how they found difficulty doing geometrical riders, and then petered out. There was rather a long silence at the end of which the same gentleman, not at all satisfied, asked what method we used.

I was speechless until someone on the opposite side came to my rescue.

'I think you probably still use the old method,' which he explained briefly on my behalf, and I nodded in vigorous agreement.

I don't think it fooled anyone, least of all John Dancy. In retrospect I was most grateful to that headmaster for I was now spared from having to perform in this subject before one of Her Majesty's Inspectors.

We got through the week, the report duly arrived, and at a common room meeting John Dancy gave us the gist of it and announced that any master who wished to come and discuss his own report could do so, 'But I won't pull any punches, gentlemen,' he added rather ominously.

I happened to be playing at Portsmouth that night so I decided to go and hear the worst and then I could enjoy the game.

'You're all right,' said John. He never showed me my report, and I didn't press to see it. 'When's your next match?'

'Tonight, at Portsmouth.'

His face lit up with a smile and he inclined his head in acknowledgement. 'I hope it goes well.'

'I hope so,' I replied and closed the door. I liked John Dancy.

We lost the game 3–6, which *The Times* reported :

In a splendid match under floodlights at Fratton Park, Portsmouth beat Pegasus by a margin of three goals, but it was sixty minutes before the superior stamina, experience, and skill of the professionals swung the game away from the amateurs.

Pegasus, indeed, took an early lead, lost it, and then recovered it to go in at half-time leading by two goals to one, and when Portsmouth rushed into the lead after only ten minutes of the second half, Pegasus recovered to level the scores at 3–all.

The football added important lessons to the pleasure of watching two intelligent sides. There was the overall brilliance of Pinner, who gave a superb exhibition of goal-keeping, uncanny in defensive anticipation and intelligently constructive in attack. Then, for all to see, was the value of matches like this for amateur sides and the importance of choosing the right opposition for the sharpening process.

Pegasus went off to a quick lead, a finely combined movement between Walsh, Heritage, and Pawson saw Tanner pounce on to the winger's lob and give Barnett no chance. Throughout, Dale was the field commander for Portsmouth; he prompted Newman and Henderson with grace and ease and he put Walsh through a searching test. His trickery, combined with Henderson's deep-playing tactics, caused Pegasus no end of trouble, and it was Dale who scored the equaliser. Pegasus regained their lead when Walsh advanced to some 25 yards from goal and his long, high cross shot passed over Barnett into the far corner of the net.

If Newman and Dale stole the first half thunder for Portsmouth, Harris, fleet of foot, evened the home attack in the second half. Paradoxically it was now that one fully appreciated the coolness and construction of Saunders at left half-back and the foraging of Heritage and Blythe. Within ten minutes Dale left Henderson with the easiest of chances, which the centre-forward took, and next Harris scored from a through pass by Dale. The tall Gunter was now making his presence felt, but in the sixteenth minute Pegasus came again. Tanner took a long ball from Pinner down the middle and out-paced both Rutter and Wilson to lob the ball past Barnett for a beautifully judged goal. At once Harris was away and forced three corners before a long cross was deflected on to Newman and into the net by a defender. Henderson scored twice more, once after a deft close dribble with four Pegasus defenders unable to tackle him

172

effectively, and the match ended on a high note with Pinner once more soaring to hold the Pegasus fort.

PORTSMOUTH – Barnett; Wilson, Mansell; Gunter, Rutter, Dickinson; Harris, Robertson, Henderson, Dale, Newman.

PEGASUS – M. J. Pinner; J. F. Raynes, G. H. McKinna; P. M. J. Walsh, K. A. Shearwood, D. F. Saunders; H. A. Pawson, S. G. Heritage, J. D. P. Tanner, J. H. Blythe, R. Sutcliffe.

The following week at Maidstone, where we lost 1–4, Arthur presented me with a brand new pair of his Slimline boots. 'See if they'll improve your game a bit,' he said, handing them to me. He wore a dark blue overcoat and a black homburg hat. His hair was silver and he looked distinguished. I thought he looked better, too.

On the last Friday of December 1955, we all met for dinner at the Zetland Hotel, Saltburn, Yorkshire.

The next morning we visited the Imperial Chemical Industries and saw the extent of horrifying industrial landscape that ran parallel to a grey uninviting North Sea. We toured a factory, saw some laboratories and in the afternoon drew 3–3 with the I.C.I. side, Billingham Synthonia.

Afterwards we were shown a film and at six-thirty met the directors over cocktails. The dinner they gave us was quite first class, not exactly true of the dance held at the Zetland Hotel much later that evening.

'Well,' said Tommy as we chatted before going to bed, 'if any of you want a job, here's your chance. I can tell you now, they'll take some of you.'

I gave it some thought, but decided no.

Came New Year's Day and on next to the Royal Hotel, Princes Street, Edinburgh, playing bridge most of the way at the back of an extremely cold bus which went like a bat out of hell on the icy roads, once skidding and hitting the curb violently, knocking the cards flying —just when I had a good hand.

'Think the bloody driver knows what he's doing?' remarked Jerry, who was in charge of travel arrangements.

The Royal Hotel was of particular interest to me since I'd last been there as a rating in 1942. I was serving aboard the destroyer H.M.S. *Montrose* which was in the *Hood*'s dry dock, Rosythe, and one afternoon, on a 'run ashore', I'd entered the place and taken a bath, a free one. It was something I had done successfully on a number of occasions and in various parts of the country, for I enjoyed a bath, a luxury not to be found aboard one of His Majesty's destroyers.

173

I'd taken my small 'pussers' attaché case containing towel and soap, walked in, gone up the stairs, and found a bathroom without much difficulty.

I lay soaking in the hot water. Once I heard someone try the door handle. Eventually I got out, dressed, and leaving everything clean and ship-shape, opened the door to be confronted by a formidable lady of the house.

'Are you staying in the hotel?'

'No, I was just taking a bath.'

'You've no business to be doing so.'

'No, you're quite right,' and I apologised profusely.

'Well, don't do it again,' and I felt her eyes on my back as I walked down the corridor to the stairs.

I looked up some of the old haunts of those days, the little café half-way up Waverley Steps, the Y.M.C.A. at the back of Princes Street, where at six in the morning we'd eaten hot bacon rolls and gulped scalding cups of tea before dashing out into the cold, dark streets of Edinburgh, to catch the train to Inverkeithing, which would get us back on board just in time to 'turn to'.

Then on next to Glasgow to play Queen's Park at Hampden. I knew the place was big, but was unprepared for the sheer vastness of the stadium. 10,000 watched, though it seemed more like 500.

And a very mixed press we got too, some of it extremely critical with headlines: 'Mistakes? We Got The Lot Here' and:

PEGASUS? CALL THEM 'CAB HORSES'

It was cab-horse stuff from the university men and Queen's Park. A drab draw, a dull game with full marks only to one man—Maurice (Mike) Pinner, the English amateur international goalkeeper.

Queen's were weakened by reserves. But they would still have been too good for the men of Pegasus, who had more initials than soccer ideas, but for Pinner.

And:

Maybe I was watching in the ranks of the visitors a future Prime Minister, or a Lord Chancellor, or an Archbishop of Canterbury, but certainly no star of the soccer firmament.

Pegasus twice in post-war years have won the English Amateur Cup, and on each occasion played to a packed Wembley. English amateur football is not exactly, on yesterday's evidence, something to boast about. I reckon a team of teenager's from our secondary juveniles would do very well in the Saxon Competition.

174

But we got some better reports and Gordon McKinna, who captained us that day, played exceptionally well and was referred to as 'a giant of a man in the true Corinthian mould.'

The Times beneath a headline 'Pegasus in Scotland' said :

Many memories were stirred at Hampden Park yesterday afternoon with the visit of Pegasus. It is a quarter of a century since the Corinthians last opposed Queen's Park in what became over the years a contest between the cream of the two countries' amateurs cherished by all who played and watched. Now Pegasus have crossed the border for the first of what may well be many visits.

After a preliminary canter at Billingham to start their New Year tour where Pegasus shared six goals with the Synthonia on Saturday the team moved on to Edinburgh. On Monday the traditional local Derby between Hibernian and Heart of Midlothian was watched at Easter Road and the impression one gained at that game in the matter of sportsmanship was certainly repeated in Glasgow.

Queen's Park, who still, of course, carry the beacon of amateur football in Scotland, at present are riding high and clear at the head of the Scottish B Division with the hopes of Glasgow for promotion. Pegasus were therefore faced with a formidable task. That they survived to hold Queen's Park to a 1–1 draw was due partly to lack of final thrust by Queen's Park, who were wearing their black and white ringed shirts outside their shorts in their distinctive and traditional manner, at the crucial moments and partly to a certain depth of covering by the Pegasus defence.

Even so, it needed Shearwood's head on the goal-line to keep Church's shot out and the intervention of the cross-bar to say nothing of Pinner's goalkeeping. Indeed, the strength of Church, a beautifully-moving and dangerous centre-forward, and the wingers Hopper and Omand, showed up the difference between the two teams. Queen's Park were faster and stronger and their wing-halves, McEwan and Robb moved the ball about quickly and sharply. Pegasus, perhaps, showed the clearer method and their pattern of play, if slower, was more deliberate.

At the outset Miller showed Savage a clean pair of heels, and two long runs on the left wing gave the Pegasus forwards clear chances which they missed. In the ninth minute Hopper headed Church's cross from the left wing past Pinner, and almost at once Trimby sent Miller streaking through and the left-winger made no mistake with a rasping drive over the advancing Crampsey. A minor Hampden roar emitted quite impartially throughout the second half indicated the crowd's enjoyment as the game moved to its close and the low clouds took on a roseate hue at the end of a most pleasurable match.

QUEEN'S PARK – F. Crampsey; G. Savage, G. Church; A. McEwan, J. Valentine, J. Robb; N. Hopper, D. McLean, C. Church, J. Ward, W. Omand.

PEGASUS – M. J. Pinner; J. P. C. Newell, G. H. McKinna; P. M. J. Walsh, K. A. Shearwood, D. F. Saunders; J. D. P. Tanner, J. H. Blythe, R. W. Trimby. G. Scanlan, D. Miller.

South to Harrogate where we stayed in a great barn of a hotel before playing the British Police on the Huddersfield ground.

I didn't play but sat with Arthur Rowe and listened.

'Look at David Miller. He'll be over that stand and into the next county before he knows where he is.'

For David was fast, extremely fast. But for most of that night there was a policeman on his tail who was not only twice his size but almost as quick. And like many a winger, before and since, David did not relish crossing the enemy's bows too often, but would make lightning tracks for the corner flag.

Of the old hands only Denis Saunders and Roy Sutcliffe played. Brian Wakefield came in for Mike Pinner and how fortunate we were to have him as a reserve goalkeeper. Though not as brilliant as Pinner, who had already played for England in the Olympics against Bulgaria and for Aston Villa, he was good enough later to be reserve for Great Britain in the 1960 Rome Olympics.

Newell, Walsh, Coe, Miller, Beddowes, Blythe, Scanlan and Land played in that last match of the tour. We won 4–1. And there was another new Oxford forward, Robin Trimby, who had played in the previous game at Hampden and was eventually to become an international.

Our final journey home was a nightmare. The bus was like an old refrigerator, the roads foggy and icy and the driver, urged on by Tommy and the odd lurid comment from Jerry, had plainly lost his nerve.

Eventually, around ten o'clock at night, the bus stopped, still some 140 miles short of London, and I dropped off with Tommy, Leslie Laitt and kit, to pick up my old Rover which I'd parked on meeting the bus at the start of the tour. It took us some time and much winding to get the thing started. Eventually we got it going and set off to drive the sixty-odd miles to Oxford where I was to stay the night with Tommy.

And what a hell of a drive that proved to be! For I was now the bus driver, on whom Tommy as pilot could turn his full attention. It wasn't long before I knew exactly how the real bus driver had felt, and why he had lost his nerve.

With no heater in the car and wipers that couldn't shift the ice, I drove with my side-window down, stopping every so often to scrape the windscreen. And all the while ceaseless instructions poured down my left ear: 'Turn left, turn right, go faster, go straight on, get over, look out man, you're on the wrong side.' I think Tommy developed cat's eyes that night and a sixth sense. He seemed quite oblivious of our dangerous skids, bumps and frequent near misses which kept Leslie sitting rigidly attentive, frozen, and bolt upright in the back seat.

We finally made Oxford at half past three in the morning.

How nice it would have been, if only for Arthur Rowe's sake, had we been successful in the Amateur Cup of 1956. *The Times* summed up the draw for the first round proper beneath a headline,

STRONG OPPOSITION FOR PEGASUS

On 14 April the final of the F.A. Amateur Cup will be played at Wembley Stadium. To-day 64 clubs set out on the first round proper of a competition which began its qualifying stages as long ago as 17 September.

The draw has provided a number of keen matches but looking down the list one will expect the majority of the following sides to find their way towards the last stages, providing of course that they can avoid one another: Bishop Auckland, the holders and once more the favourites; Wycombe Wanderers, semi-finalists last year; Kingstonian; Pegasus, winners of 1951 and 1953; Hounslow; Hendon, beaten in the final at Wembley last year; the Corinthian-Casuals, and perhaps Willington.

The eyes of many in the South once more will be on Pegasus, who also begin with a hard-looking match against Barnet. Pegasus field five men in this year's university match: M. J. Pinner (goal), D. Hancock (right-half), and D. Miller, R. W. Trimby, and G. Scanlan in attack. There are possibilities about them again with further talent in the background, if required. It is about time, too, that the Corinthian-Casuals made a stir. Since the return of J. Laybourne to centre-forward, just before Christmas, they have been scoring freely and they should now deal with Sheppey United at the Oval.

There is thrust and skill in attack, with M. J. Stewart, the Surrey cricketer, outstanding at inside-left, and if things go their way the Casuals may well raise the cheers down Kennington way. Their team will be:

P. Ahm; F. C. M. Alexander, D. W. Newton; G. M. Shuttleworth, R. Cowan, R. C. Vowels; D. J. Insole, J. Sanders, J. S. Laybourne, M. J. Stewart, N. Kerruish.

Incidentally, Alexander, Cowan, Vowels and Laybourne won Cup winners medals with Pegasus in the past. In passing, one would like also to see some success fall to the Northern Nomads and Yorkshire Amateurs, clubs who have done much for the game in the north.

The correspondent did not add that Guy Shuttleworth, Doug Insole and Norman Kerruish had also played for Pegasus. All seven from Cambridge, they had chosen to abide by the one-year rule, and good

177

luck to them. But one couldn't help speculating how strong we'd have been with their services.

Barnet, our opponents, were a young side, average age twenty-one. Their centre-forward Tommy Lawrence, an amateur with West Ham, had scored twenty goals to date '... but not enough,' the *Express* wrote, 'to stop Pegasus winning.'

And just as Les Allen had done when Briggs Sports knocked us out of the Cup in the fourth round of 1954, so Lawrence played deep and presented me with the same old problem of whether to be drawn up field, or let him go, in the hope that he'd be picked up by one of our mid-field men. My going left a gap behind me, staying placed an extra burden on Denis and Paddy Walsh. If one of these should fail to pick Lawrence up—and each had their opposing inside-forward to mark—the centre-forward was then free to come at me with the ball. In such circumstances I could but hope to contain him before committing myself somewhere outside the box. I did a bit of both that afternoon and had an uncomfortable match of it, creating problems not only for myself, but for my colleagues. Fortunate we were in possessing a goalkeeper of the calibre of Mike Pinner.

The Times reported :

PEGASUS 2, BARNET 0

The blue sky and bright sun of the early morning over Oxford faded all too soon to be replaced by a cold, drab squall. Thus did the elements exert their influence at Oxford.

The almost continuous rain, the sharp cold, and the greasy playing surface, however, though occasionally causing mistakes, did not prevent both teams from setting a high standard of football. Barnet, to be sure, seemed happier in the conditions in the first half. Lawrence—whose deep play worried Shearwood— Cannon and Mercer, readily fed by Cooper and Ridley, repeatedly drove the Pegasus defence back, but there was too much lateral emphasis in the Barnet attack, and Saunders and McKinna often had time to cover up the gaps.

Once Pegasus settled down methodically—and method was the key difference between the sides—the result was never in doubt. The critical point of the match came two minutes after the interval. Barnet were then one goal down, for Sutcliffe had beaten George, an heroic goalkeeper, in the seventh minute with a long cross from the edge of the penalty area. Now Mercer sent Cannon streaking through the middle behind Shearwood, and the inside-left's shot was brilliantly anticipated and diverted by Pinner for a corner-kick. This was a truly great save. Barnet forced three more corners in quick succession without effect. But from then on Pegasus were on the home stretch.

In the opening spell there had been narrow misses by Trimby and Scanlan, the latter also denied a goal by George, and a glorious chance spurned by Blythe from Miller right in front of goal and just before half-time. In the second half there was Sutcliffe's shot blocked by a defender, and his header which flew past the post—both from Miller's centres—and there was Scanlan's raking drive which struck Barnet's crossbar.

The second goal, however, made up for much. This was Trimby's, and it was a beauty. It rounded off a movement begun deep inside the Pegasus half and carried on by Scanlan and Blythe, a creative centre-forward, with incisive precision. It cut the Barnet defence wide open straight down the middle, and Blythe's final pass, which left Trimby clear of all opposition, was the best of the afternoon. The sprightly Pegasus forwards, swift on the move and imaginative in their approach, are going to take some holding.

PEGASUS – M. J. Pinner; J. P. C. Newell, G. H. McKinna; P. Hancock, K. A. Shearwood, D. F. Saunders; D. Miller, R. W. Trimby, J. H. Blythe, G. Scanlan, R. Sutcliffe.

BARNET – B. George; C. Stevens, M. Cooper; G. Mole, A. D'Arcy, D. Ridley; R. Mercer, D. D'Arcy, T. Lawrence, R. Cannon, B. Ridley.

On hearing the draw for the second round my heart began to beat slightly faster, for despite it's being a home tie, we'd drawn Wycombe Wanderers again. A glance at their playing record was enough to show that they were an even better side than the previous year. Top of the Isthmian League with eleven wins, three draws and three defeats, they'd scored fifty goals and conceded nineteen. And just as when we'd drawn the Corinthian-Casuals in 1953, so now we knew a lot about Wycombe and that fluent, well-supported forward line of theirs: Worley, Trott, Truett, Tomlin and Bates. Well, it was up to us to stop them, up to our complete Cambridge forward-line to score some goals.

The match was to be played at Iffley Road, on 4 February, but because of frost it was postponed. When we met the following week the ground was still treacherous, with an east wind that cut like a whetted knife. Inside the old changing-room a big coke fire glowed red. Outside in the chill entrance hall the referee, a big, tall man who exuded authority stood talking to his small son. 'Would he like to come into our dressing room and keep warm by the fire?' a suggestion the father promptly accepted. 'Might do us a bit of good', I thought, showing them through the door and into the referee's room, which was off ours. 'Might make him think twice and save us from a harsh decision.' I should have known better.

They were out first, Syrett their goalkeeper, in a tracksuit, their players wearing gloves and rubber studded boots, a wise precaution. Our leather studs drummed on the hard slippery surface. No chance here for a defender to turn quickly; every opportunity for mistakes.

179

Straight from the kick off their forwards began pressurizing us, in particular Mike Pinner, harrassing him as they followed through on their shots in the hope he'd mishandle. He never did. Yet so fiercely did they come at him that on more than one occasion the Wycombe forward ended up in the back of our net having first had the ball whipped brilliantly from off his feet. They raided us from every quarter, laying the ball in behind our backs for their front men to run on to, measures not easily counteracted in such conditions other than by cover in depth.

Then, midway through the first half, much to our dismay, and mine in particular, John Newell brought Truett down and the big referee blew and pointed authoritatively.

Waiting for the kick to be taken I thought of the penalty Ben had saved at Highbury in those closing minutes of the 1951 semi-final against Hendon, of the gratuitous award from which they'd scored a week later at Crystal Palace, and the crucial one we'd been awarded against Hayes that had sent us on our way to Wembley in 1953—the slings and arrows of outrageous fortune.

Now, not even Pinner could save us, and we came off at half-time a goal down to try and sort out our problems with Arthur Rowe.

The small boy, still warming himself by the fire, greeted his father a good deal more cheerfully than I felt like doing at that particular moment of time. For though no doubt the referee's decision was correct, it was also unquestionably a very tough one—they invariably are on the receiving end. John Newell had never intended a foul, but had simply lost his feet and collided with Truett. Not altogether surprisingly Ken Aston, who was later to referee the Cup Final of 1963 when Manchester United defeated Leicester City 3–1, and become Chairman of the F.I.F.A. Referees' Committee, had not been swayed one least bit by my little stratagem.

The sudden hope that Peter Hancock's equalizing goal gave us eight minutes from time was almost immediately dashed in our faces as the Wycombe centre-forward, Paul Bates, scored their winning goal and knocked us out of the 1956 Amateur Cup. The biggest crowd of the nine ties, 6,500, saw the exciting finish. It was my thirty-sixth and last cup-tie for Pegasus, of which *The Times* commented :

PEGASUS 1, WYCOMBE WANDERERS 2

Wycombe Wanderers' splendid victory over Pegasus showed them to be a strong and well-balanced side poised for honours this season. Wycombe, whose colours ironically are light and dark blue, could point to their forwards as the afternoon's heroes, supported by their probing wing-halves Lawson and Moring. Bates and Truett, who have switched positions from last season, together with the forceful Trott—in spite of the fact that Saunders was the best Pegasus defender—made the running.

The Pegasus right flank was their essential weakness, for Newell, who played a storming game, was constantly exposed to a dual thrust by the frailty of Walsh, whose tackling and passing were poor indeed. Moreover, Miller declined for most of the match to use one outstanding asset, namely, his speed. The pitch at the Iffley Road Running Ground, Oxford, looked deceptively faithful; it was in fact treacherously slippery and though neither side relished the difficulties Wycombe were less inconvenienced than Pegasus. Even so, Pegasus might have snatched something from the bitter afternoon, made more unpleasant by a strong icy wind.

Five minutes after the start Blythe showed the way with a snap shot from the edge of the area which struck Syrett's left-hand goal post at the other end. After four Wycombe corners and a glaring miss by Bates in the middle Truett came cutting in only to be brought down by Newell. Truett took the penalty kick himself and Wycombe went in with a slender lead.

Pegasus, with the wind behind them, began the second half in more determined fashion and after Pinner had safely held Trott's free kick came the turning point of the game. Scanlan, now more in the picture, and Blythe always worrying the uneasy Darvill into mistakes, held the key. Thrice Scanlan came within an ace of scoring, once with foot and twice with head, and then Blyth, in the ninth minute, had a glorious chance. He chased a loose ball, beat Darvill who slipped, and as Syrett came out he lobbed the ball over the bar. It ought to have been a goal.

Almost at once Wycombe recovered their balance, and Trott and Truett were denied goals by Pinner. Here, indeed, was the critical difference in attack : Wycombe could point to Pinner's hands denying them goals, but Pegasus had only themselves to blame.

With eight minutes to go the persistent Hancock dribbled through the middle and unleashed the shot of his life which Syrett never saw. But it served only to goad Wycombe into exerting their authority. Within two minutes Tomlin's short pass was taken by Bates—it was these two players who sealed Wycombe's victory against Pegasus last year—and before Shearwood or Mckinna could tackle the ball was moved up to take Wycombe's twelfth corner-kick and in the end there was no denying that the more determined and balanced team won.

PEGASUS – M. J. Pinner; J. P. C. Newell, G. H. McKinna; P. M. J. Walsh, K. A. Shearwood, D. F. Saunders; D. Miller, P. Hancock, J. H. Blythe, G. Scanlan, R. Sutcliffe.

WYCOMBE WANDERERS – D. Syrett; M. Wicks, F. Westley; F. Lawson, B. Darvill, J. Moring; L. Worley, C. Trott, P. Bates, J. Tomlin, G. Truett.

The *Telegraph* correspondent remarked of Ken Aston's decision :

I thought the penalty after twenty-five minutes was a little harsh, particularly as earlier on a similar incident took place in the Wycombe penalty area, but for this only an indirect free kick was awarded.

The drive back was interminably long, cold and depressing, the road icy, with thick fog lying in patches between Guildford and Horsham. And as always on those journeys I reflected on the match. Long before I reached home I had come to the conclusion that even if I was still required, it was time to call it a day.

Eight marvellous years of football I'd had with Pegasus during which I was ever aware of my good fortune—there were plenty of others who could have done just as good a job at centre-half, if not better. Now, like all things, the scene had changed and of the team that had just played against Wycombe only Denis and I remained from the 1951 side.

And Denis? *The Times* correspondent was correct in his estimation of him. How well he'd played. Tall and as thin and imperturbable as ever, he'd got hold of the ball with those long spindly legs, and searching, found space and time to support his forwards with telling passes and still defend, winning as usual most things in the air. Even then he must have been as good an amateur wing-half as any in the country.

We played out what was left of the season, losing at Cambridge in the final of the Cambridgeshire Invitation Cup 0–2 to Wisbech Town, somewhat redeeming ourselves by once more reaching the final of the A.F.A. Cup for the fourth time—we'd already won it three times—after defeating Cambridge Town 3–2.

But our eyes and many others' were now fixed on the Corinthian-Casuals, who, with their seven ex-Pegasus players, all from Cambridge, were going from strength to strength. Sheppey United, Wimbledon, St. Albans City and Hitchin Town had all fallen to them. In the semi-final they'd met Dulwich Hamlet, at Stamford Bridge and won 3–1, playing for seventy minutes with only ten men, for Jack Laybourne had been carried off with a severely cut leg which required eight stitches.

Then, at Wembley they'd met our old opponents, Bishop Auckland, and after extra time had drawn with them 1–1 before a crowd of 82,000.

Before the replay took place on the Middlesbrough ground, Ayrsome Park, the Casuals' committee telegrammed Jim Swanton, Port of Spain, Trinidad, where his cricket side was touring, requesting permission that their inside-forward Micky Stewart be allowed to fly home and play in the final. Unfortunately severe head winds delayed the plane and after a dramatic rush by car from Prestwick, he arrived just too late to take the field, but in time to see his side lose to the Bishops 4–1.

What, I wonder, might have been the outcome if Pegasus and the Corinthian-Casuals had pooled their resources?

18 Some Selling and Writing

About this time, I was approached by a small, rather old-fashioned—in a nice sort of way—clothing manufacturing firm in the Midlands, to represent them in London and try to open some accounts with the big stores. For doing so I was to be paid three pounds a day plus my expenses.

Before Easter, I went to stay for a week at their factory of 500 employees to learn something about the clothing trade. They were all very friendly, especially the two senior directors who each had their own private aeroplanes. When the week was up I returned to Lancing having really picked up very little, but prepared to have a go. I had at least been measured and presented with a new suit, for the firm considered it would be a good advertisement for me to wear one of their own make.

Soon my samples began to arrive : a man's overcoat and lamb's wool jacket. Two men's Harris tweed jackets and terylene trousers. There were youths' jackets and blazers, trousers and shorts. They were accompanied by numerous swatches, heavy bunches of different shades and grades of cloth, to be shown the buyers when they had, as we all hoped, presented me with an order.

I went into Worthing, bought the biggest Revelation expanding suitcase that I could find, and one warm day towards the end of April bade Biddie farewell and set off by train for London.

At Victoria I caught a bus to Kensington, my huge, heavy suitcase only just fitting beneath the stairs. For a first port of call I had decided on Pontings, which I considered might prove not too awe-inspiring.

I felt hot and conspicuous as I entered the crowded store and made for the lift. Nearby a middle-aged shop assistant wearing a smart black dress was demonstrating a product to a group of shoppers, working away deftly, occasionally glancing over the heads of her onlookers with an air of bored detachment. I watched idly until the lift doors opened. Then, as I bent to pick up my suitcase, one end of the handle came clean adrift and I had no alternative but to clasp the case in my arms—which didn't particularly endear me to the liftman or the occupants already packed in tightly. 'Men's clothing,' I murmured and seconds later staggered from the lift still holding the wretched case.

I put it down and approached the assistant. Walking across the carpet I was vaguely aware of the muted sound of traffic pouring along Kensington High Street far below. I was thankful there wasn't much activity in the department.

'I'd like to see the buyer if possible,' I stated, as nicely as I knew how.

'Mr. Crawford's still at lunch. He shouldn't be long. Have you got a card?" I gave him one, which for some unaccountable reason had on it the telephone number of Sam Jagger, one of my colleagues at Lancing.

Twenty minutes later the assistant gave me the signal that Mr. Crawford had returned from lunch and was willing to see me. Picking up the suitcase once more (it was far too big to put under my arm) I went towards the buyer, a short elderly man whom I warmed to at once.

'You seem to be in some trouble,' he remarked as I put the case down.

'I am; it's brand new. I only got it yesterday.'

'Looks as though you've a soft rivet there old man,' he remarked, examining the case. 'Your best bet is to take it straight back to their place at Chiswick and they'll give you a new one. You can get there by bus.'

I nodded. 'May I show you what I've got?' I asked tentatively.

'I'll have a look at it. I know your firm, I've dealt with them in the past.'

This sounded encouraging.

I took out the overcoat, a soft, long, very heavy dark-grey crombie. I showed him the jackets and the trousers and the youths' stuff. He quite liked the man's lamb's wool jacket. But he gave me no order.

'I'll give them a ring at Chiswick and tell them you're coming,' which was nice of him. 'Come and see me again,' he suggested holding out his hand.

It proved a long bus journey to Chiswick and all the while the sun shone down hotter than ever. Eventually I arrived, unpacked my clobber and repacked it into a new case. At least I had learnt how to fold clothes. Then I set off for Victoria and caught a crowded train back to Lancing, standing for most of the journey. I made out my report and expenses and decided to try Gorringes the following day—they ran our school shop.

I had visited Gorringes last in 1930 when my mother had taken me there to be fitted out for my preparatory school, Maidwell Hall in Northamptonshire. As far as I could see the store had changed very little. For a while I hung around watching an assistant indulging a concerned parent whose bored young son seemed to be going through much the same performance as I had done some twenty-five years earlier.

Eventually I was summoned to see the buyer, a man in his fifties who had a round slightly florid face beneath a head of flat yellowish thinning hair. His blue eyes looked at me keenly through steel rimmed spectacles.

I decided on a different tack this time.

'Let me put my cards on the table,' I began. 'I'm very much a novice at this game, only doing it part-time. I'm really a schoolmaster by profession.'

He glanced at my card.

'Lancing College?'

I nodded.

'I can't do much for you at the moment, but we'll have a cup of coffee,' and I followed him past the young boy who was now trying on a blazer and looking more bored than ever.

Mr. Kenyon was friendly, enquired about Lancing and announced that he would be down later in the term to see the bursar. He had a brief look at my samples and showed some interest in the men's terylene trousers, but presented me with no order. He wish me good luck and told me to call again in a month.

I telephoned Harrods next and spoke to an unpleasant upper deck voice in the buying department who, on hearing of the firm I was representing informed me with curt rudeness that we were not for them.

'And bollocks to you,' I managed to get in before the phone clicked the other end.

I went down to Whiteleys in Bayswater humping my suitcase, which this time did not have a soft rivet. I sought anonymity in the crowded store and felt more at home. Eventually, after waiting a very long time, the buyer gave me a couple of minutes and I thought showed some interest in the boys' blazers, but gave me no order.

I visited amongst others, Barkers, Derry and Toms, Elys at Wimbledon, Bentalls at Kingston, and Chiesmans at Lewisham. As I sat in the latter store drinking a cup of coffee one morning Colin Cowdrey came in with another.

'It's all right, I haven't got the sack from Lancing,' I assured him as he greeted me in passing my table, at the same time glancing curiously at the suitcase. 'Just trying to do a little business with you,' which needless to say I did not achieve.

And then the summer term began and my merry-go-round temporarily ceased though I did manage to slip up occasionally to keep some continuity going.

Once, of an evening, John Dancy popped in to see us, just when all my samples were suspended on coat-hangers round the sitting-room picture rail. As he sipped his cup of coffee I watched him more than once cast a curious eye at the strange array of ticketed garments festooning our walls; but he made no comment.

The sun shone; May, June and July came and went and another summer term slipped quietly away, leaving behind us as relics of some distant age, a Founder's Day, the written sweat and worry of all those dreadful 'O' and 'A' level examinations, and a host of mixed memories to remind the leavers that their school days were over—to remind the rest that they still lay ahead. But, for most of us, and in the immediate future, there now stretched the golden prospect of eight glorious weeks of holiday.

We spent all August in our caravan down on the farm at Treveague, Gorran, the home of the Whetters. Our field was beautifully situated on National Trust ground, high above Hemmick and close to the Dodman. We looked across a wide expanse of sea, flanked by cliffs and headlands, with the Gull Rock standing out distinctly and the distant loom of the Lizard visible on clear days. On bad days we'd watch the sou'westerly gales gathering over the Goonhilly Downs, before driving across the dark, white-capped waters, eventually smothering our field in sea mist, while the wind shook our frail van and the rain beat fiercely upon its aluminium roof.

On one such day we drove down to Lamorna Cove to visit Biddie's cousin, Susan, wife of J. H. Williams, author of *Elephant Bill*.

'Why don't you write a book about your experiences as a fisherman?' he urged me before we left. 'You've a book there all right.'

As we drove back to our caravan, the wind buffeting the car, I considered his advice. And the more I thought about it the more determined I became to start.

I began to write *Whistle the Wind* the following day, scribbling down the story in a cheap exercise book and enjoying doing it. I wrote whenever I could and wherever I was. Distractions around me didn't worry me in the least; I simply shut myself off. I was to write on the Brighton Belle, going to and from London as I tried unsuccessfully to sell clothes. And between unprofitable calls I would sit in the sunshine on a park deck-chair and forgetting the world, scribble away in an exercise book, using my suitcase as an arm rest.

Returning from that summer holiday I gained an introduction to John Lewis and saw their buyer, a Mr. Tallon, who was most considerate to me.

One afternoon just before the start of the winter term, I called at their offices situated in Draycott Avenue, off the King's Road, and was given the break I had been awaiting.

'The single weft satin lining in that jacket of yours is no good. Apart from being expensive it threads,' and he picked up the lamb's wool jacket—still my best exhibit—and showed me what he meant.

'Now,' he said, 'I want you to make some sample men's jackets.'

I took out my pencil and notebook and waited with some excitement and a good deal of gratitude.

'Right,' he continued, having examined the swatches most carefully and given me the cloth number, sizes and price. 'I want your firm to make sixteen men's Thornproof jackets, three button, single vent, with a Marsdon Wilsdon lining. And then,' he said, smiling and getting up from behind his desk, 'provided they are up to standard, we should be able to do some business.'

Delighted, I went out and found the nearest telephone box and put through the order. The firm was pleased and the following week I had an encouraging letter from one of the directors.

Two weeks later I called again on Mr. Tallon knowing that the sixteen jackets had been despatched.

He was standing by the window when I went in. Turning, he shook his head and I knew the worst.

188

'Their make simply isn't good enough,' he said. 'I'm sorry,' and I could see he genuinely was.

'That's all right,' I told him, trying to hide my disappointment, 'but would you show me where they've gone wrong?'

'Well, to start with the lapels are too heavy and the jackets need to be more waisted. The pocket lines are not as clean as they should be nor is the sleeve head.' He told me a lot else, all of which I reported to the firm.

They wrote back and asked if I would come up as soon as possible and discuss the matter with their cutter, which I did. But it was now clear to me that I was representing a firm whose articles were simply not good enough for the London market. However, I was prepared to persevere and they seemed happy that I should do so. And the money was a great help.

The Michaelmas term of 1956 began with the usual batch of new boys' tea parties, and as assistant housemaster to the Reverend Henry Thorold I attended one of these.

Such occasions are always fraught with tension and Henry's presence ensured that the Gibbs new boys' tea party was no exception.

'Keep them standing,' he'd say of the parents. 'Never let them sit.'

Around the walls of his drawing-room hung some fine pictures, a Poussin, a large sporting painting of two horses by J. F. Herring, and two family portraits by Reynolds, both looking remarkably like Henry.

When the parents began to arrive, he'd greet them with a limp handshake and a broad smile, his long fair hair swept back, his full black cassock encircled by a thin, worn leather belt extended to its last notch. Then the fun would start.

'Here,' he'd say introducing me, 'is our house tutor. He is the most distinguished amateur footballer in England,' a statement which caused me acute embarrassment and completely nonplussed the parents.

A little later, when one of them rashly broached the subject of work, I found myself even more heavily committed, as Henry, drawing himself up and seeming to inflate as he did so, suddenly announced to his astonished audience 'In this house we do no work, do we, Ken?' To which 'gobstopper' I'd muster an idiotic grin of acquiescence while Henry continued to sail in and out amongst his guests with smiling composure.

On another occasion when conversation was somewhat wilting—

Henry made statements, not conversation—a slightly hysterical mother began relating how her nephew's housemaster at Clifton was a very keen outward bound type of man, who organized all sorts of exciting expeditions for his boys. 'Once they had to cross the Avon Gorge at night without using the bridge,' she enthused, while Henry listened saying nothing. 'Don't you think it was a good idea?' she finally ended in near desperation.

'Yes,' said Henry firmly. 'A very good idea. But in this house,' and he fixed her with an amused, beady eye, 'we're inward bound.'

In mid-October I took Nick Evans and Graham Sharman, two of the Lancing side to watch another of our floodlit games with Portsmouth. Throughout the match the rain sheeted down and by the end we'd lost by eight clear goals.

'You're not only over the hill,' announced Arthur Rowe, putting his hand on my shoulder, 'you're bloody well half-way down Porlock Hill, mate.'

'I know Arthur,' I replied.

In fact it hadn't been anything like such one way traffic as the score suggested, for the goals, most of them snap shots of tremendous power, were all beautifully hit yet could so easily have gone wide of the mark.

Before leaving Portsmouth I called on, and had a cup of tea with, Jack and Moyra Mansell. The former had just played against us and was still helping me coach at Lancing.

When we eventually set out again the rain had lifted and the night was fine. Everything was going well until suddenly, between Arundel and Worthing, the engine began making a most alarming noise.

'What the hell's that?' I asked slowing down and in some dismay.

'Sounds like a big end,' suggested one of the boys cheerfully.

I thought so too and promptly switched off the old Rover engine. It was one o'clock in the morning. A light shone from a downstairs room in a house across the way. I went over and knocked discreetly. The door opened and I saw in the hall a policeman's helmet. We were in luck and the man kindly allowed me to use his telephone. Then I went and sat in the car and wondered how much it was going to cost.

The moon had risen and I watched wearily as the two lads kicked a tennis ball about on the empty wet road which glistened in the moonlight.

190

We waited a long time. Eventually a van arrived and towed us into Worthing. It was well gone three a.m. before we finally got back to Lancing.

I worked hard that Christmas holiday trying to sell clothes and get on with the job of writing *Whistle the Wind*, a task I found a good deal more enjoyable than the former. When I had written something Biddie would read it, we'd then discuss it and she'd remind me of episodes and encourage me to write more.

By now I had got to know the buyers much better and included several schools on my visits, Dulwich, Alleyns, and one at Reigate where an order always seemed in the offing but never quite materialized. And I seemed at last to be getting somewhere with the buyer at Barkers; but then, just as an order seemed imminent, the House of Frazer stepped in and bought the wretched store so I had to begin all over again with a new buyer.

I did not go on the 1957 New Year tour with Pegasus which began with a resounding 7–2 victory over Harwich and Parkeston in the first round of the A.F.A. Cup. A new centre-forward from Oxford, Martin King, scored four of the goals.

On New Year's Eve in a 3–1 floodlit win over Bury Town, the same player scored all three Pegasus goals. A week later at Iffley Road he played another big part in the defeat of the British Police by hitting a further three goals. He was small but exceptionally skilful and quick, and very elusive. He was already playing a bit for Colchester United and was eventually to turn professional for them.

So, with a full measure of confidence Pegasus faced Romford at Iffley Road in the first round of the 1957 Amateur Cup only to find themselves trailing at the end by the odd goal in three and out for another year.

I read the result in the evening paper and shared their disappointment. I consoled myself that at least I did not have to face that long and tiring drive home.

The Times correspondent wrote :

PEGASUS 1, ROMFORD 2

Pegasus departed from the F.A. Amateur Cup at Iffley Road on Saturday, victims of their own making, at the hands of Romford who, before the match, had been awarded no chance of survival. But such is the uncertainty of cup-tie football, and Romford, without question the less distinguished side in a disappointing game, took what the gods had to offer.

They snatched two quick opportunist goals soon after Pegasus had opened the scoring in the seventeenth minute and hung on to their lead through an interminable second half. Theirs was a triumph of defence over persistent pressure, in which Taylor and Rogers, centre-half and goalkeeper respectively, played their part to the full. Pegasus, however, played largely into their hands by persisting in their close passing game when obviously out of touch and failing to thrust home their opportunities when they came.

Certainly Pegasus began as if they meant to run away with the game. In the fourth minute an angled ground pass from Beddows was flicked on by King for Trimby to shudder the Romford cross-bar, then Sutcliffe drove wide when King's challenge of Rogers in the air for a centre by Blythe left him in an easy position. But Trimby soon put matters right with an innocent looking header just inside the far post from a corner forced on the right and Pegasus were in the lead. But two minutes later Romford were on terms when a deep through pass by A. Taylor caught the Pegasus defence out of position and Bee gave Pinner no chance. Then, at the twenty-fifth minute, Andrews seized on to a clearance by Newell; a neat chip to Tiffin was hooked back from the by-line and there was Abbott to shoot home at close range.

For the remaining twenty minutes of this half Pegasus hammered at the Romford goal without respite—or success. First a run and ground shot by King was saved at the foot of the post, then a drive from Blythe was pushed round for a corner. Soon afterwards Blythe cut inwards out of a pass from Trimby only to shoot across the face of the goal. A minute later Rogers somehow turned aside a shot by Trimby taken on the half-volley and before half-time Pegasus were to squander two further chances.

With the resumption the pattern began to change. Pegasus were seldom out of Romford territory but they were now being held more at arm's length. Their chances became fewer and farther between as the game progressed and Romford resorted to delaying tactics—until finally Romford, incredibly, had won the day.

PEGASUS – M. J. Pinner; J. Dougall, J. P. C. Newell; J. Beddows, B. A. Coe, D. F. Saunders; J. H. Blythe, R. W. Trimby, M. N. G. King, G. Scanlan, R. Sutcliffe.

ROMFORD – E. Rogers; N. Appleton, M. Cooper; J. Whitecross, D. Taylor; G. Andrews, K. Abbott, C. Tiffin, B. Barber, J. Bee.

And once again the eyes of many were now turned on the Corinthian-Casuals, who went from strength to strength only to lose to Wycombe Wanderers in the semi-final.

19 A Disappointment

One Saturday in early February 1957, I'd taken the Lancing side to Eton and was having tea after the match when my opposite number, Tolly Burnett, casually remarked to a small man sitting opposite me, whose son had once played for Eton and was now at Oxford, 'Ken has a business side-line.'

'Oh,' said Rudolph Palumbo, 'what do you do?'

'I represent a clothing firm, and I'm trying to open a few accounts for them in London,' I replied a little flippantly, handing him my card with the wrong telephone number. He looked at it carefully.

'Do you know Edward Merrell of Whiteaway and Laidlaw?' he asked looking up.

I shook my head. He continued to stare at me thoughtfully.

'I know the managing director of the Army and Navy Stores very well. I'll have a word with him. Could you manage to have lunch with me at the Savoy one day next week and we can then talk about it?'

I said with alacrity that I could. Shortly afterwards he left.

'Who's Mr. Palumbo?'

'Rudolph?' said Tolly. 'He might be able to help you. He's a millionaire.'

The following week I duly had lunch at the Savoy with Rudolph Palumbo and on several occasions later. He was always extremely kind and did all he could to help me.

I visited Whiteaway, Laidlaw and Co. Ltd. in the City and showed them my samples which they examined carefully, saying very little, but shaking their heads frequently. 'Is that one of their suits you are wearing?'

I nodded, feeling more like a fish out of water than ever.

'They should make you another. It's not good enough. A very bad advertisement.'

'The clothing trade's a tough business,' explained Edward Merrell gently. 'The cut and make of your samples are not good enough.'

I telephoned the Army and Navy Stores using the introduction Rudolph Palumbo had given me. It worked like magic but I detected a certain wariness in the voice at the other end.

I was not long kept waiting in that famous store. Very shortly after I had presented my card, a well-dressed man with a superior manner swept towards me as though he wished to get the whole matter over and done with as quickly as possible. I opened my case and showed him the lamb's wool jacket which he bore away over his arm, disappearing behind a frosted glass door. Very shortly he was back, walking quickly and shaking his head, holding the jacket at arm's length—disdainfully I thought—and making strange sinister indrawn hissing sounds.

I beat a hasty retreat to Kensington and the friendly old buyer at Pontings, who did something to restore my morale. But the truth of the matter was that I had now lost confidence in the firm and my samples.

One afternoon, I met Rudolph at the Grosvenor and drove down in his magnificent chauffeur-driven Rolls-Royce to watch his son play for Oxford in an end-of-season away match at Witney. Peter was a useful player but did not get a Blue. I think he was inhibited by his wealthy background and lacked confidence, which was a pity, because he was extremely fast and direct and had the makings of a good winger.

We arrived at the ground only to find that his son was unable to play at the last moment because of an injury. I introduced Tommy to Rudolph and after the game Penelope joined us for a late dinner at the Mitre.

Long gone midnight I set off for Lancing sitting in the back of the Rolls with Rudolph, stopping first at his country house in Tetworth Ascot, where we arrived at two o'clock in the morning.

I was invited in and after we'd had a drink and he'd shown me the house and its beautiful paintings and possessions, I set off once again in the Rolls. This time I sat in the front with the chauffeur, looking down the car's long glistening bonnet to the graceful silver emblem which now seemed to be winging its way towards the first faint shafts of light that were breaking in the east. It was a drive I shall always remember, for the great black car sped quietly and effortlessly along the empty road, the speedometer needle every so often creeping well over the hundred mark.

When we arrived at Timberscombe the Reverend Henry Thorold's car was standing outside, as upright and distinctive as a dowager duchess, its ancient body clad in fabric.

The chaffeur got out and walked slowly round the old car smiling to himself as he examined it carefully.

'Look,' I said, 'why not leave yours and take that one back instead?'

We went inside and had a cup of tea. Then I saw him off.

Standing outside with Kim I sniffed the fresh air. The sun was up, the sea reflecting its golden light. It was a perfect morning to herald the start of another summer term at Lancing.

It was to prove a particularly full one, what with a heavy timetable, coaching the school cricket XI, which took many hours, and playing a bit at the weekend. To make matters worse, I have always suffered badly from hay fever and at the height of the season would sneeze my head off, doubling up and making a high-pitched slightly hysterical scream which at least had the merit of keeping the form awake on hot sleepy afternoons. 'Won the south of England sneezing championships for three consecutive years,' I'd casually inform them, 'was twice runner-up in the all England championships.'

'How did they judge the best sneeze sir?'

'Volume and tone. But it's the quality of the sneeze that really counts,' and I'd give them another just for good measure, which convinced some and caused others to stare incredulously.

For some time now we had been hiring out two small caravans, bought on the never never, to help supplement our income. 'Why not call it King Ken's Caravan Company all spelt with a K?' Henry had suggested as I set about drawing up some sort of brochure.

We did quite well with these two very basic and cheap caravans, a Berkley Argosy and a Paladin Pixie, but things did at times go wrong. Once I set off to play cricket with the towing ball still attached to the back of the car, leaving Biddie to explain and find another for the new customer.

On another occasion an enormous inspector of police and his wife arrived to collect the Paladin Pixie. He said very little as he viewed the tiny caravan, walking slowly round it several times, gently pointing out its deficiencies and one illegality. By the time he'd finished I thought we stood a very fair chance of being arrested. However, the two couldn't have been more friendly and whilst on holiday sent us a postcard. Later, when I was playing for Pegasus in an away match, an official stuck his head into our changing-room to say that someone was asking for me in the main entrance. Going out I was delighted to find it was the same inspector of police. I hope he reads this book.

But on Founder's Day we did face a real crisis. One of the vans had failed to return and the new customers, a family of four, were already waiting, and quite understandably far from pleased. All day, in academic dress, I kept dashing to and fro by car, doing what I could to support Biddie, who spent most of the time bringing out incessant cups of tea and food as the hours ticked by and no van appeared. Eventually, to ease a situation that was fast becoming completely out of our control, I promised to knock a pound off every hour they'd had to wait. At last when the light was beginning to fail and it seemed there was every likelihood that we'd be putting them up for the night, our van finally hove into sight and the family set off on what had now become virtually a free holiday.

Towards the end of that summer term I received a letter from the secretary of the Lancing Town Football Club asking me to coach them. I wrote that I'd like to do so, but could do nothing until the latter half of August. The Town were in the Second Division of the county league, had a fine large ground of their own with ample parking space and a covered stand that seated five hundred. They seemed to have an abundance of enthusiasm and plenty of players.

Returning from the West Country I watched them for the first time lose the opening league game of the season. To me the main problem that afternoon seemed to lie with the captain and centre-half, a tough fearsome looking player who, urged on by a vociferous home crowd, never failed to belt the ball indiscriminately, and not only the ball I might add.

But after a couple of training sessions I suggested to the selection committee, which met regularly in a singularly depressing and dingy room of the Railway Hotel, that we made some changes, and in particular dropped the captain.

We won the second match, but at the next meeting the large railway works at Lancing presented us with a signed petition demanding the reinstatement of the captain. To make matters more awkward still, the captain himself turned up demanding to meet the selectors and know why he had been dropped from the first side. We explained again—I had already told him why he had been dropped as gently as possible—and sticking to our guns left him out of the next game which we duly won. After that there were no more petitions and we won the league handsomely and gained promotion to the First Division. At the annual dinner the players presented me with an inscribed cigarette case, while the secretary—though more discreetly—slipped an envelope into my hand which contained a cheque for fifty pounds. I was surprised and extremely grateful.

Meanwhile Pegasus had begun the 1957–8 season in great style, after an afternoon's coaching at Iffley Road, on 29 August, under Jack Mansell. We were looking for a coach and I knew Jack would have loved to do the job. The club badly required a man who could go on to the field and actively inject fresh ideas and method into our play, which was tending to become stereotyped. We needed someone decisive, to take charge, widen our horizons and select our sides. For the world of amateur soccer had not stood still and many clubs, following our example and using coaches, were—apart from paying their players highly organized on a thoroughly professional basis. If we were to keep abreast of the times we needed to plan carefully for the future. When I heard that Jack had been officially invited to come up to Oxford and have an afternoon with Pegasus I was pleased.

He put on an excellent session, the players occupied and interested as they worked in tight areas and small groups, gradually developing into lengthier and positive attacking patterns, with balls knocked in and laid off and players coming at defenders.

It was exciting stuff to watch, in advance of its time. For Jack Mansell, besides being a fine player, was a highly skilled, intelligent and articulate coach who knew exactly what he was doing and what he wanted. Unfortunately he possessed a certain abrasive toughness of character and sharpness of tongue which tended to cloud the brilliance of his work—for some.

Two incidents that afternoon were to illustrate this side of his character.

He had been working with the players for some time when John Tanner, who was not now playing for Pegasus, came running onto the Iffley Road ground, full of beans.

'Where do you want me, Mr. Mansell?' he enquired.

'Over there until we're ready,' said Jack, who was deeply engaged demonstrating a point.

He didn't mean to be curt, but such brevity didn't help.

197

Meanwhile Tommy, who had been watching everything most closely from the touchline, suddenly called across, 'What about doing some attack v defence, Mansell?'

Jack gave a perfunctory wave of acknowledgement and continued with what he was doing.

Five minutes later Tommy called again, 'Are you going to do some attack against defence, Mansell?'

This time Jack called things to a halt and turned towards Tommy.

'Doctor Thompson,' he said, 'we've been practising attack against defence at Portsmouth for the last eight months and we still haven't scored a goal.'

Tommy said nothing.

But I knew then that this would be the last time Jack would ever be asked to coach Pegasus—and it was. And more was the pity, for he would have been so good for us, then, or at any time, always provided that he had the time and was given a completely free rein, the only way in which a coach can operate effectively.

Even so, though he was never to coach us again we proceeded to win our first seven matches against Coventry, Newbury, Oxford City, March Town, Ilford, Eastbourne and Worthing, scoring thirty-one goals, conceding ten. Martin King played in six of these games and scored twelve times.

I played in the game at Worthing and was able to have a good look at him as he knocked in another four. His style was economic and I was impressed by his skill as he moved swiftly forward, sleeves flapping loosely about his wrists, leaving defenders floundering in the wake of his fluent control. Trimby, Sutcliffe, Miller and Walsh all helped themselves to a goal each that afternoon making it eight. With Pinner in goal and with players of the calibre of Dougall, Harding, Beddows and Hancock to cover him, I thought the side looked good. And it needed to be, for the draw was an extremely hard one, away against Walthamstow Avenue, who had reached the first round of the F.A. Cup, conceding only two goals in three cup-ties against Bedford Town and Coventry City.

On the day, Pegasus were soon in dire plight and by half-time, with the slope to face and two goals to make good, looked finished. That they survived, scoring twice in ninety seconds was a measure of their potential. Norman Ackland, always a great friend of Pegasus had this to say :

A spirited rally early in the second half, after they had been subjected to heavy pressure nearly all through the first half earned Pegasus a replay at Iffley Road, Oxford, next Saturday.

During this attacking spell Pegasus scored twice in under two minutes, and although towards the end of this exciting first-round tie Walthamstow Avenue were attacking again, their forwards were unable to beat Pinner.

Pinner alone was consistently safe in the Pegasus defence. Dougall and Harding were often out-paced and out-manoeuvred by the speedy Harvey and the tenacious Groves, and McKinna found it difficult to turn on the heavy slippery pitch.

Morever, the Pegasus tactical plan soon went awry in the first half. Then it became evident that King, normally a most dangerous centre-forward, was held in check by the Olympics centre-half Prince, it would have been advisable for the Pegasus half-backs to divert their ball-supply to the wings.

Their close-passing, too, was not nearly so effective as the long-passing exploited so skilfully by their opponents.

So it was Walthamstow, faster, better-balanced and more confident, who were usually in control in the first half.

After twenty minutes Walthamstow jumped into the lead when Sully scored with a shot that went in off the bar.

The Avenue were now almost complete masters, and after Pinner had saved two great shots from Sully, Daines scored their second goal from Harvey's low centre.

Pegasus suddenly swarmed into attack at the start of the second half, and English crashed the ball through a crowd of players for it to strike the Walthamstow right-half, Keenes, and rebound into the net.

Before the Avenue defenders could recover English had the ball in the net again. It struck Farrer en route but this made no difference; it was obviously a goal from the moment it left the Pegasus inside-left's boot.

Now the game truly sprang to life. Pegasus nearly scored again when a movement between Sutcliffe and Scanlan ended in King shooting straight at Wells.

Then, with Walthamstow regaining the midfield mastery, Pinner's abilities were tested by Barber, Sully and Hall before the finish.

WALTHAMSTOW – D. Wells; D. Clarke, L. T. Farrer; T. Keenes, S. Prince, D. Hall; R. Groves, B. Barber, S. Daines, J. Sully, B. Harvey.

PEGASUS – M. J. Pinner; J. Dougall, J. Harding; P. Hancock, G. McKinna, D. F. Saunders; R. Sutcliffe, G. Scanlan, M. N. G. King, R. English, R. S. Hurren.

Before the replay, Tommy as chairman, John Tanner as treasurer and George Ainsley, who was now coaching the side again, met to decide who should play on the right wing. It was a question of whether to bring in Jimmy Potts, who was now the secretary of Pegasus. Leslie Nichol had this to say about the problem:

Confronting them: Jimmy Potts, former England amateur winger, once ranked

199

in the £10,000 League class. Potts, one-time Oxford Blue, has played only three games this year after a long lay-off.

But Jimmy is also a member of the varsity team's selection panel. Says Mr. Potts: 'I shall tell my colleagues I am as fit as I can be and leave the decision of whether I play or not to them.'

If Potts plays he faces the shrewdest, strongest left-back in the amateur game—Avenue skipper 33-year-old Tom Farrer, of bygone England and Olympic fame.

Farrer, who captained Bishop Auckland in the 1950 Amateur F.A. Cup-final, forms the power-point which can explode the power-packed Pegasus parade.

Problem No. 2 for Pegasus: John Harding or John Newell at left back? Harding will have a fitness test in Hyde Park this morning. Whoever is selected takes on tearaway Avenue right-winger Reg Groves, brother of Arsenal's Vic.

But I go nap on Pegasus and include them in my star challengers for Wembley—alongside Corinthian-Casuals, Wycombe Wanderers, and Woking.

In the end Jimmy was not selected for the replay at Iffley Road which took place on 18 January 1958 about which *The Times* wrote :

PEGASUS 3, WALTHAMSTOW AVENUE 1

Pegasus rounded off some unfinished business at Oxford on Saturday when they beat Walthamstow Avenue in an F.A. Amateur Cup first round replay and so qualified to meet Ferryhill Athletic—winners over Evenwood Town—on the same ground next Saturday. The measure of Pegasus's achievement is that Walthamstow reached the first round proper of the F.A. Cup this year and then succumbed by a single goal, unluckily by all accounts, to Coventry City on the professional club's own ground. It was, then, probably the hardest draw that the first round had to offer, and Pegasus may well look forward to still better things.

The strength of both Pegasus and Walthamstow, on Saturday's evidence, is their defences, and the game suffered accordingly as a spectacle, for neither set of forwards, further hampered by a strong wind, could make much headway. In fact, there were only two co-ordinated forward movements of any note during the afternoon, and each produced a goal, one to either side, in the first half. First, after 25 minutes, Harvey and Sully attacked down the left, and for the only time in the entire match Dougall was outmanoeuvred. Harvey's centre was squared back by Groves, and Daines's final touch was a formality. Walthamstow's lead lasted a quarter of an hour before Hancock, Hurren and English opened the way for Trimby.

This was a shrewd blow for Pegasus only five minutes before the interval. A second was to follow a minute after it, when King beat Prince fully 40 yards out, made for goal at top speed with the ball expertly in control, and lashed it imperiously past Wells.

From that moment one sensed that Walthamstow's bolt was shot. It is, of course, too early to talk in terms of a Pegasus tradition—unlike the American university whose principal decreed that from the following Monday it would be a tradition that nobody was to walk across the lawn—but they already have

200

a reputation for resilience and strength of recovery, and somehow one felt that Walthamstow's task was now beyond them.

Walthamstow did in fact achieve one or two near misses, notably when Daines's header hit the crossbar and when Pinner saved desperately on the goal line after the wind had played tricks with Harvey's free kick. But it is goals, not near misses, that count and another came Pegasus's way before the end. King once more exercised his royal prerogative over Prince and dispatched Trimby on an errand of anything but mercy. The trusty messenger was toppled in the target area and McKinna, summoned to exact retribution from the penalty spot, did so with a thunderous blow. It was altogether fitting that the Pegasus defence should provide the final stop.

PEGASUS – M. J. Pinner; J. Dougall, J. Harding; P. Hancock, G. H. McKinna, D. F. Saunders; R. Sutcliffe, R. J. English, M. N. G. King, R. Trimby, R. S. Hurren .

WALTHAMSTOW – D. Wells; D. Clark, T. Farrer; T. Keenes, S. Prince, D. Hall; R. Groves, D. Barber, S. Daines, J. Sully, B. Harvey.

There was jubilation in the Pegasus camp. King's goal was a match-winning classic and Dick Lucas, Walthamstow Avenue's coach and their secretary Jim Lewis agreed that this goal won the match for Pegasus.

George Ainsley, as delighted as anyone, remarked to the press 'I have seen Pegasus six times since I took over this season and I am certain they are outstanding prospects for Wembley. As the competition progresses so the side will become stronger and stronger. If we reach Wembley I am certain we will win the Cup.'

George was paid a bonus of thirty pounds for helping us defeat Walthamstow Avenue and it was agreed that for subsequent F.A. Amateur Cup-ties, he should receive a fee of ten pounds and ten pounds for all other matches, provided the club was still competing in the Cup. There was to be no bonus for wins in rounds two, three and four of the Amateur Cup, but if the club reached the semi-final, he was to receive an additional bonus of two hundred pounds. If the club reached the final, a bonus of three hundred pounds. If the club was eliminated from the Amateur Cup he was to be paid seven pounds a match for the rest of the season.

It all looked so promising and confidence ran high as the side prepared for the next cup-tie at Iffley Road against Ferryhill Athletic, the Northern League side. Two changes were made; Potts came in for Sutcliffe and Scanlan for English.

I couldn't believe my ears when I heard the result, which *The Times* confirmed on Monday morning :

Pegasus withdrew from the F.A. Amateur Cup with some loss of dignity at Iffley Road, Oxford, on Saturday. In the first half they assumed command as though by right, but could not score; in the second they lost authority and assurance in turn and became persistent prey to an offside trap that worked like a charm. Meantime Ferryhill, having shuffled their three inside forwards at the break, first shook off their preoccupation with defence, then rebounded with energy and purpose from their moral hammering of the first half.

It was largely a question of confidence and initiative, flowing first from one team then from the other, as though the gods who govern these things were having a little game of their own. The change had a tactical effect, anxiety and aplomb coming to the surface in short and long passing respectively. The second was the order of the day, for the pitch, hard underneath, was greasy and treacherous on top, while around it the waterlogged running track glistened in the pale sunshine as though the Isis was playing out of position for the afternoon.

The strength of Pegasus lay in their defence, where McKinna was a commanding influence in the middle. In attack their wings were clipped on a day when they were needed; on one flank Hurren could accomplish little and on the other Potts seldom had the ball at all. King missed chances—several of his own making—and often was offside, but in approach work his gifts were evident. His positioning kept Ferryhill on edge and his deft ball control was remarkable on such a pitch.

Ferryhill's short and often square passing indicated their state of mind in the first half. They were slower to the ball than Pegasus and did not hit it hard enough to move it far. Seldom could they penetrate the Pegasus penalty area, and from time to time Pinner trotted round it to keep warm while his colleagues swung the ball about gaily to make seven openings from which two or three goals should have accrued. After the interval it was different. Ferryhill realised that, with the offside trap functioning smoothly, they might have a chance after all. With Pegasus the seeds of doubt had been sown; no longer were they using the ball so quickly or so well; their buoyancy had gone. The first goal emphasised the new trend, and in this half the openings were about four to one in favour of Ferryhill, who were now hitting the ball harder and playing it with purpose, while Pegasus time and again were arrested and charged with offside when in full cry for goal.

The essential difference was that Ferryhill did not spurn their chances and on such a pitch it was in the natural order of events that their wings should have a say in the goals, scored after 59 and 82 minutes. First Heslington, on the right, gathered a long crossfield pass, cut in and shot; Bell deflected the ball on to a likelier route, Pinner could only parry it, and Leach did the rest. Next Broom, from the left, put over a hard cross that was headed in smartly by Smith. Pegasus could blame no one but themselves—the prize had been theirs for the taking.

PEGASUS – M. J. Pinner; J. Dougall, J. Harding; P. Hancock, G. H. McKinna, D. F. Saunders; H. J. Potts, G. Scanlan, M. N. G. King, R. W. Trimby, R. S. Hurren.

FERRYHILL ATHLETIC – R. Robinson; J. B. Hunter, R. Norman; G. Masters, W. Nesbitt, H. Bell; R. Heslington, R. Kilcran, A. Snaith, T. Leach, G. Broom.

And for the third year in succession the Corinthian-Casuals did well in the Amateur Cup, losing to Crook Town in the quarter-finals this time.

Martin King played only four more games for Pegasus after that cup-tie with Ferryhill Athletic, yet still managed to score a further twelve goals. But by the following season he had left Oxford to play professionally for Colchester and we never saw him again.

I played once more for a scratch Pegasus eleven against Eton when we scored fourteen goals! Strange to recall that once their old boys had won the F.A. Cup. Their school side is somewhat better now!

Under floodlights at Headington we defeated Oxford City 3–0 in the final of the Oxfordshire Invitation Cup and lost in the semi-final of the Cambridgeshire Invitation Cup to Wisbech Town. Of late we were having to rely on our performances in these other cups for our continued exemption from the preliminary rounds of the Amateur Cup.

In the last match of 1958 we went down 1–3 to the F.A. Schools, and with a strong side at that. But perhaps we might be allowed a slight grain of comfort in believing that the club's achievements during the last ten years had done something to stimulate the game in the schools.

In June the committee met at the Morris Motors Athletics and Social Club, Cowley. We had a new secretary, Jimmy Potts, and the meeting was very short. Glancing through the minutes of the treasurer's report I noticed that Leslie Laitt's honorarium had fallen from fifteen guineas to fifteen pounds!

And then, business over, we went out into the sunshine to play our annual cricket match against Morris Motors.

20 A Titanic Struggle

Early in the summer of 1958 I finished writing *Whistle the Wind* and sent the manuscript up to Peter Lewin, a literary agent, to whom I had been recommended. He wrote back :

I think you have made an excellent job of this and it is a wonderful change to read a story of this sort with its natural charm and modesty. I think it would suit a number of publishers, but I am sending it to Rupert Hart Davis to start with.

I felt tremendously encouraged, for it had passed its first hurdle.

Towards the end of June I heard again from Peter Lewin, this time informing me that Rupert Hart Davis wanted to publish the book but was unhappy about the title and felt the book was a shade long.

I was delighted with this news and so was Biddie. So also was 'Elephant Bill', who wrote in a warm letter :

I must remind you, this is when you start writing another. Plant a tree, build a house, beget a son and write a book is a man's job in life I have been told.

The title had certainly proved something of a problem and I had eventually plumped for *A Dog in the Sky*, the Cornish fisherman's expression for that small round rainbow which can at times be seen just outside the sun and is a sure portent of bad weather. Look closely and sometimes two 'dogs' can be seen 'mocking the sun'.

Unfortunately, however, at that precise moment of time the Russians sent up a dog called Leica to orbit the earth which promptly put paid to this idea.

We thought of a good many other titles before eventually settling on *Whistle the Wind*. I chose it because I used to enjoy whistling to myself when we were out at sea fishing. But one of the crew, George Pearce, a great bull of a man and a fine fisherman wouldn't have it at any cost 'There's enough wind without your whistling', he'd grunt, steadily hauling the line hand over hand, every so often turning his head to send a long stream of dark tobacco spittle over the side.

I visited the offices of Rupert Hart Davis at 36 Soho Square, and met them all and they couldn't have been more friendly. Over lunch David Hughes, who was married to Mai Zetterling, told me that they wished to cut some ten thousand words from the book and indicated the passages that should go—a task for the coming holiday.

When finally the summer term came to an end we faced yet another move, this time into the college itself, for John Dancy had asked me to become a housemaster.

All day it took moving our possessions into a very large room in Sanderson's House, our new abode, which my predecessor John Handford, who was still in residence, had kindly emptied for us. The move was made doubly difficult and expensive, because the van could not get under the arch into the inner quadrangle and everything had to be carried round its perimeter—a long way.

Finally, quite exhausted, we closed the door on an empty Timberscombe, hitched on the caravan and set off late in the evening for Cornwall, stopping after some hours' driving to sleep.

Arriving in our field the following afternoon we found Bill Kennard, our pathologist friend and family, the only other occupant. His young son came running towards us. 'Have you heard the news?' he called breathlessly. We had no idea what he was talking about.

'You didn't see it in the papers?' enquired his father, rather anxiously I thought, as he came across.

I shook my head. We hadn't bought a paper that day.

'Oh dear. I'm afraid your friend "Elephant Bill" died yesterday on the operating table.'

We stared at him in disbelief, shocked and saddened.

Six weeks we spent in our caravan that holiday and then, ten days before the term began, we returned to find the house in an awful state. We hadn't been able to return earlier because John Handford, through no fault of his own, had not been able to move sooner.

At once we set about humping everything from the big room into the other rooms and a hell of a task it proved. We had also insisted, to make our new living quarters reasonably tolerable (though we were strongly opposed by the bursar) that an internal staircase from the enormous kitchen to the upstairs should be put in and this was still in the process of being completed.

Somehow we managed to get things shipshape for the beginning of the term. There had been no decoration done in any room and I even had to fight the bursar to get a lid to the lavatory in the bathroom.

Just before the term started we entertained our first guests, David Hughes and Mai Zetterling, who was as delightful as she was beautiful. David presented us with a copy of a novel he had written called *A Feeling in the Air*, inscribed 'for Ken and Biddie'—a set book for the upper sixth and in return I presented him with the corrected manuscript of *Whistle the Wind*. Then we were ready for our first new boys' tea party.

Fourteen of them, there were, and apart from getting the parents' names all mixed up, in particular introducing the wrong one as the admiral, it seemed to go all right, though it's an occasion that nobody in their right senses can possibly even remotely enjoy.

Later Henry came in to enquire how we'd got on. 'Did you make your how d'ye do's?'

He had spent his customary first two nights with us, the first sleeping on the kitchen window-seat with our labrador as company, the second on the window-seat in the dining-room. He'd shifted his berth because the intermittent rumblings of the huge and ancient school refrigerator (we had no larder) and the dog's regular visits to see how he was faring had not helped his night's rest. He had been unable to use our spare room as the floor was still up.

So I came into house-mastering, with no preconceived ideas other than that there should be no corporal punishment by me or anyone else, the personal fagging (underschooling at Lancing—I hate hierarchy) was to be got rid of, and that our own door would be open at all times to any boy. We were fortunate in having a mature and humorous head of house, Christopher Saunders, who in due course was to be twelfth man for Cambridge at Lords in 1963 and gain Blues at Oxford for both soccer and cricket the following year. I found the job absorbing, enjoyable, full of problems, some funny, some not so funny, and by the end of the term, very, very tiring. But that's another story; my concern is still Pegasus and those closing years that were finally to mark the end of the road for the old Flying Horse.

1958–9 was the last fully recorded season in the Pegasus Minutes' Book in which twenty-seven matches were played.

I took part in one of these at Iffley Road, the last time ever, when the 1951 XI played the 1958 XI, of which *The Times* wrote:

PEGASUS 1958 XI 2, PEGASUS 1951 XI 1

The Iffley Road running ground at Oxford was the scene of a notable reunion on Saturday. The Pegasus team which had carried off the F.A. Amateur Cup in 1951 reassembled almost in its entirety—J. F. Platt, whose place was taken by Heritage, was the only absentee—to meet the challenge of their successors of 1958.

Dr. Thompson, the club's founder and chairman, most fittingly acted as referee, and the intimate atmosphere was enhanced by a cheerful crowd who seemed to welcome back each player as an old friend.

The game began in driving rain which perhaps, influenced the decision to play 40 minutes each way. Yet in no time, as the weather brightened, the veterans were recapturing their old coherence. With Pawson and Potts bemusing the defence on either flank, and with Shearwood, as ever, a formidable barrier, they continually delighted the spectators with clear reminders of their former prowess.

Three times in the opening half only Pinner's agility kept out strong shots by Saunders, Pawson, and Dutchman. Their opponents' only comparable counter was one flowing move, originating in their own penalty area, which ended in Hurren's volleying the final centre past the post. It came as no surprise when, one minute before the interval, Carr put his side ahead with a powerful ground shot.

As long as the sun shone the cup-winning team prospered, but as the pitch grew heavier beneath darkening skies their younger rivals came increasingly into their own. With Trimby the chief prompter they laid siege to Brown's goal, and soon Sutcliffe's centre from the left was lobbed back by Handscomb for Grayson to head the equaliser. Still it looked as if the 1951 side would achieve the draw they well deserved, but with only two minutes left and the rain pelting down Hurren drove hard from 25 yards to deal the decisive blow. The masters lost, but not before they had given their lessons.

PEGASUS 1951 XI – B. R. Brown; R. Cowan, J. Maughan; S. G. Heritage, K. A. Shearwood, D. F. Saunders; H. A. Pawson, J. Dutchman, J. D. P. Tanner, D. B. Carr, J. H. Potts.

PEGASUS 1958 XI – M. J. Pinner; J. Dougall, J. Harding; P. Hancock, M. J. Costeloe, K. Garland; M. J. Handscomb, R. W. Trimby, D. Grayson, R. S. Hurren, R. Sutcliffe.

Referee – Dr. H. W. Thompson.

T. Churchill was now the coach and the New Year tour took place once again in the Channel Isles where the side drew their two matches.

Drawn at Oxford against Kingstonians in the first round of the Amateur Cup the club got through by the single goal of the match, a typically headed goal by Denis Saunders from a Sutcliffe corner.

A week later, on 24 January 1959, the same eleven : Pinner, Dougall, Harding, Hancock, Edge, Saunders, Race, Trimby, Barber, Scanlan and Sutcliffe, travelled to Bishop Auckland and drew 0–0, surviving magnificently on a cruel, rutted and frozen pitch.

With one change, Grayson for Barber, the side drew again at Iffley Road the following Saturday 0–0, watched by the correspondent of the *Oxford Mail*.

207

Pegasus and Bishop Auckland, two of the most glamorous names in football, have now extended their F.A. Amateur Cup second round clash to 210 minutes, and part three of the serial will be under floodlights at Sheffield on Wednesday when another attempt will be made to decide who shall entertain Redhill in the third round.

When the teams first met at Bishop Auckland, Pegasus were a little fortunate to survive in a grim, exciting struggle.

On Saturday it was another hard, relentless battle, but the big mystery to all of the 3,056 spectators was how Pegasus failed to win.

Bishop Auckland had two spells with only ten men on the field. After 14 minutes goalkeeper Harry Sharratt twisted his knee and not until 11 minutes had passed in the second half was he able to leave his substitute, inside right Lewin, while during extra time right-back Marshall had five minutes off to have a cut over his right eye patched up.

But the handicap of playing a man short brought the best out of Bishop Auckland and their extra fight and determination were such that they never looked like a team deficient in numbers.

Nevertheless, Pegasus could and most definitely should have had the match in their pocket even before the Bishops' injuries started, for in those opening minutes, three wonderful scoring chances were wasted.

Sutcliffe gave a return pass to the unmarked Scanlan, who from five yards could only push the ball weakly at Sharratt and then Scanlan gave to Trimby, who had a most unhappy game and he fired wide of a gaping goal.

The most serious and unforgivable lapse, however, was by Saunders. He tried to place his penalty kick, but there was so little power behind it that Sharratt easily moved across and pushed the ball away.

The injury to Sharratt should have been the signal for Pegasus to pile on the pressure, but the combined university side eased off.

If the verdict goes against them under the Hillborough floodlights on Wednesday, Pegasus will have paid dearly for Saturday's missed chances.

And most dearly did they pay, but let *The Times* tell the story :

The drawn-out contest between Bishop Auckland and Pegasus for the right to receive Redhill in the third round of the F.A. Amateur Cup competition ended after 300 minutes when Bishop Auckland won worthily by 1–0 under the floodlights at Hillborough last night. As the teams had previously been locked in conflict for 210 minutes without a goal being scored, it was a swift release for the Auckland when Wilkinson scored in the fifth minute.

To write that Wilkinson scored is perhaps stretching a point in spite of the intense enthusiasm with which his successful effort was received by his team. It would be nearer the truth to say that the centre-forward, who was not many yards from the touchline, swept in a speculative centre which dropped over the head of the goalkeeper and into the net. Pinner certainly was at fault with his judgment. He advanced too far from his goal and left himself powerless to do anything but turn and dismally watch the ball dropping into the net.

Doubtless the Auckland counted their blessings thankfully, but such was their superiority in skill, marking and tackling in the first half that no one could have quibbled at their half-time lead. Certainly Pegasus hardly could complain after Dougall had missed a penalty in the 33rd minute, though it must be conceded that Wilkinson had the look and authority of a marksman just before he was fouled in the penalty area. With painful memories of the failure of Saunders to score from the penalty spot on Saturday, Pegasus had, before the match, nominated Dougall for the job if it was necessary this time. Saunders had, it is understood, rolled his kick; instructions to Dougall were 'to have a real go' and he certainly did, driving the ball high and wide of the bar into the gloom of the Spion Kop. This was anything but a happy match for Dougall, for too often he was in trouble against the live-wire Todd.

Pegasus did much in the reorganisation of their resources and strategy in the second half, during which they were considerably more powerful in attack. There was, for instance, a splendid shot by Sutcliffe which Hewitt was pleased enough to punch away for a corner.

The crowd was not disappointed in its hopes of seeing these two well-known amateur teams play the game in freedom of style and movement. One fitting Yorkshire testimony came in these words: 'That's reight good football, lads.'

BISHOP AUCKLAND – C. Hewitt; T. Elliott, C. Barker, R. Thursby; L. Brown, C. Perkins; G. Bromilow, D. J. Lewin, J. Wilkinson, G. Greenwood, K. Todd.

PEGASUS – M. J. Pinner; J. Dougall, J. Harding; P. Hancock, G. D. Edge, D. F. Saunders; J. A. Race, G. Scanlan, D. W. Grayson, R. J. English, R. Sutcliffe.

Missing those two penalties and failing to take the chances that came our way, particularly in that first replay, cost us dearly.

Beneath the floodlights of Hillsborough, after eight years of memory and five hours of titanic struggle, the Bishops finally wiped the slate clean and took their revenge on us for Wembley 1951.

Early that March I received the proofs of *Whistle the Wind*, which I corrected and returned. By the end of April I was sent six advance copies. On 14 May, I heard from Harry Townshend, one of the directors, who wrote :

Just a line to greet you on publication day. We have sold slightly over 1,000 copies of *Whistle the Wind*; quite a good start and I am sure that when the reviews appear it will really start moving.

The edition was only 3,500, but it did have some surprisingly good and lengthy reviews, nineteen in all—including a third of a column in the *Sunday Times* by the poet Charles Causley.

As a family it gave us great pleasure that summer, seeing the book displayed in Mevagissey and knowing that the fishermen liked it. It has since been reprinted, and it gives me just as much pleasure to know that it is still being read by the families of those skippers, alongside whom—for a short while—I once fished for my living.

So to the last few years of Pegasus, the events of which are not easy to piece together. The picture is blurred and only by a close examination of the Minutes' Book—some of which are missing—and putting together what records I can lay hands on, does the end become at all clear.

On reflection it now seems inevitable that the wheel should have turned full circle and we'd find ourselves once more back where we'd begun—an undergraduate club—but sorely pressed.

For the constitutional cracks that had appeared first as early as 1949, when the one-year rule had been voted out, never healed. By the mid-fifties we'd built up a mature team with a lot of experience of the rough and tumble of cup-ties, but the passage of players to the Corinthian-Casuals : Shuttleworth, Cowan, Doggart, Insole, Laybourne, Dutchman, Platt, Vowels, Alexander, Pretlove, Adams, Harrison and others, had split our forces. By the end of the fifties the average age of the team had fallen from twenty-six to twenty as the old guard of Brown, McKinna, Saunders, Pawson, Tanner, Potts, myself, Carr, Lunn, Sutcliffe, Blythe and Hancock, gradually fell by the wayside. Never was the need for unity and understanding between the two universities more essential to the future of Pegasus. But it was never attained, and the minutes reveal best the reason why.

At the Annual General Meeting of November 1959, held at St. John's College, Oxford, our President, Harvey Chadder, began by paying tribute to the late vice-president and former treasurer W. V. Cavill. Genial and rotund, once headmaster of Hymer's School, Hull, he had a deep booming voice that could be heard on a winter's afternoon like the warning blast of some great foghorn. He was a life-long Rotarian and had journeyed with us to Hong Kong, boots, braces, trilby and all, uttering frequent, outrageous puns and much wise council. He was missed.

And at the end of these minutes there was an ominous hint of some of the troubles that lay ahead, when Tommy stated that since he was unable to see many Pegasus games owing to other commitments, he would make it a condition of his re-election as chairman that the committee would agree to the following :

(a) Immediate analysis of the club's activities.
(b) Re-distribution of administrative duties.
(c) Centralized administration in Oxford.
(d) Holding bi-weekly meetings in Oxford.

Nor did our treasurer, John Tanner, exactly brighten the occasion when he announced that we'd made a net loss of £322.2s.5d. and the special Commissioners of Inland Revenue had rejected the club's tax claim with the consequence that we were liable to pay £4,000 in income tax—a fact which perhaps does something to explain why Leslie Laitt's honorarium dropped even further to £10.10s.10d.!

The start to the 1959–60 season was not made any easier by the departure of some good players, Paddy Walsh and George Scanlan to Southall, Bob English to Walthamstow Avenue, Robin Trimby to Corinthian-Casuals, John Beddows to Harwich, Mike Pinner temporarily to Queen's Park Rangers. Nevertheless of the thirty-two matches played fifteen were won, six drawn and eleven lost. The goal-scorers were : Jackson twelve, Bushell eleven, Palmer ten, Randle nine, Hancock and Race four, Jacobs, Scanlan, Grayson and Wilson two each.

Trevor Churchill was again the coach and the tour took place in the south with games against Worthing, Eastbourne United, and Brighton and Hove Albion. I watched these matches and against Eastbourne United, player-coached by Jack Mansell, I brought over two Lancing Town players since the Sussex club was hit by injuries. Afterwards, having talked with Tommy, I drove back along the coast with a feeling of impending doom, which, I quickly reminded myself, was only to be expected if one took too seriously his views on the club's future. Nevertheless, the storm-clouds were gathering.

On 9 January 1960, Pegasus defeated Alton Town away 2–1 in the first round of the Amateur Cup, but were knocked out of the competition, 1–4, a fortnight later when visiting the northern side, Norton Woodseats.

However, although we lost the final of the Oxfordshire Senior Cup that year, losing to Oxford City after a replay, we did finish on a good note, winning the Cambridgeshire Invitation Cup by defeating Ely City in the final, on the Cambridge City ground.

Before the final of the Oxfordshire Senior Cup took place, the committee had met on 16 April, at the Dolphin Lecture Room, in St. John's College and this time there was trouble. It arose over the selection of the side for that Oxfordshire Senior Cup final, when three members voted for Mike Pinner to keep goal (Thompson, Saunders and Theobald) and five for Newsome (Dougall, Harding, Weir, Potts and Tanner). Upon the result of this vote Tommy, as chairman,

211

immediately resigned. And there was more to come—three hours of it! I quote from the minutes :

There followed a long discussion about the future of the club which hinged on two main points:
(a) Apathy, and lack of loyalty and enthusiasm among the undergraduates.
(b) Lack of administrators and senior members at the universities with sufficient time to help the club.
 Dr. Brown felt unable to assist in administration; the secretary, H. J. Potts, had already advised that for business reasons he would be resigning at the end of the current season; and the treasurer, J. D. P. Tanner, had increasing business commitments which meant that the extent of his assistance would be more limited. Despite the chairman's resignation (he would be abroad in July and August of this year) he would be able to play little or any part in the club's affairs, even if he withdrew his resignation. At Cambridge there seemed little hope of practical assistance within the university.
 Without resolving the administration problem, more as an act of faith in the future of the club, three proposals were discussed for the future.
 1. To use the White City as a London ground for eight to ten matches.
 2. To play Isthmian and Athenian League clubs once per season, against each club on their own ground with a third of the net gate going to the club. No final decision was reached on this proposal.
 3. To attract promising school players in the north and south, particularly the latter, in order to minimise the influence of other clubs, but again no formal decision was reached as to the ways this should be implemented.

A month later at the Hawk's Club, Cambridge, the discussion on the future of the club continued and various views were expressed :

 1. That the club needed a fixed base and a stronger fixture list.
 2. That an order of playing priority between the universities, colleges, and Pegasus should be laid down, although in the last analysis it was felt bound to be a matter for the individual's choice.
 3. Whilst no one in the universities felt that the club should wind up, and there was in fact a strong feeling that it should continue, no one seemed able to do anything about it in the sense of active administration.
 4. For the 1960 programme, it was finally agreed that the club should play:
  (a) Approximately six games at the White City, two before the Michaelmas term and four during the Christmas vacation.
  (b) Four games during the Michaelmas term, two midweek floodlit matches and two against the universities.
  (c) The club should enter for the F.A. Amateur Cup and the Oxfordshire or Cambridgeshire cups.

At the Annual General Meeting on 29 May held at the Hawk's Club, Cambridge, Tommy was elected the new president as Harvey Chadder wished to resign, John Tanner the general secretary, and

212

Colin Weir of Oxford and F. Skelton of Cambridge, assistant secretaries. Sydney Bayliss, who had already given the club a great deal of help, was treasurer with W. J. Sartain as assistant treasurer. The committee members were Saunders, Jackson and Harding for Oxford; Hancock, Dougall and Race for Cambridge.

Finally the question of membership policy was raised and Reg Vowels stated :

The lack of loyalty to the club was due principally to the constitution in relation to its membership policy and that the re-introduction of the one-year rule for playing members would restore the loyalty of undergraduates.

Ralph Cowan had circulated 34 members of the club who were also members of the Corinthian-Casuals. Of the replies received 22 approved of the Casuals' views concerning Pegasus's reversion to the one-year rule.

A long discussion followed with John Tanner replying to the argument of the Casuals' representatives.

Other contributions were made by Harrison (D. G.) Bateson, Hancock, Weir, Potts, Bushell, Dougall, Bayliss and Gillard.

Palmer stated that Pegasus could have no legitimate claim to players' loyalties, as it was open to all players, undergraduate and graduate, and must stand in the same position as any other club.

It was finally proposed by Cowan and seconded by Vowels and carried unanimously by the meeting that the committee examine in detail the playing policy of the club with regard to the re-introduction of the one-year rule.

On 13 June the executive committee comprising Tommy, Bayliss, Brown, Sartain and Tanner met at the Bridge Hotel, Bedford, where the following policy was agreed :

1. During the Michaelmas term, the university clubs at Oxford and Cambridge must have first claim on all players with the proviso that the respective captains should do their best to co-operate in the provision of suitable players for inevitable Pegasus obligations such as county cup-ties.

2. Thereafter, Pegasus should have first claim on all junior members of either university while in residence.

3. Out of residence, each man should please himself whether or not he played for Pegasus, though by the rules he would continue to be eligible to do so.

It was agreed that certain difficulties of choice were unsettling for undergraduates, but it was considered impossible to eliminate these entirely.

It was thought impossible to legislate for college cup-ties, Centaurs and Falcon matches or even Arthur Dunn cup-ties, except under the simple rules set out above; and it was recognised that the final decision should rest with the player himself.

It was agreed that the secretary should write to Ralph Cowan as chairman-elect of the Corinthian-Casuals F.C. and put forward the views of the committee in greater detail. Messrs. Brown, Sartain and Tanner were deputed to represent Pegasus F.C. at any subsequent meeting between the two clubs that might arise. Their task would be to help negotiate some settlement between Pegasus F.C. and Corinthian-Casuals F.C. if this seemed possible. But they would not have pleni-potentiary powers and any finally negotiated terms would need to be referred back for approval.

On 3 July the executive committee met again, this time at Oxford where, amongst other things, it was agreed that a contract be signed with the White City Stadium to play at least four matches during the 1960–61 season. It was agreed at the end that a meeting be called as soon as practicable, probably the following month, August. But it was never called. The next official meeting recorded in the Minutes' Book was the A.G.M. over a year later, held again in the Dolphin Room at St. John's, Oxford on Sunday, 22 October 1961. Between those dates I renewed my acquaintance with Pegasus.

21 With Pegasus Again

I had now completed two years as a housemaster and John Dancy's initial impact at Lancing, which had brought about much coming and going of staff and had been referred to by some as 'Dancy's inferno', had gradually softened with time as the school not only flourished but was full to overflowing. Many of the old guard had left and—at last all those preposterous marks had been discarded for a tutorial system which was infinitely preferable and beneficial to all concerned.

I was still coaching the town as well as the school and had got both sides playing a four-two-four formation, twin centre-forwards, full-backs wide, double cover in the centre of the back line and two link-men in the middle. I couldn't understand why other clubs, apart from England under Walter Winterbottom, were so slow to adopt this system. No one in the county league of Sussex was using it nor any of the schools. I asked George Curtis, manager of Brighton and Hove Albion (I'd been with him on that F.A. tour of the Channel Islands back in 1949 and hadn't seen him since) why he didn't adopt it. 'You need special players,' he assured me. You need special players in any system, I thought.

Before Lancing played Winchester that season I rang Hubert Doggart under the guise of a retired Wykhamist naval officer.

'Haven't been down to the place for a long while. Wondered if you'd a game of soccer coming up?'

'We have,' said Hubert, 'we've got a school match this Saturday.'

'Splendid. I'd like to come and watch. Who are you playing?'

'Lancing College.'

'Never heard of 'em. Never played 'em in my day. Are they any good?'

'Not bad,' said Hubert, 'they're playing a four-two-four system.'

'Four-two-four? We never used to do any of that sort of thing. Do Winchester play it?'

'No,' said Hubert emphatically.

'Have you got a good side this year?'

215

'Yes,' said Hubert, 'I think we have,' and he began warming to his subject. 'We've got a good strong centre-forward and a very fast outside-right.'

'What's the goalkeeper like?'

'Weak on crosses and a bit slow off his line, but otherwise adequate.' Gradually, without giving the game away, I drew from him a clear picture of the Winchester side.

Eventually, satisfied I had found out all I could, I revealed my identity. 'Thank you, Hubert,' I said and heard an explosive snort at the other end.

But he had the last laugh, for right on time we lost by the only goal of the match. Jeremy Nichols, the Lancing captain and centre-half, now running the soccer at Eton (successfully I might add), with no pressure at all, proceeded to put through his own goal and give them the game.

I was still popping up to London whenever I could, trying hard to sell a few clothes. Once I had a near squeak. I was showing some men's terylene trousers, when I suddenly spotted in a mirror a senior member of my house approaching. 'Just a moment,' I said quickly, and sliding over the counter hid behind a screen before the astonished buyer could open his mouth. However, on this occasion, and to my amazement, I received an order for fifty pairs of men's terylene trousers. Upon this climacteric note I decided to call it a day, 'hang up' whatever one does in the clothing trade, and end my career as a part-time salesman.

Pegasus had now been granted permission to use the White City Stadium and for the inaugural match, our old foe from the North, Bishop Auckland, travelled South and defeated us, 4–2. It was the sixth and last game the two clubs were ever to play, and a good one at that, which deserved a much larger crowd. As Harry Sharrett, the Bishop Auckland and England goalkeeper remarked 'There was no atmosphere out there. It was like a morgue.' Less than 500 watched the match in a stadium that could hold 65,000. Yet wrote Leslie Nichol :

100,000 cheered the same clubs when Pegasus beat the Bishops 2–1 in the classical 1951 Amateur Cup final at Wembley. The 'gate' on Saturday amounted to around £50. Bishops had a guarantee covering the cost of the trip, which must amount to much more than £100.

Pegasus hope to make White City the showpiece of Southern amateur football. They deserve better support—the soccer was excellent.

David Grayson gave Pegasus the lead, then Bishops raced ahead through Seamus O'Connell, Terry Francis and Cyril Gowland, Roger Jackson retaliated and George Sharp made it 4–2.

Wakefield, Sharp, Harding, Hancock, Dougall (capt.), Pearce, Race, Jackson, Grayson, Randle, Ogden, played for Pegasus on that occasion.

One evening during the Michaelmas term of 1960 the telephone rang and out of the blue I was asked by John Tanner to coach Pegasus. I was amazed, delighted and honoured, particularly the former, for I had no F.A. preliminary coaching badge, though I had been repeatedly urged by Jack Mansell to get one. But time was always pressing and I was deeply involved with the town side as well as the school, and in constant touch with Jack who had succeeded Ron Greenwood as player-coach at Eastbourne United.

I first officially met the Pegasus players on the 29th of December, at 2.45 in the Great Northern Hotel, Peterborough, where we had a long talk before playing the British Police that night under floodlights. Several faces I knew, but a lot were strangers to me. There were two first class goalkeepers in Pinner and Wakefield; three backs : Sharp, Harding and Dougall; five mid-field players : Saunders, Pearce, Beddows, Hancock and Moxon; and six forwards : Jackson, Carlisle, Ogden, Race, Randle and Smith.

Pinner was an Olympic goalkeeper and had already, as an amateur, been helping out Queen's Park Rangers, as he was later to do for Aston Villa, Sheffield Wednesday, Manchester United, Chelsea and Leyton Orient—for the last club he eventually turned professional. Harding had captained the England amateur side and was now playing for Kettering Town. Saunders and Dougall were both internationals and Carlisle had played for Scotland. Wakefield, Jackson and Moxon were all to become internationals and there were five former captains of Oxford and Cambridge in the party. They looked to me a pretty good lot and I felt most honoured to be their coach.

After John had briefly introduced me, I considered it wise to make clear from the start the way in which I might possibly be of any assistance to them as a coach. I was most aware of succeeding such distinguished professionals as Vic Buckingham, Reg Flewin, George Ainsley, Leslie Compton, Joe Mercer, Arthur Rowe and Trevor Churchill. Under all but the last I had been a player, so at least I

217

had that experience to hand on. Even so, I was only an amateur, of no great distinction, and I knew if I was to gain their confidence, I had to convince them I had something more to offer. Above all, that I believed in what I was propounding and was capable of carrying it out on the field in practical coaching sessions. I explained that I had been coaching men for some years now and had been fully involved in plenty of cup football, the F.A. Cup, the Amateur Cup, and local Sussex cups, as well as a full county league programme in which ex-professionals could play. The experience gained had been supplemented by a close-working alliance with Jack Mansell. It was this I hoped to pass on and in doing so to promote a professional approach —the only approach—since it represents above all the very highest aspect of the game.

I was keen to play a 4-2-4 formation straight off that evening and after I had discussed it thoroughly with the players they seemed happy to do so, though Denis Saunders I knew was a little dubious and so was John Tanner. They felt we'd lose the mid-field, and that it was asking too much of the link-men.

I contended that if this was so, one of the centre-forwards could drop back and lend a helping hand; so also could one of the centre-halves move forward to strengthen the middle or contain any on-coming threat. In the latter case it would be up to the appropriate full-back to pivot round and cover the centre as of old. And there was nothing, I argued, to stop the unengaged winger from moving inside and so helping out the mid-field. Any formation should be fluid. There was strength too where it mattered most, down the length and centre of the field involving seven players, two strikers, two link-men, two centre-halves and the goalkeeper. Above all, in a 4-2-4 system one did not need to anchor defenders rigorously, but could free them. Who better to go forward than unmarked players—defenders—in particular wing-backs?

So we put Denis Saunders into the back four to play alongside Jack Dougall at centre-half. It would take some of the pressure off him and his skill and ability to read the game would be invaluable. Jack Dougall, the captain, an enormous chap, taller than Denis, and physically very strong, was a more orthodox centre-half. With Mike Pinner behind I thought they'd be well capable of holding the fort and winning everything in the air.

We drew 1–1 with the British Police on Peterborough United's ground that night and I was delighted that our goal was the direct

218

result of Harding at left-back attacking freely. What a good player he was—so elegant and composed. It surprised me not a bit that he'd captained England.

Then we travelled back to the Melville Hotel, Oxford (our head-quarters for the New Year Tour), talking as usual most of the way. It was like old times, but I missed Jerry, who was now living in Paris and had just been promoted to the rank of Counsellor of the European Nuclear Energy Commission, and Tommy, who was in America, and our old treasurer Bill Cavill, no longer with us, who had once with booming geniality and headmasterly firmness refused Mike Pinner's demands for his girl friend's breakfast expenses.

We did a long stint of training at Iffley Road the next day trying to develop a pattern of play on the flanks, with wingers coming at opponents and plenty of support and movement off the ball. I was particularly looking for someone who could break fast from the middle and head for the heart of an opposition. I was looking also for skill—but then who isn't!

On the last day of 1960 we travelled to the White City and defeated the Sussex F.A. 4–2. I knew most of their side, having watched them playing in the Sussex county league. In particular I knew about Nigel Wigglesworth, who was the Lancing Town goalkeeper. Beneath a headline 'Pegasus 4-2-4 Off to Promising Start' the press wrote :

Pegasus and Sussex, who both face stiff examinations later this month, gave each other a preliminary test in the echoing vastness of the White City stadium on Saturday. They earned good marks, too—Pegasus because of their mobility, team-work and resilience, Sussex because the less experienced players in their experimental team clearly benefited from a demanding match.

Sussex, runners-up in the Southern counties amateur championships last season, play Oxfordshire on 14 January for a place in the quarter-final round, and for Saturday's match fielded a blend of regular county players and promising reserves.

Because of this, and the fact that they are not used to this sort of pitch, they took a long time to settle down and never completely overcame their disadvantage in team-work in spite of reorganising their attack in the second half. In addition, they too often took their passes at a standstill and suffered for it.

Yet Sussex played well in the period astride the interval, pulling up from 0–2 to 2–2 with goals by Sowter and Worth, and must have been particularly encouraged by the work of Igglesden, Knight, Stubbs and Tappin. Because of injury there is a vacancy in goal, but Wigglesworth hardly advanced his claims.

Pegasus, in fact, may well have been slightly—but only slightly—flattered by their final tally, though their goals were well taken. Carlisle and the lively Jackson, the two-edged sword in attack under the 4-2-4 scheme, each scored

219

twice and each had another shot blocked on the line by a back. But early in the second half the attack had a frustrating time, confusing each other and obscuring the path to goal by keeping the ball too close.

This ominous phase passed and Pegasus reasserted themselves. They deserved to win, because they were quicker both to and on the ball, kept it down, and found their men in a fluidity of movement that Sussex lacked. Wakefield had a particularly good match in goal, but J. Harding and probably E. L. D. Sharp, who were not available on Saturday, will have to be found places in front of him. And the right-wing position must still be in doubt.

Finally, but not least important, a few thoughts on the adoption of the 4–2–4 formation, which Pegasus used for the first time when they drew with the British Police at Cambridge last Thursday and retained on Saturday. It has had a successful start, which should give them confidence in it; too many teams lose that confidence because of early failures before they have had time to accustom themselves to the new fashion and wear it to the best effect.

There is room for doubt, however, in the question of timing, because Pegasus have only two more matches—including a Draconian examination— before they visit Erith and Belvedere on 21 January in the first round of the Amateur Cup. That means the scheme will be based on only four matches, plus training, before being put to the test in the searching fires of the Cup. Only a bold club would take the plunge like this, but if one expects boldness anywhere in football, one expects it from Pegasus.

PEGASUS – J. B. Wakefield; P. Hancock, J. Dougall (captain), D. F. Saunders, H. Moxon; R. A. Pearce, J. Beddows; B. J. Randle, R. J. Jackson, R. Carlisle, G. J. Ogden.

SUSSEX – N. Wigglesworth (Lancing); D. Ranger (Rye United), D. Studds (Littlehampton Town); R. Knight (Worthing), G. Tappin (Eastbourne) (captain), F. Cottis (Seaford Town); A. Selway (Hastings United), V. Worth (East Grinstead), D. Laffar (A.P.V. Athletic), M. Sowter (Haywards Heath), J. Igglesden (Rye United).

Then back again to Oxford and some more training on Sunday at Iffley Road.

At the White City a week later, we drew 0–0 with a Draconian side containing eight Welsh internationals. Our defence looked good, but we needed another forward and I was trying to get hold of David Jacobs, a current Cambridge player who I thought would fit the bill.

Before journeying to play Erith and Belvedere—our opponents in the first round of the Amateur Cup—we defeated London University at Oxford by the only goal of the match. After watching the game I was more certain than ever that we needed something extra to support the thrusting speed of Jackson, a match-winner, given the right service. So I telephoned David Jacobs again—he was playing in the Eastern Counties League—this time successfully.

I felt confident now that the side was capable of giving a good account of itself. But I knew too well the pitfalls of Erith's ground, and remembering our last cup game with the Kent club in 1950, when we'd precariously hung on to a 1–1 draw, I warned the players of the dangers they'd find themselves in if they attempted to play short stuff. 'Cut out the tip-tapping today; get power and length into your passes.'

Ideally I wanted the back four to by-pass our mid-field, the backs to get it in early to the wingers, the centre-backs to find our two front men, who could then lay it off to the link-men. Under such glutinous conditions I hoped to bring our midfield into the game from the front and not from the back.

The referee had looked in. Time was running out. 'No ball watching,' I urged as the team prepared to leave the dressing-room. 'Goal-side when they're in possession and remember, no ceremony. Win it and whack it—that's the order of the day. All the best.' And then they were gone and I was left with Leslie Laitt in a strangely quiet and empty changing-room. 'Up to them now, Les.'

'Yes,' he said, unperturbably putting things into his bag. He still wore his hat, the same brown trilby.

There's not much to be said with effect in the last stages before a match. A word in an ear here and there, a bit of reassurance, but too much directive is unsettling. In any case it should all have been done before.

Sitting on the touchline I felt the old pre-match tension seeping out of me and hoped it had not shown earlier. As the two sides kicked around at each end I could see the ball was already beginning to stick, in and outside both penalty areas. John Tanner, the secretary, quietly pre-occupied, was chewing his upper lip watching the scene closely. Colin Weir, team secretary, an habitual dark blue scarf wound round his neck, sat tall and upright chatting concernedly to Sydney Bayliss, our treasurer. How much these three had done for Pegasus. Tommy, of course, was in America. Then the whistle blew. Ninety minutes later we were still in the Cup, but only just as *The Times* reported :

ERITH AND BELVEDERE 3, PEGASUS 3

Whatever else Pegasus may lack these days, their fighting heart remains. This was made abundantly clear as they clumped their way through the mud at Belvedere on Saturday and, with more grit than guile, but with a defence that performed wonders in the second half, forced Erith and Belvedere to an F.A.

Amateur Cup replay which almost certainly will be at the White City next Saturday.

On the day Erith were slightly the better side, more methodical and balanced in attack, with a defence that obscured its limitations by its quickness in the tackle. But happily for the melodious little knot of their supporters in a wing of the stand, Pegasus refused to look these—and other—facts in the face. The pattern of the afternoon went thus: Pegasus, two up in four minutes, thanks to the quick wits and sure eye of Jackson, were pulled back to 2–2 by the interval, and went 2–3 behind soon afterwards. Then, as Erith moved in for the kill and as our minds went back a year to Dronfield, Norton Woodseats and the last time a Pegasus cup challenge was lost in the mud, there came a magnificent twist. Against all the odds Pegasus equalised. A quick free-kick by the right touchline to Jackson; a long cross-field pass like an arrow to Ogden; he swept past his man, cut the ball over to his right foot and planted it, by way of Jarrett's fingertips, just inside the near post.

This splendid goal and escapes at both ends in the remaining 20 minutes spring more easily to mind than the defiant, if, perhaps, too negative Pegasus defensive action that had gone before. Yet it was here in the first part of the second half that the match was decided. Throughout this testing period, with Erith make opening after opening, Saunders, quite unflappable, and Dougall, just as solid, were pillars of wisdom and authority at the rear of the Pegasus 4-2-4 defensive formation; and one should not forget Harding at left-back, who was kept at full stretch by the wiles of West.

But all this could not hide the fact that the Pegasus attack must be sharpened if only as insurance against the rainy day when Jackson is not himself. At the moment he is, perhaps, one of the most effective forwards in the amateur game, a point he quickly made on Saturday. First he took his chance from a poor Erith clearance; then, with the home defence in hot pursuit after being caught hopelessly square by Wakefield's long clearance, he dribbled half the length of the field before slipping round Jarrett to score again. With Race injured just before half-time—he was little more than a pained spectator afterwards—and with Jacobs and Beddows out of touch, little Ogden was Jackson's only ally.

Erith were well served by their wing halves, Heritage and Danks, and it was Heritage who hammered in a quickly taken free-kick by Martin after 24 minutes that put his side back in the hunt. West equalised with a remarkable volley just before half-time, and Neylen's goal after 49 minutes then paved the way for that exciting climax.

ERITH AND BELVEDERE – H. Jarrett; R. Dack, D. Crawford; F. Heritage, J. Hurlock, R. Danks; T. West, B. Martin, C. Neylen, D. Shreeve, K. Jenman.

PEGASUS – J. B. Wakefield; E. L. D. Sharp, J. Harding; P. Hancock, J. Dougall, D. F. Saunders; J. A. Race, D. Jacobs, R. Jackson, J. Beddows, G. Ogden.

On Monday when the draw for the second round was announced we learnt of our tough assignment—Bromley away. But we had first to defeat Erith and Belvedere. We read also in the *Oxford Mail* of that same day a criticism of the match being played at the White

City, criticism that I think we all felt was justified and understandable, for Oxford had given us such tremendous support.

On the actual morning of the replay, the *Sports Mail* produced another long article written by A. J. C. Roche, entitled 'Pegasus and the White City', concluding :

The misfortune is, of course, that should Pegasus go out of the Amateur Cup this season without playing here, Oxford will then have had two seasons in succession without a cup-tie to stimulate the very considerable potential support which still exists for the club. For this, of course, the draw rather than the club has been to blame.

I do not believe that the 12,000 who saw Pegasus play Bromley on the Running Ground in the fourth round in their first season or the 7,000 who saw them, as today, replay against Erith and Belvedere, in the first round in 1949/50 on the White House ground, are figures easily to be repeated.

However—writing in advance of events and chancing my arm on today's gate at the White City—with Oxford United and Oxford City away, as they were this afternoon, I believe it could have been comfortably exceeded on the Running Ground.

Not since 1954/5 have Pegasus gone beyond Round 2, but at their zenith they took half Oxford's male population to Wembley with an appeal as irresistible as the Pied Piper's

Here a successful Pegasus can command the scene in an atmosphere which inspires success. That could never be at the White City.

Finally, let me emphasise that mistaken as today's arrangements may seem to many in Oxford, it would be wrong to deduce that Pegasus are unappreciative of past support or irrevocably committed to a White City future.

For the replay we made two changes, Flann and Randle for Race and Jacobs (the latter had a septic foot). I was glad that Randle was in, for he was the type of player we were looking for, direct, very quick into his stride and with a good deal of skill. He played well that day. *The Times* wrote :

PEGASUS 2, ERITH AND BELVEDERE 0

Two goals, both scored within five minutes of the end of extra time, enabled Pegasus to oust Erith and Belvedere from the Amateur Cup in their first round replay at the White City on Saturday. But that the issue should hang in balance for so long was largely of their own making, for Pegasus had sufficient of the play to have won comfortably long before.

Pegasus favour the 4-2-4 formation, with Saunders in defence alongside Dougall and Beddows linking with Hancock to supply the attack. But hard as they both worked, neither had the flair to inspire the attack, which was left to create its own openings. Here Jackson and Randle, severally and together, occasionally produced the answer only to disappoint as often. They suffered, too, from the lack of real thrust down the wings, so that their approach **was** mainly through the middle, where they were pinched out by the workmanlike Erith defence.

Indeed, Erith fought a defensive battle and relied on the direct, open attack in the hope of a goal. But only Jenman on the left wing looked capable of finding a way through and in the later stages he was surprisingly changed to the other wing, where he more than met his match in Harding, who had an outstanding game.

But Erith had their chances, although they were largely on the defensive. In the eighteenth minute Jenman beat Sharp on the inside and slipped a short pass to Brown, whose shot beat Wakefield only for Harding to clear off his goalline. Again, at the half-hour, Jenman hit the crossbar from the edge of the penalty area, and West headed the rebound over, with Wakefield out of position.

Pegasus had two good chances to open the scoring early in the second half, but first Jackson's left-footed drive was saved and then Randle ran himself into a cul-de-sac. Once Harding broke through to try his luck, but at the other end Wakefield was nearly in trouble with a back pass which failed to travel.

With five minutes of extra time remaining Hancock burst through the edge of the penalty area and hit the Erith crossbar with his drive; the ball rebounded to Ogden, who doubled back and shot for the far top corner with Jarrett beaten at last. A despairing hand pushed the ball aside and Randle scored from the penalty. Within minutes Randle sent Flann down to the by-line and Ogden was up to drive home from close range.

The future of Pegasus at the White City is still indefinite. Only about 700 to 800 spectators supported this match and such a gate is no recommendation to the G.R.A. to continue their experiment of attracting Association football to the White City.

PEGASUS – J. B. Wakefield; E. L. D. Sharp, J. Harding; P. Hancock, J. Dougall, D. F. Saunders; P. Flann, B. J. Randle, R. F. Jackson, J. Beddows, G. J. Ogden.

ERITH AND BELVEDERE – H. Jarrett; R. Dack, D. Crawford; F. Heritage, J. Hurlock, R. Danks; T. West, B. Martin, C. Neylen, W. Brown, K. Jenman.

It had been too close for any of our liking, but I felt that Randle's inclusion as one of the link-men had given us a good deal more thrust and chance of creating opportunities. Above all he took some of the pressure off Jackson who was now a closely-marked man. For Randle had speed and control to take on defences, though he had a problem of knowing when to release the ball. Beddows the other link-man was a slower, stronger and more orthodox wing-half, whose task it was to win and use the ball early and support his forwards. Denis too was a key factor, for he was free to go forward and initiate attacks and plug any gaps left by abortive mid-field thrusts.

But our chief difficulty lay in adapting to positional interchange and recognizing the opportunity of a quick break from defence to

224

attack. But it was beginning to come and I certainly did not share Syd Cox's pessimism when he wrote in the *Oxford Mail*:

If there were any Bromley officials at the White City Stadium on Saturday they will almost certainly report back that there is no cause for undue alarm over the visit of Pegasus next Saturday in the second round of the F.A. Amateur Cup.

A colleague who saw Bromley beat Tooting and Mitcham 3–2 in the first round at Tooting reckoned the chances of Pegasus reaching the third round as very remote, even allowing for the uncertainties of cup-ties.

However, there was little doubt in any of our minds that we faced a stiff task. For Bromley were top of the Isthmian League, having played twenty matches, won thirteen, drawn five, and lost only two, with 58 goals for, 29 against. But I liked the look of our side and felt we could do it. Ogden on the left was a neat player, Jackson with Jacobs alongside would prove a dangerous pair, while Carlisle on the right, if he lacked stamina had craft. A lot would depend on Beddows winning the ball, and Randle's thrust from the middle. I had no worries about the back four or our goalkeeper, Brian Wakefield.

Very quickly the week passed and we found ourselves at Hayes Lane, and there were Helen and Guy Pawson making for a section of the main stand which had been reserved for Pegasus supporters. It was good to see them both and I chatted briefly with them before going to our changing-room.

We began unpacking our gear and suddenly those two faithful supporters, Chedder Wilson and Doug Margates, stuck their heads round the door and wished us good luck. It was twelve years ago that we'd lost to Bromley 4–3 at Oxford when the Kent side had gone on to win the Amateur Cup, beating Romford 1–0 at Wembley. Now only Denis, aged 34, remained of that 1949 Pegasus side, only Reg Dunmall, 38, of that Bromley side. Once again they faced each other in what *The Times* considered a 'Gripping Tie at Bromley'.

BROMLEY 1, PEGASUS 1

Having survived a record of a Scottish reel on which the needle several times got stuck—once for fully two minutes—it seemed that nothing Bromley and Pegasus could do in the following 90 minutes would stretch our nerves so completely. But the gripping last 20 minutes of this second-round F.A. Amateur Cup-tie at Hayes Lane on Saturday proved us to be wrong.

Pegasus, against the odds and considerably against the run of play, had gone ahead just before half-time, inevitably through Jackson, and although Bromley, proudly leading the Isthmian League, continued to have more of the game, and with it some atrocious luck near goal, it was not until 11 minutes from the end

225

that they drew level. And after this the match might have gone either way half a dozen times. It was stirring, full-blooded football, and there is the promise of more in the replay at Iffley Road next Saturday.

Once more Pegasus leaned heavily on their defence. But again Dougall and Saunders, central figures at the rear of the 4-2-4 formation, had an answer for almost everything—although Dougall once had Wakefield diving across his goal to catch a sliced clearance—and on either side of them Harding, plucky and decisive as ever, and Sharp played their full part.

What is more, there are signs that this defensive burden might soon be lifted for in Beddows and Randle Pegasus seem to have found an effective link between defence and attack, and it will prosper still more if Randle learns to release the ball a little sooner. In attack Jackson chose to show an England selector but one shining example of his ability, but it was good to see Jacobs at last playing himself free of a bad spell.

Still, for all their shortcomings up front, Pegasus proved in the thirty-seventh minute that the Bromley defence, even with the experience of Wallis and Dunmall—whose legs seemed to get longer and longer as he cut off passes to Ogden—and the power of Norman and Nelson, could be stretched to breaking point. Wakefield, catching the second of two quick Bromley corners, not for the first time found Carlisle with an accurate throw; a gallop down the right, a low centre to Jacobs, passed on to Jackson, and there was the ball sailing wide of Price from 25 yards.

It says much for Bromley that their eagerness did not turn to desperation as they tried everything they knew to beat the Pegasus defence—and their own run of bad luck. As the minutes ticked away Saunders cleared off the line from Viney, Nash had a surprise shot well saved by the dependable Wakefield, Nottage headed against a post and once even Dunmall rumbled up into the firing line, brushing aside all the Pegasus lightweights until he met his match in Dougall. Then 11 minutes from the end a Bromley free-kick over on the right by Hall reached Keats, unmarked near the far post, and his header saved the day for Bromley, and at the same time acted as a sharp reminder of how little margin for error the Pegasus forwards are giving their defence these days.

BROMLEY – F. Price; R. Dunmall, D. Norman; G. Nash, H. Wallis, L. Nelson; D. Hall, A. Viney, P. Sheckles, E. Nottage, B. Keats.

PEGASUS – J. B. Wakefield; E. L. D. Sharp, J. Harding; D. F. Saunders, J. Dougall, J. Beddows; R. Carlisle, B. J. Randle, R. F. Jackson, D. Jacobs, G. J. Ogden.

'D'you think Pegasus will beat Bromley sir?' the form asked me on Monday morning.

'I think we've every chance,' I replied.

'What went wrong on Saturday, sir?'

'We didn't sufficiently exploit their weakness,' I explained and began to tell them (it was what they wanted, of course, and plenty

226

of it!) how we'd tried to get out left-winger to run Dunmall in the second half. 'It was clear early on that the Bromley right-back lacked pace, and—I suspected—wind. He gave our left-winger a tremendous amount of room—using all his positional wisdom to save his legs and not commit himself. He waited for us to make the mistakes. We should have come at him, run him into the ground and buried him. Instead (and he must be given credit for it) we played it the way he wanted us to play, to the extent we even made him look good.' I refrained from telling them that if we'd had Pat Neil, the brilliant Cambridge outside-left, it would have firmly tipped the scales in our favour and we'd have won the match first go.

But we still lived to fight another day, and a week later, at Iffley Road, Oxford, on a gusty Saturday afternoon in early February 1961, before an official crowd of only 2,001—nearly 10,000 less than had watched Bromley conclude our first-ever venture into the Amateur Cup of 1949—we lost once again to the same club, 2–1. 'Bromley Clip the Pegasus Wings' wrote *The Times* correspondent :

Bromley had a few anxious moments while overcoming Pegasus at Oxford on Saturday in a replayed second round F.A. Amateur Cup-tie, and won on their merits by hard, uncompromising football. Only for a brief period did Pegasus look capable of saving the day when, with a quarter of an hour remaining, Randle reduced Bromley's two-goal lead and conjured up the possibility of extra time. However, Bromley's tall, strong defence were not to be caught again. The Pegasus effort had come too late in the game to hold out any real hope of survival.

It was a difficult afternoon for football, with a high wind blowing straight down the pitch towards Iffley Road. Bromley winning the toss took full advantage of this and with the sun at their backs laid siege to the Pegasus goal from the start.

The first half quickly developed into a question of how well the defensive formation favoured by Pegasus could stand up to Bromley's repeated attacks. They succeeded in this, mainly because Dougall was always in the heart of the battle, but for a single goal scored at the half-hour.

Bromley perhaps were fortunate then, for Norman, their full-back, storming through on the left, was challenged as he centred and the ball was deflected by a defender and swept by the wind over Wakefield's head and under the cross-bar. So, encouraged by two promising moves by their forwards, one felt at half-time that Pegasus had a more than even chance.

But with the change of ends the expected pattern of the game did not materialise, for the Bromley forwards, strongly supported by Basham and Nelson, continued to make inroads into the Pegasus defence by keeping the ball on the ground in a series of quick, short passes. But for over-anxiety they could have made the game safe, for within minutes Viney and then Nottage blazed over the Pegasus bar from close range.

Eventually Bromley forced a corner on the right and Nottage ran in un-challenged to head past Wakefield. Meanwhile, at the other end, the Pegasus forwards had been firmly held at arm's length and only a thirty-yard drive from Jackson had caused Price a moment of anxiety. With the game as good as lost, Pegasus suddenly produced a good crossfield move which Jacobs carried on down the left wing, beating his man cleverly to centre deep over the Bromley defence for Randle to hit home.

PEGASUS – J. B. Wakefield; E. L. D. Sharp, J. Dougall (captain), D. F. Saunders, J. Harding; B. J. Randle, J. Beddows; P. Flann, R. F. Jackson, D. Jacobs, R. Carlisle.

BROMLEY – F. Price; H. Wallis, D. Norman; L. Nelson, D. Joyce, A. Basham; D. Hall, A. Viney, P. Sheckles, E. Nottage, B. Keats.

On the day we simply were not man enough for the job, and a power-headed corner in the second half seemed somehow to ram the fact home. I felt a powerless shrinking feeling as I watched the side strive for an equalizer that never really seemed within their grasp.

Driving back on my own to Lancing, I relived the game as I'd done so many others. To ease my disappointment I took some consolation in the knowledge that I'd been with the club for eight matches and we'd only been defeated once. It did something to help.

I never saw Pegasus play again.

22 Into Cold Storage

We were now under a new headmaster, E. W. Gladstone, who had succeeded John Dancy, the latter having become Master of Marlborough. John Dancy (we were to reap the harvest he'd sown by gaining 40 Oxford and Cambridge awards in four years), had done great work at Lancing, and Biddie and I were far from being the only ones saddened by the departure of him and his family. We missed his friendship and enthusiasm, though the latter had once provoked Henry Thorold to exclaim : 'I can stand lying, I can stand cheating, I can stand downright evil, but I cannot stand enthusiasm.'

Willie Gladstone, great-grandson of the prime minister, did not particularly want the job as he was about to become a housemaster at Eton. The Lancing post had not been advertised and it was done under the usual old-boy network. The inner ring of the H.M.C., the Ushers' Union, knew of someone who in their opinion would fit the bill, and abracadabra there it was; we had a new headmaster. It was one way of doing it, I suppose, but there was something slightly distasteful about it all.

A few years later when the headmastership of Eton came up—it was not, of course, advertised—I decided to put in for the job. There had been much speculation in the papers as to the likely candidates and the name of Willie Gladstone (he like myself got a third in history) had been proferred as a possible and certainly suitable one, but for the fact that he'd only been at Lancing for a short while. So I wrote my letter :

Dear Provost,
   Despite what Peterborough and the *Daily Mail* write, I feel that I'm your man. I would be most grateful if you would send me the relevant documents concerning the post of headmaster of Eton. I make this request as so far no notice has appeared on our common-room notice board. I shall look forward to hearing from you.
                    Yours sincerely,
                         Ken Shearwood.

I did hear—indirectly and very shortly—for the Provost of Eton promptly telephoned Willie Gladstone, who wrote to me :

Dear Ken,

I should be most grateful if you would discontinue your correspondence with the Provost of Eton—please !

Yours,

Willie Gladstone.

Which made my hackles rise somewhat.

'The trouble is, Ken,' explained Willie on the telephone, 'there are so many important people concerned in this appointment that it could do our cause harm.'

My hackles rose even more.

'And it's all this nepotism that I so heartily dislike,' I replied with some heat.

'You're bang right,' agreed Willie before hanging up.

And bang right he was about important people being involved, for Tony Chenevix-Trench, at the time headmaster of Bradfield (we'd overlapped at Shrewsbury) had first to visit the Rt. Hon. Harold Macmillan, at Number Ten, before finally being appointed headmaster of Eton.

And talking of Bradfield, Paul was now at this school, and I shall not forget in a hurry their new boys' tea party for it dragged on interminably.

First we all had to go to the school shop and buy their games' clothes, which I found tedious and irritating, particularly when I saw their balloon shaped soccer shorts, which smacked of the other game. We stood in a long queue (I was told this was to help the parents to get to know each other !) while a stupid mother at the front held us all up as she fussed ostentatiously around her unfortunate son. The man in front of us (I discovered later he was in the Foreign Office) blew immaculate smoke rings and fiddled so nervously with his match box that it suddenly exploded in his hand and for one brief moment it looked as though the Bradfield school shop might be burned to the ground.

By now Tommy had returned from America and on 22 October 1961, the A.G.M. was held. It was the first meeting of the club for fifteen months and Tommy as president commented on the fact that there were no recorded minutes of meetings held since 3 July 1960. He explained that in March 1961 he had received a letter from John

Tanner saying that there had been a serious loss of interest in the club after the defeat by Bromley.

On 14 May Tommy had met Bayliss, Wilson, Tyrell and Harrison at Oxford, and after a thorough discussion—chiefly concerning the loss of Pegasus players to other clubs—it was approved that twenty-five draft forms of registration be sent to each university captain for distribution among resident players. These registration forms were prepared and despatched by Tommy after his departure again for America on 8 June.

Then he had received a letter from John Tanner, and another from Ralph Cowan of the Corinthian-Casuals, accusing him of some indeterminate conduct in sending out registration forms, all of which he strongly refuted.

On his return from America on 1 September, it was decided, because of several early defeats and the impossibility of raising adequate sides, to have no further matches until mid-October. The president stated that he found it impossible to obtain answers to letters, and more important, that other clubs and the fixture bureau were now becoming unwilling to co-operate as regards fixtures.

The final minutes of that Annual General Meeting make ominous reading :

The president then gave an exact account, with dates and correspondence, of the circumstances leading up to the difficulties with the Cambridge captain, Mr. D. Wilson. On 9 October he had written to Messrs. Wilson and Jackson (the Oxford captain) proposing a match for 21 October when both universities were free. Jackson agreed, Wilson failed to reply. On 14 October Ilford F.C. had telephoned suggesting a match on 21 October. Before accepting it the president had telephoned to Wilson, who agreed to play and bring several other Cambridge players. The match was then arranged. On 17 October Wilson had written saying that he could not play, and intended to play for Harwich. After repeated telephone discussions with both Wilson and Harwich, Wilson agreed to play at Ilford, but made it clear that he intends now to resign.

The members present unanimously endorsed the president's action in this matter.

The president also wished it to be known that in the course of these discussions the Cambridge captain had stated that resident Cambridge players could not play for Pegasus before consulting the Corinthian-Casuals F.C.

The president gave it as his view that it would be impossible to continue without proper club loyalty and a decision by players to honour their promises. He felt that the resident players might not fully appreciate the importance of the club for the future of the game at the two universities and that if it lost prestige too far, other more serious effects would follow to the great disadvantage of future undergraduates.

231

A lengthy discussion took place after which the president was asked to take over the affairs of the club for the time being and to arrange future matches. It was agreed that Mr. S. W. Bayliss should be reappointed honorary treasurer, and Mr. C. J. Weir assistant secretary. Members of the committee could not at present be selected owing to uncertainties about their intentions.

By now our difficulties were well known and on 10 December Brian Glanville voiced them in *The Sunday Times* with an article headed 'Pegasus in Danger' :

Is it too late to save Pegasus, the winged horse which has apparently flown too near the sun? It would be a tragedy for British football were it to disappear, for such a club can give soccer, in time, the administrators it so desperately needs.

And yet—ironically—the crisis of Pegasus appears to be itself a crisis of administration. The old spirit of the team—largely composed of ex-Servicemen— that twice won the Amateur Cup seems dead. Younger players appear to have been discouraged and alienated to such an extent that, this season, the match against Cambridge University had to be cancelled because Pegasus couldn't raise a team.

The case of this year's Cambridge captain, Wilson, who left the club because he was refused permission to play in a match for his local side, Harwich and Parkeston, is especially sad and symptomatic. Nor was there any reason why Pegasus should have lost that other gifted half-back, Paddy Walsh, now playing happily for the Corinthian-Casuals.

John Tanner, the Oxford and amateur international centre-forward who worked so hard for Pegasus both on and off the field, resigned from the committee this year. Ken Shearwood, their former centre-half, who coached the side last season with great ability, tells me he's ... 'heard absolutely nothing from them.' Yet his enthusiasm for the club is as great as ever, and he's sure that Arthur Rowe, the Crystal Palace manager, who once coached Pegasus, would gladly give his help again.

The deep irony of it all is that Dr. 'Tommy' Thompson, who founded and inspired the club, now finds himself president of a vanishing entity. There can be only two solutions : either Pegasus must be governed by younger men, wholly in sympathy with the present generation of undergraduates, or it must die—and a similar club can then take its place. Let us hope that this does not become necessary.

Such was the situation when the club faced Hendon at Iffley Road before a crowd of only 1,100 in the first round of the Amateur Cup on 20 January 1962 of which *The Times* wrote :

Although this fixture had been imbued with a certain morbid poignancy by those prophets who forecast the death of Pegasus this season, it proved to be a rousing rather than funereal affair, with the combined universities giving such a good account of themselves against the 1960 Cup winners that they are entitled to hold high hopes for the replay next Saturday.

But for weak shooting and ebbing stamina, two factors which betrayed Pegasus at Iffley Road, Oxford, there would be no need for the pilgrimage to Hendon. Even before the match began a candid appraisal of the fitness of the Pegasus team was available from J. Carver, a coach of international repute, called in by Dr. H. W. Thompson, the enthusiast behind the present Pegasus quest for better times. Solemnly he reported that his team were not as fit as Hendon, or as sharp in their understanding as a side playing regularly together.

Events proved him right, but not before Pegasus had revealed something of the spirit and tenacity, if not the imperious quality of the play which brought them Amateur Cup triumphs at Wembley in 1951 and 1953.

Spector won the toss for Hendon and elected to advance with the wind, a useful ally for himself and Aldridge in their sudden eruptive bursts of speed down the wings. Williamson, consistently brilliant in the Pegasus goal, won many duels with Farrell, although he had Turnbull to thank for a goal-line clearance after a drive by Aldridge. But for most of the half he was given ample protection by a cool, relentless Pegasus defence.

Jackson, Thomson and the bearded Flann chased or conveyed the ball great distances, but they lacked the discipline that tells a forward when to stop dribbling and start shooting.

Having held their own against the fury of Hendon's assault, Pegasus proceeded to box Hendon in their own territory for the first 20 minutes of the second period. There were times when Hendon, with three reserves in defence, seemed about to crack, but always Pinner was positioned to gather the ball with aplomb. With a stronger Hendon defence promised for the replay, Pegasus must produce a marksman or come to grief on Saturday.

PEGASUS – R. Williamson; C. Turnbull, K. Saxby; P. Vaughan, J. Dougall, D. Saunders; P. Thomson, T. Wood, R. Jackson, P. Flann, A. C. Smith.

HENDON – M. Pinner; W. Fisher, D. Bolton; H. Ashman, G. Riddy, C. Murphy; K. Aldridge, C. Sells, M. Farrell, D. Bell, M. Spector.

Psychologically it could not have helped seeing Mike Pinner in the Hendon goal. And he was there the following week when Hendon took ample revenge for that sunny afternoon back in 1951 when we'd defeated the London club 3–2 at Crystal Palace. Beneath a headline 'Pegasus Upset by Pitch' *The Times* wrote :

HENDON 6, PEGASUS 1

On a glutinous morass at Claremont Road—which before the game began was the subject of an official protest by Pegasus to the Football Association—the more physically powerful and experienced Hendon team overcame a Pegasus side, dismayed by the conditions and lacking a marksman. From Pinner in goal to Spector at outside-left, the home team relied on long, hard-hit passes, quick breakaways, and switches of direction—tactics which were the only practical ones on such a day.

Territorially Pegasus must have had 60 per cent of the game, and for the first half-hour, in spite of losing a goal to Spector after five minutes, Pegasus looked the more accomplished footballers. Vaughan and Saunders were setting up probing attacks. Thomson was showing his paces on the right wing, and Flann, with his clever footwork, was more than a handful for the Hendon defenders, two of whom resorted to tactics which did their side no credit.

As the minutes ticked by and no equaliser came, Hendon grew more confident, realised their power, and scored twice more through Bell and Spector, with a finely controlled chip shot over the advancing Williamson.

The second half followed much the same pattern. For half an hour Pegasus tried all they knew to pull themselves back into the game, urged on by Dougall, and plied with through passes by Turnbull, the most accomplished back on the field. Time and again they reached the Hendon penalty area, only to be stopped there by mud, a misdirected pass, or a desperate tackle.

So Hendon weathered the storm, two more goals from Bell and a third one driven in from 25 yards by Spector saw them home to avenge their defeat in a semi-final match in 1951. Now they are ready to meet St. Albans next Saturday.

A penalty goal by Smith was the only reply that Pegasus could manage on the day, but the perceptive spectator might well see, when he looked at the spirit of the universities' XI and considered the undoubted talents of such young players as Williamson, Turnbull, Vaughan and Flann, that out of such a heavy defeat a new and successful Pegasus side could emerge.

One left the ground with that thought—and that even though the victims of Gilbert's Mikado were asked to play 'on a cloth untrue with a twisted cue, and eliptical billiard balls,' they were not asked to play football on porridge.

HENDON – M. Pinner; M. Williams, D. Bolton; R. Walker, G. Riddy, C. Murphy; K. Aldridge, C. Sells, M. Farrell, D. Bell, M. Spector.

PEGASUS – R. Williamson; C. Turnbull, K. Saxby, J. Dougall, D. Saunders; P. Thomson, T. Wood, R. Jackson, P. Flann, A. C. Smith.

All good things come to an end and the last Annual General Meeting of the club was held in the Hawk's Club, Cambridge, on Saturday, 10 November 1962, with Dr. H. W. Thompson, C.B.E., F.R.S., M.A., the president, in the chair. Those present were : Messrs. C. J. Weir (acting hon. sec.), S. W. Bayliss (hon. treasurer), Dr. B. R. Brown, Messrs. K. Saxby, C. J. Turnbull, J. Dougall, E. A. Evans-Jones, M. M. L. Barnwell, M. Bristowe, B. A. Hardcastle, M. Ralph, F. I. Parker, S. Szemerenzi, G. Clayton, R. P. Ritch. After the minutes of the previous A.G.M. had been read and signed by the president and business arising from the previous minutes dealt with, the secretary's report was heard :

Mr. Weir said that there had been a discussion among senior members of the club about whether or not efforts should be made to continue the club. It was decided that these efforts should be made, and, as a result, a meeting had been held in London in the summer between the acting hon. sec., M. Ralph (captain

O.U.A.F.C.) and H. Moxon (captain C.U.A.F.C.) to plan a programme of matches in preparation for the Amateur Cup match in December, as the club had not this year been granted exemption from the Qualifying Competition. Both universities had agreed to leave a number of Saturdays free in the Christmas term so that Pegasus could play. It was decided not to play matches in September because of the expense involved.

Mr. Weir then gave details of the results of matches played so far this season and said that the club had entered for the F.A. Amateur Cup, the A.F.A. Invitation Cup, the Oxfordshire Senior Cup, the Cambridgeshire Invitation Cup and the Smith Memorial Cup. Pegasus had been drawn against Northern Nomads in the second of these, Henley Town in the third, Exning United, against whom they had lost 3–4 that day in the fourth and Oxford City in the last.

Mr. Weir then went on to speak about the absolute necessity of university players putting the interest of Pegasus above other clubs, particularly college football clubs, if success was to be achieved and the objects of the club fulfilled. It was essential players in reserve should not drift off to other clubs, as it was impossible to produce a good Amateur Cup XI without being able to call on the full strength of the two universities.

He said that the agreement on the availability of players signed jointly by Pegasus and the Corinthian-Casuals F.C. two years previously was still in force and that Pegasus had kept strictly to it.

The president said that the Corinthian-Casuals had flagrantly broken the agreement in the current season. Mr. Weir agreed that this had been so, but said that he thought it was proper for him to work for an agreement with Mr. W. Wickson, the hon. sec., of Corinthian-Casuals F.C. to the benefit of both clubs in view of the increasing 'shamateurism' in the game.

So the 1962–3 season began with a match against Walton and Hersham away, on 29 September, culminating in a resounding defeat for the club by six clear goals. A week later the side lost again to Southall away 0–2. A single match was played in October, at Iffley Road, against Croydon Amateurs resulting in a one–all draw, our goal, a penalty, scored by Dougall. Two more matches were played in November, both away games, at Berkhamstead Town, where we won 3–2, and at Exning, where we lost 3–4 in the first round of the Cambridgeshire Invitation Cup.

Such was our short and undistinguished playing record when, on 15 December Pegasus met Windsor and Eton in the fourth qualifying round of the Amateur Cup. Fourteen years ago, almost to the day, we'd begun our first venture against Enfield in the same round, knowing we had to win to survive. Now we were back once more where we'd begun and the players faced the same critical situation.

I'm glad I did not see the match about which *The Times* wrote : 'Illustrious No Longer — Sad Decline of Pegasus'.

235

There is a stricken look about the once illustrious Pegasus after the sombre happenings in this rather tasteless encounter at Iffley Road, Oxford. The price of defeat may be loss of all exemption in the Amateur Cup next season, which would almost certainly force Pegasus to drop out of the competition. They could not call on Oxford and Cambridge players much before the university match in December.

The days of soaring success, with Amateur Cup triumphs at Wembley in 1951 and again in 1953 are gone. The crowds who warmed to the Pegasus ideals and acclaimed their arrival in Amateur football fifteen years ago are gone too. Nearly all the meagre crowd on Saturday were loyal to the Delphian League club. Even the spirit of Pegasus is flagging, now that some of the best players at both universities prefer to represent other teams in the competition.

Ten years ago it would have been unthinkable for Pegasus to have played a man short for the first twelve minutes of a Cup-tie with no reserve available to take his place. Yet this happened against Windsor and Eton, Saxby arriving late and the official reserve having cried off. It is the enthusiasm and labour of a few officials which has kept Pegasus intact, but the present crisis may be beyond even their resources.

The misfortune that dogs Pegasus these days deprived them of a potential match-winner in G. Clayton, the Cambridge forward, who was injured in the University match in a tackle with Ralph—the outside-left he should have partnered against Windsor. His loss was felt by an attack which moved jerkily, like actors with half-remembered lines, through the humiliation of the first half and the disappointment of the second.

Pegasus were overwhelmed in the opening twenty minutes. Facing a fierce wind and boisterous opposition, they were made to defend desperately, and respite in the form of breakaways came only three times. All the Windsor forwards were prodigal with their chances, but at least Goodland turned in Bristow's corner. Incongruously Hardcastle levelled the scores with a speculative effort from the wing.

Owen swiftly restored Windsor's lead, yet for a time, Pegasus, with Ralph, Fitch and the deep-lying Parker playing well, moved with more wit and invention. The hopes were scuttled by an ill-timed back-pass by Dougall which sailed over the head of Hingley and into the Pegasus net. Like the stray shot which blows up an arsenal this single kick shattered the Pegasus effort. The second half was a drab formality, nothing more than another sad chapter to the Pegasus story.

PEGASUS – P. Hingley; C. J. Turnbull, K. Saxby; M. Bristow, J. Dougall, P. H. Vaughan; L. M. L. Barnwell, R. P. Fitch, F. Parker, B. A. Hardcastle, M. Ralph.

WINDSOR AND ETON – R. White; H. Reynolds, P. Badcock; M. Hill, J. Millbank, P. Knibbs, G. Rowley; C. Owen, K. Lunnon, W. Goodland, C. Bristow.

On Saturday, 9 March 1963, a meeting of the committee was held in Dr. H. W. Thompson's room in St. John's College, Oxford, at which the following were present : Dr. H. W. Thompson (president), Dr. B. R. Brown (chairman), Messrs. C. J. Weir (hon. sec.), S. W. Bayliss (hon. treasurer), M. Ralph, H. Moxon, D. F. Saunders, R. D. Williamson, B. A. Hardcastle, J. Dougall, K. Saxby, P. H. Vaughan and C. J. Turnbull. Apologies for absence were received from F. I. Parker (O.U. Centaurs) and P. F. Varey (C.U. Falcons). The single item on the Agenda was 'The future policy of the club'. I quote from the minutes :

The president, who took the chair, gave a brief outline of the facts and activities of the club since its formation in 1948, and said he was sure no other amateur club had had such a formidable record in so short a career. He had now, however, come reluctantly and sadly to the conclusion that Pegasus could no longer continue to play competitive football, and that a way must be found of putting the club into 'cold storage'. There were many factors that had led to the present unhappy situation and the president enumerated some of them : It had always been difficult to get full support and co-operation from Cambridge University and since 1959 each succeeding Cambridge captain had left the club, taking other members of the C.U.A.F.C. with him; there had been attempts by other clubs, among whom he named the Corinthian-Casuals, to deprive Pegasus of players who ought to have played for a combined universities' club; there had been the situation at Christ's College where loyalty to the college football club was put before loyalty to Pegasus; and finally there was a growing apathy among all undergraduates concerning Pegasus affairs, and an unwillingness to shoulder burdens of responsibility in the only way which could lead to success. Faced with this situation the president could see no other solution than to suspend activities. He was at pains to point out that if Pegasus did stop activities now, it would never again be possible to enter for the F.A. Amateur Cup and that no one should be under any illusions that the club might be granted any exemption in future. If Pegasus was ever revised as an Amateur Cup club, it would have to start at the very beginning of the competition.

Dr. B. R. Brown (chairman) concurred with what the president had said and thought it right that the club should now cease operations, particularly as there was no one who was willing to run the club in face of apathy and defections.

Mr. D. F. Saunders remarked that things need never have reached the present pass if only players in the previous five years had been loyal to the club. There had been a wealth of talent at both universities and indeed the standard of play had probably been higher than in the early years of the club. But players had not stayed and instead of helping both Pegasus and themselves —for many would surely have gained international caps—they had drifted away.

Mr. C. J. Weir (hon. sec.) said that the last few years had been a tale of broken promises from players, and increasing difficulty in fielding a representative XI. He too, thought that the club should now cease operations, and asked whether in fact there was any support for Pegasus at Cambridge.

237

Mr. K. Saxby reported that there was no support for Pegasus at Cambridge. Mr. B. A. Hardcastle said that there was interest in and support for Pegasus at Oxford, but agreed that it would be impossible to run the club successfully without full support from both universities.

Mr. P. H. Vaughan remarked how disappointed he and others would be if the club finished and said that he had been wondering whether entry to a league competition might save Pegasus. But he now realised that even this was impossible.

Mr. J. Dougall said that he thought the president's remarks had been rather hard on the present undergraduate members of the club, and that had they known success as the founder members had done, all might have been different.

After further discussion it was agreed by the committee that:

1. There should be no further entries for competitive football .
2. The club should be put into 'cold storage' i.e. it should remain in being as a club, but should not play matches for the moment, and that its affairs and financial matters should be entrusted to a small body of members to be appointed later.
3. The following brief statement should be issued to the *Oxford Mail* for transmission to the Press Association:

> The committee of the Pegasus Football Club discussed the present and future activities of the club at a meeting on 9 March 1963. A detailed statement of future policy will be prepared by the officers and issued in the near future.

At the end of the meeting, the honorary secretary told the members that one of the oldest and staunchest supporters of Pegasus, Mr. Frank Weedon of Cholsey, had died earlier in the month. Mr. Weedon had travelled many hundreds of miles to see the team play and had been present at the last cup-tie on 15 December 1962. The secretary had written a letter to Mrs. Weedon to express the club's sympathy with her in her loss.

The meeting was adjourned at 7.45 p.m.

The last recorded match that Pegasus played was on 6 April 1963, against Marston United in the third round of the Oxfordshire Senior Cup, which they won by a single goal scored by G. Clayton.

Those who played were: P. Hingley; C. J. Turnbull, K. Saxby; W. Groves, J. Dougall (capt.), D. F. Saunders; C. Feeman, J. P. Payne, G. Clayton, R. P. Fitch, R. S. Hurren.

And Denis Saunders, once captain and sole remaining player of those two Amateur Cup-winning sides of the early fifties—with well over two hundred matches under his belt—was still present that afternoon at Iffley Road, playing quietly on as though determined to see Pegasus through—right to the bitter end.

In Conclusion

So, what began as a combined football venture by Oxford and Cambridge undergraduates, inspired by Tommy, finally foundered on a difference of opinion that became apparent as early as 1949 when the one-year rule was rescinded. It created a gulf that was never bridged, a contention never resolved.

By and large players at Cambridge—and a few at Oxford—stuck to the now extinct one-year rule, and after being down a year, moved on and played for the Corinthian-Casuals. The London club had attended that first meeting of Pegasus to discuss the formation of an Oxford and Cambridge Football Club, and had supported Tommy in his important and successful bid for exemption. Understandably they opposed the abrogation of the one-year rule, for in their eyes Pegasus had now suddenly become a rival—a club that could retain university players who would otherwise have found their way to the Casuals' camp.

Right from the start it had been evident that a link existed between the Corinthian-Casuals and Cambridge that was not to be found at Oxford. But then at Oxford there existed a link between Tommy and the university that was not to be found at Cambridge. And this was significant, for it explains why the Cambridge players tended to view Tommy in a different light from us at Oxford. To them he represented the 'auld enemy'; brilliant, arbitrary, and sometimes most disconcerting. Fundamentally Tommy was a pragmatist. His policies and his pursuit of them were not always compatible with diplomacy. But as Pegasus soared higher and ever higher during those early years such matters were of no real consequence for we had the world behind us. Towards the end of the fifties, however, when our wings had been well and truly clipped and we were falling fast, the Cambridge players—a good deal younger at both university—viewed the club more and more critically, the distant figure of Tommy with increasing incomprehension.

But still the real question remains—should the one-year rule have been abolished? Most of us at Oxford believed that it had to go and

239

that Tommy was right and justified in striving for its abolition. Hypothetical though it may be, Pegasus would not, I think, have survived and won the Amateur Cup in 1951 and 1953 had the club quickly lost the services of that post-war generation of players with their pre-university experience. And from our success, it should be remembered, the Casuals rejuvenated themselves and later reaped the benefit of experienced Pegasus players who helped them in their own successes of '56, '57 and '58.

What a pity that the two clubs could not have amalgamated in some way, sunk their differences, and pooled their resources, but it was simply not practicable.

In the final count then, no one was really to blame. The club's early demise was an inescapable fact. The real reason lay not solely with the players, Tommy, differences of opinion, problems of administration, the Casuals, or the attitude of a new generation of undergraduates, although all were contributory factors.

The real reason lay in the timing of Pegasus's inception. Its growth and success, in the aspiration of men who came to Oxford and Cambridge, not as typical undergraduates, but as older and mature students, something that Tommy recognized and used to such telling effect.

Was there ever then the basis for a permanent club once this generation had gone? I don't think so. Nor really did Geoffrey Green, who wrote in his book, *Soccer in the Fifties* :

Pegasus came and went like a shooting star. But in their short life they shed a bright light on the game as a whole. They were something different.

And if there is one name that has earned a permanent right to be associated with Pegasus first and foremost, then it is surely that of Professor Sir Harold Warris Thompson, Commander of the British Empire and Fellow of the Royal Society, more simply known to us all as Tommy.

As for myself—have I any regrets? None—which isn't strictly true : there is just one—that I never played for England as an amateur. But then had Rob Tillard not elected to shoot pheasants on that particular Saturday back in October 1947, I might never have played for Oxford, let alone Pegasus. So who knows ... who knows?

List of players

Abbott, D. B.
Adams, J. G.
*Alexander, F. C. M.
Balderstone, B. L.
Bamford, P. W.
Barber, P. J.
Barnwell, L. M. L.
Beddows, J.
Bigley, B.
Bishop, M. H.
Blythe, J. H.
Boddy, B. H. P.
Bolton, D.
Bonsell, R.
Bowyer, R. E.
Brett, J.
Bristow, M.
Brough, D. W. T.
*Brown, B. R.
Bufton, I.
Burgess, J. H.
Burnham, D. W. L.
Burrage, D. J.
Burton, G.
Bushell, M. J.
Caddick, R. H.
*Carlisle, R.
Carr, D. B.
Chadder, R. H.
Cheshire, C. S.
Chukwudebe, B. N.
Clarke, D. A.
Clayton, G.
Clegg, J.
Coe, B. A.
*Cowan, R.

Costelo, J. M.
Crisp, J. G.
Dean, A. O.
Dewhurst, T.
Doggart, G. H. G.
*Dougall, J.
Dryborough, C.
Duck, M.
Dunn, D. H.
*Dutchman, J. A.
Dyson, T. K.
Edge, G. D.
English, R. J.
Evans-Jones, E. A.
Feeman, C.
Fish, H. R.
Fitch, R. P.
Flann, P.
Fletcher, P. K.
Foster, A.
Fordham, J. J.
Gadsby, N. E.
Garland, K. J.
Gibson, A.
Gibson, I.
Gillard, R. G.
Gorton, J. D.
Grayson, D. W.
Green, D.
Groves, W.
Haigh, J.
Hall, R. W.
Hancock, P.
Handscomb, M. J.
*Harding, J.
Hare, B. J.

Hardcastle, B. A.
Harrison, D. G.
Head, W. R.
Heritage, S. G.
Heslop, R.
Hewitson, G.
Heywood, J.
Hingley, P.
Hornby, R. P.
Howlett, J. E.
Hurren, R. S.
Hutson, P.
Igglesden, J. A.
Insole, D. J.
Ions, E. S. A.
Irvine, G. H.
Jacobs, D.
Jackson, E. W.
*Jackson, R. F.
Jarvis, P.
Jones, J.
Jones, P.
Joynt, H. W.
Keighley, D. W.
Kenny, J.
Kerruish, N.
Kidd, J. M.
King, M. N. G.
Knightly-Smith, W.
Laidler, T.
Land, R.
Lanyon, D.
Lawson, T.
*Laybourne, J. S.
Leyden, P. J. R.
Lewington, G. J.

241

Liddington, J.
Loader, D.
*Lunn, R. G.
Lupton, T.
*McKinna, G. H.
Madison, J.
Marsh, S.
Maughan, J.
May, P. B. H.
Miller, D.
Mitchell, A. M. D.
Moncrieff, J.
*Moxon, H.
Murphy, T.
Needham, B.
Newell, J. P. C.
Newsome, A. T.
Norfolk, D. E.
Notley, K. J.
Norgrove, C. J.
Ogan, D.
Ogden, G. J.
Osborne, H. W. G.
Palmer, P. E.
Palumbo, P.
Parker, F.
Pass, L. G.
Patrick, J.
*Pawson, H. A.
Payne, J. P.
Peagram, R.
Pearce, R. A.
Pearson, J.
Peet, F. A.
Pellow, G. S.
Pepper, E. J.
*Pinner, M. J.

Platt, J.
Platts, W. G. C.
*Potts, H. J.
Power, J. M.
Pretlove, J. F.
Race, J. A.
Ralph, M.
Randle, B. J.
Raynes, J. F.
Reeve, W. B.
Rhys, H. R. S.
Richards, D. M.
Ries, M. A.
Roberts, A.
Robinson, J. S.
Robinson, M. T.
Ryan, M. A. J.
*Saunders, D. F.
Saxby, K.
Scanlan, G.
Senior, A.
Sharp, E. L. D.
Shearwood, K. A.
Sheret, W. B.
*Shuttleworth, G. M.
Skelton, F.
Sleddon, G. J.
Smith, A. C.
Smith, A. R.
Smith, J. W.
Smith, P. J.
Sorley, T. I.
Stamp, M. A.
Steward, M. R.
*Sutcliffe, R.
Sweeney, P. D.
Szemerenyi, S.

*Tanner, J. D. P.
Taylor, K.
Theobald, M. J.
Thomas, S. H.
Thompson, P.
Tillard, J. R.
Tordoff, C. G.
*Trimby, R. W.
Turl, A. R.
Turnbull, C. J.
Tweddle, E. B.
Tyrrell, J. M.
Tyson, C.
Utley, D.
Vaughan, P. H.
*Vowels, R. C.
Waddilove, C.
Wade, M.
Wakefield, J. B.
Walsh, P. M. J.
Walton, P.
Waters, R. H. C.
Weir, C. J.
Whitefield, G.
Whitehouse, R. A.
Whitworth, A.
Williamson, L. J.
Williamson, R. D.
Wilson, D.
Wild, E. H.
Wittekind, G.
Woodacre, E. E.
Wood, T.
Woodley, F. J.
Wright, D. J.
Young, A. G.
Young, C. M.

Honours

Winners, Football Association Amateur Cup.
1950–51, 1952–3.
Quarter-Finals, Football Association Amateur Cup.
1948–9, 1953–4, 1954–5.
*   *   *
Winners, Amateur Football Alliance Invitation Cup.
1951–2, 1953–4, 1954–5, 1956–7.
Runners-Up.
1950–51, 1952–3, 1955–6.
*   *   *
Winners, Oxfordshire Senior Cup.
1949–50, 1957–8.
Runners-Up.
1959–60.
*   *   *
Winners, Cambridgeshire Invitation Cup.
1959–60, 1960–61.
Runners-Up.
1955–6.
*   *   *
Winners, Ben Warner Cup.
1957–8.
*   *   *
Winners, Sudbury Invitation Cup.
1958–9.

1950 – 51 AMATEUR CUP

First Round		Second Round		Third Round		Fourth Round		Semi-finals		Final	

First Round

- Pegasus — 4
- *Gosport Boro' Athletic — 3
- Slough Town — 1
- *Poole Town — 1
- Brentwood & Warley — 3
- *Westbury United — 1
- Rawmarsh United — 1
- *Ferryhill Athletic — 2
- *Oxford City — 4
- Erith & Belvedere — 4
- *Metropolitan Police — 4
- Saltash United — 2
- *Crook Town — 0
- Yorkshire Amateurs — 1
- *Harwich & Parkeston — 5
- Hounslow Town — 7
- *Tooting & Mitcham — 1
- Letchworth Town — 1
- *Edgware Town — 2
- Kingstonian — 2
- *Jack Mould's Athletic — 2
- *Woking — 3
- Wimbledon — 3
- *Shepley United — 0
- Bungay Town — 4
- *Histon Institute — 3
- *Hendon — 0
- Smethwick Highfield — 0
- *Cheshunt — 0
- Dagenham — 4
- *Wycombe Wanderers — 2
- Walthamstow Avenue — 3
- *Ilford — 1
- Briggs Sports — 0
- *Walton & Hersham — 3
- Salisbury — 1
- *Willington — 0
- Marine (Liverpool) — 1
- *Moor Green — 2
- Romford — 0
- *Evenwood Town — 3
- Bishop Auckland — 2
- *Shildon — 2
- Bearpark C.W. — 1
- *Whitby Town — 3
- Hallam — 1
- *Cambridge Town — 3
- Clapton — 1
- *Hitchin Town — 4
- St. Alban's City — 1
- *Barnet — 1
- Worthing — 0
- *Eastbourne — 4
- Barking — 1
- *Sheffield — 3
- Penrith — 2
- *Leytonstone — 0
- Wealdstone — 5
- *Boldmere St. Michael — 2
- Hayes — 1
- *Billingham S.R. — 0
- Norton Woodseats — 0
- Bromley

Second Round

- Pegasus — 3
- *Slough Town — 1
- *Brentwood & Warley — 5
- Ferryhill Athletic — 1
- *Oxford City — 4
- Metropolitan Police — 2
- *Crook Town — 4
- Hounslow Town — 2
- *Tooting & Mitcham — 4
- Kingstonian — 2
- *Woking — 1 2
- Wimbledon — 1 3
- *Bungay Town — 0
- Hendon — 3
- *Dagenham — 0 1
- Walthamstow Avenue — 0 3
- *Ilford — 1
- Walton & Hersham — 3
- *Willington — 3
- Moor Green — 1
- *Bishop Auckland — 3
- Shildon — 1
- *Whitby Town — 1 1
- Cambridge Town — 1 0
- *Hitchin Town — 2 0
- Barnet — 2 3
- *Eastbourne — 2 2
- Sheffield — 2 0
- *Leytonstone — 1
- Hayes — 4
- *Billingham S.R. — 1
- Bromley — 3

Third Round

- Pegasus — 3
- *Brentwood & Warley — 2
- *Oxford City — 2 2
- Crook Town — 2 0
- *Tooting & Mitcham — 2 1 1
- Wimbledon — 2 2 1 3
- *Hendon — 0 2
- Walthamstow Avenue — 0 0
- Walton & Hersham — 1
- *Willington — 0
- *Bishop Auckland — 7
- Whitby Town — 2
- *Barnet — 6
- Eastbourne — 1
- *Hayes — 0
- Bromley — 2

Fourth Round

- Pegasus — 3
- *Oxford City — 0
- *Wimbledon — 1
- Hendon — 2
- Walton & Hersham — 1
- *Bishop Auckland — 2
- *Barnet — 0
- Bromley — 2

Semi-finals

HIGHBURY & SELHURST PARK
- Pegasus — 1 3
- Hendon — 1 2

AT LEEDS
- Bishop Auckland — 2
- Bromley — 0

Final

Wembley 100,000
- Pegasus — 2
- Bishop Auckland — 1

244

Final

Pegasus 6 — Harwich & Parkeston 0

Wembley
100,000

Semi-finals

AT HIGHBURY & CRAVEN COTTAGE
Pegasus 1 2 v. Southall 1 1

AT BRENTFORD
Harwich & Parkeston 3 v. Walton & Hersham 1

Fourth Round

Pegasus 2 v. *Slough T. 0

Romford 1 1 v. *Southall 1 2

Harwich & Parkeston 4 v. *Leytonstone 3

*Tooting & Mcham 0 0 1 v. Walton & Hersham 0 2

Third Round

Pegasus 5 v. *C Casuals 0 1 4

*Willington 2 v. Slough T. 1 1 2

Romford 3 v. *Wycombe W. 2 1 2

Wealdstone 0 0 v. *Southall 0 2

Harwich 3 v. *Clevedon 5 2

Hallam 0 0 1 v. *Leytonstone 3

Tooting & M. 4 v. *Hounslow T. 1 1 2

Evenwood T 2 1 v. *Walton & H. 1 2

Second Round

Pegasus	4	
*Hayes	2	
*Cockfield	3	
Sheffield	2	
Erith & B.	0	
*Finchley	2	
Brentwood	5	
C Casuals	0	
*Willington	3	
Salts	0	
Bromley	2	
Kingstonian	1	
*Barking	1	
Leyton	3	
Slough T.	4	4
*Eastbourne	4	4
Romford	0	
*St. Albans	0	
Ilford	1	
*Carshalton	3	
Barnet	2	3
*Woking	0	3
Hitchin	0	0
Wycombe W	1	1
Moor Green	6	1
*Wealdstone	3	3
Walthamstow Ave.	2	
*Wimbledon	1	
Shildon	1	2
*Bishop Auckland	4	2
Saltash	2	2
Southall	1	2
*Whitton	1	1
Harwich	4	1
Billingham	2	
*Harrogate	1	
Clevedon	4	
*Biggs S.	0	
Histon	3	3
Dartmouth	3	3
*Dulwich H.	0	
Ware	2	2
*Redhill	1	1
Hallam	1	1
*I.C.I.	1	
Leytonstone	6	
*Ferryhill	5	
Frome T.	0	
*Leytonstone	1	
Tooting & M.	2	
Oxford C.	1	
Anstey N.	4	
*Cambridge C.	0	
*Hendon	3	
Boldmere	2	
Hounslow T.	0	
Sutton U.	1	
*Evenwood T	0	
Whitby T.	2	
Crook T.	1	0
*Marine	0	0
*Yorkshire A.	0	
Whitley Bay	1	
Tilbury	1	
*Walton & H.		

*Signifies drawn at home.

245